ROMAN ROADS OF EUROPE

ROMAN
ROADS OF
EUROPE

N.H.H.SITWELL

CASSELL
LONDON

CASSELL LTD.

35 Red Lion Square, LondonWC1R 4SG
and at Sydney, Auckland, Toronto, Johannesburg,
an affiliate of
Macmillan Publishing Co., Inc.,
New York.

First published 1981

ISBN 0 304 30075 6

2-colour maps by Peter McClure
© N. H. H. Sitwell
Other maps by Neil Hyslop
Line drawings and design by Sarah Jackson

Filmset by SX Composing Ltd., Rayleigh, Essex
Printed and bound in Hong Kong

To T. McL. Chartered Accountants
with whom this book was begun
and B.B. Chartered Accountants
with whom it was finished

N.H.H.S.

CONTENTS

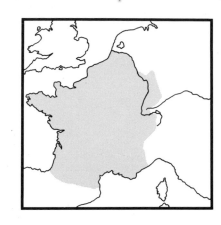

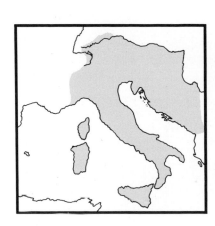

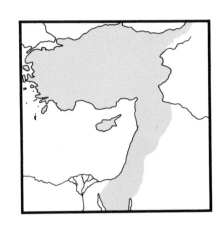
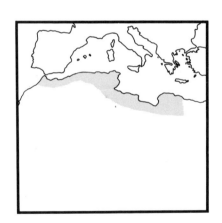
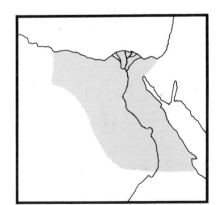

ILLUSTRATIONS

I

EUROPA
IMPERIUM ROMANUM

The Road goes ever on and on
Down from the door where it began.
Now far ahead the Road has gone,
And I must follow, if I can,
Pursuing it with eager feet,
Until it joins some larger way
Where many paths and errands meet.
And whither then? I cannot say.

J. R. R. Tolkien, *The Lord of the Rings*

THE MEDITERRANEAN SEA, round which three continents meet, was the centre of the ancient world. In the middle of the Mediterranean lies Italy. About in the middle of Italy, though rather to the west of centre—one side of the country has more harbours and a pleasanter climate than the other—stands the city of Rome. At the centre of Rome is the Forum, once the heart of a mighty road network, later abandoned save as grazing for cattle, now dug up to reveal a baffling array of broken columns and battered arches. And in the Forum once stood the heart of hearts, the centremost centre, of a world's communication system—the *milliarium aureum*, the Golden Milestone.

How many roads once radiated from this milestone! North and west from Rome a traveller could follow the Aurelian Way to Pisa, then the Way of Aemilius Scaurus to Genoa, then the Julian-Augustan Way, skirting the awkward edges of the Alps, out of Italy into France. The Domitian Way carried him on through the south of France into Spain; then the road went on and on, up and down, up and down the Spanish hills, and brought him to Cadiz—a city older than Rome, long used to exporting to the civilized East the grain and oil, the horses and cattle, the gold and silver of the half-barbarian West. Not far beyond Cadiz lay the edge of the known world, where the sun (it was said) could be heard hissing as it plunged into the sea in the evening, like a giant horseshoe quenched in a giant bucket.

Or if he wished the traveller could turn off Rome's 'Great West Road' in southern France, and instead journey north. He would leave the happy Mediterranean lands of long sunshine and short sharp rain-storms to enter a new and soggier world, where trees grew everywhere and the rain seemed to fall as if it would never stop. Yet even in this depressing country—'Hairy Gaul', it had once been called—Roman civilization had put down roots, and through it the road ran ever northward. From the small Gallic port of Boulogne a determined traveller could cross the Outer Ocean itself, defying its mysterious tides and currents, to the even smaller port of Dover, in an island that his ancestors had long regarded as half-mythical. This too now obeyed the orders of a Roman emperor.

Opposite: The Roman Forum

Roman Gaul's eastern boundary was the Rhine, then as now one of Europe's greatest highways. Roman roads followed it; Roman boats moved up and down it; Roman bridges crossed it. The river was a barrier, however, as well as a highway. Beyond it lay the wilds of 'Greater Germany', whose people, despite numerous Roman attacks, would not acknowledge the Emperor's authority. But though Roman government, Roman planned towns and Roman paved roads stopped at the Rhine, the far side was not the trackless wilderness that at first sight it seemed to be. Through Germany's gloomy woods and swamps well-defined routes led the Roman trader forward with his wine and pottery, and back again with the amber and furs he received in exchange.

Or instead the traveller could go south from Rome and take ship to Africa. Here another network of Roman roads awaited him, and flourishing cities with all the comforts of home life. Behind the familiar, though, lurked the exotic. North Africa was the Ancient World's safari-land, teeming with wild beasts and unusual plants: the mysteries of the 'Dark Continent' in those days reached almost to the Mediterranean. Beyond Rome's African frontier lay the desert, beyond that a country where almost anything might happen. There were tales of cannibals, of men with heads like dogs' or no heads at all, of men covered with hair, of mountains miles high that burned with strange fires or remained mysteriously snow-covered despite the incredible heat. The Roman soldier and the Roman businessman were slowly replacing fantasy with fact, but the African legend always seemed to stay one jump ahead of them. *Ex Africa*, as the elder Pliny remarked, *semper aliquid novi*—'out of Africa always something new'.

The road to the east was the most fascinating of all. To west and north and south Roman civilization confronted the 'barbarians'—people with everything to learn from Rome's example

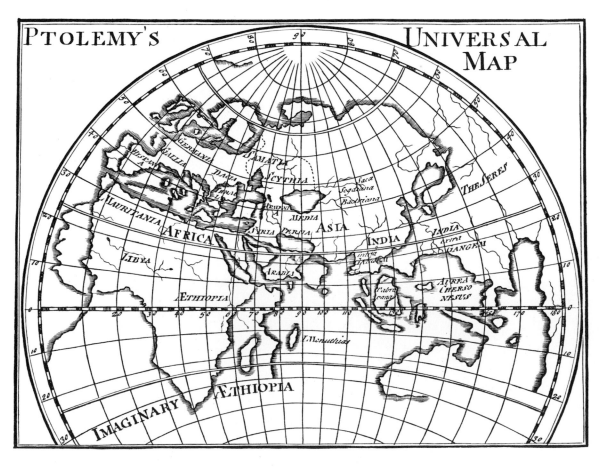

and little or nothing to teach in return. East, however, were lands from which Rome herself had learned civilization, peoples compared with whom the Romans themselves were the 'barbarians'. Here were the Greeks, who had brought civilization to half Europe; now, under Roman rule, they were supplying the Empire with artists, architects, musicians, doctors, scientists, scholars—and, as conservative Romans like Juvenal sourly remarked, a fair number of swindlers and social climbers.

> What do you take
> That fellow's profession to be? He has brought a whole bundle
> Of personalities with him—schoolmaster, rhetorician,
> Surveyor, artist, masseur, diviner, tightrope-walker,
> Magician or quack, your versatile hungry Greekling
> Is all by turns. Tell him to fly—he's airborne.

Beyond Greece were Rome's Asian provinces, where life became more complex still for the simple-minded Westerner. Here the Roman soldier, the Greek philosopher, the Anatolian bandit, the Syrian merchant and the Jewish rabbi met, quarrelled and fought—each quite unable to see the other's point of view. Instead of the sharp black and white of the western frontiers, with civilized Romans on one side and benighted barbarians on the other, the East was a many-coloured tapestry of interwoven ideas and habits. Some Romans liked it; many detested it; none could afford to ignore it.

Further east still were lands that resisted Roman arms as well as Roman ideas. There was Persia, with a centuries-long tradition of hostility to the West. There was India, which had

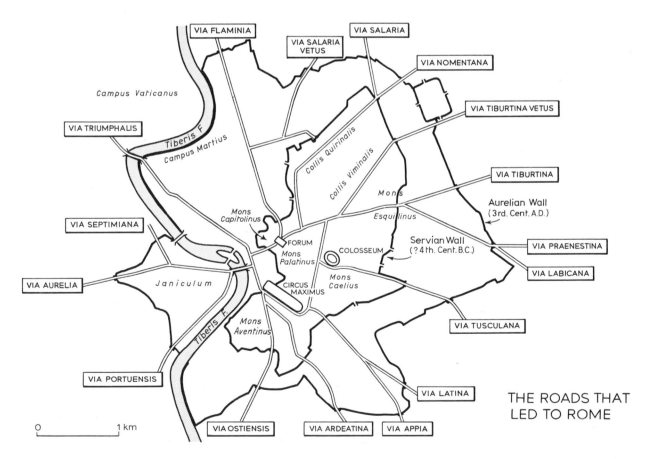

THE ROADS THAT LED TO ROME

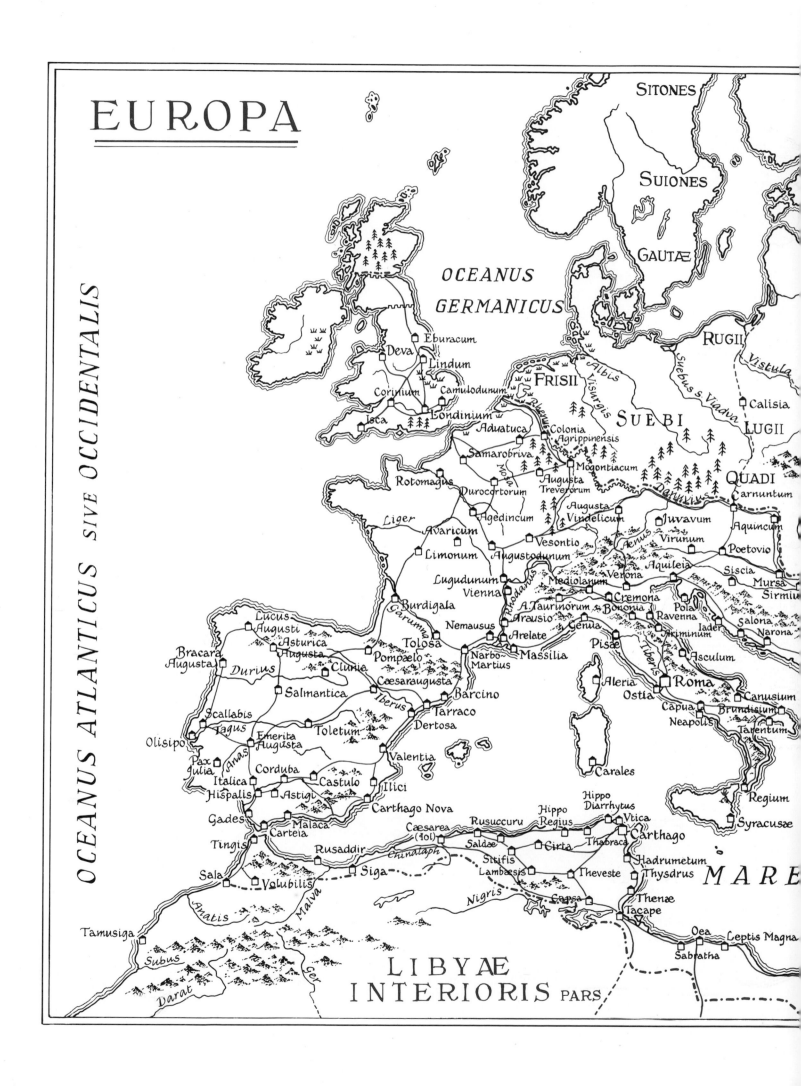

EUROPA

SITONES

SUIONES

GAUTÆ

OCEANUS
GERMANICUS

RUGII

Vistula

Suebus s. Viadua

Albis

Visurgis

FRISII

SUEBI

LUGII

Calisia

QUADI

Carnuntum

OCEANUS ATLANTICUS SIVE OCCIDENTALIS

Eburacum

Deva

Lindum

Corinium

Camulodunum

Isca

Londinium

Aduatuca

Colonia
Agrippinensis

Mogontiacum

Mosa

Augusta
Treverorum

Samarobriva

Rotomagus

Durocortorum

Augusta
Vindelicum

Juvavum

Aquincum

Liger

Avaricum

Agedincum

Vesontio

Aenus

Virunum

Poetovio

Limonum

Augustodunum

Lugudunum

Vienna

Rhodanus

Mediolanum

Verona

Aquileia

Siscia

Mursa

Sirmiu

Lucus
Augusti

Burdigala

Garumna

A. Taurinorum

Arausio

Genua

Cremona

Bononia

Pola

Ravenna

Salona

Narona

Asturica
Augusta

Tolosa

Nemausus

Arelate

Pisae

Ariminum

Iader

Bracara
Augusta

Durius

Pompaelo

Clunia

Narbo
Martius

Massilia

Tiberis

Asculum

Salmantica

Caesaraugusta

Iberus

Barcino

Aleria

Roma

Canusium

Scallabis

Tagus

Toletum

Tarraco

Dertosa

Ostia

Capua

Brundisium

Olisipo

Emerita
Augusta

Neapolis

Tarentum

Pax
Julia

Anas

Corduba

Valentia

Italica

Castulo

Ilici

Carales

Hispalis

Astigi

Regium

Gades

Carthago Nova

Hippo
Diarrhytus

Vtica

Syracusae

Carteia

Malaca

Caesarea
(Iol)

Rusuccuru

Hippo
Regius

Carthago

Tingis

Rusaddir

Chinalaph

Saldae

Cirta

Thabraca

Hadrumetum

Sala

Siga

Stifis

Lambaesis

Theveste

Thysdrus

MARE

Nigris

Capsa

Thenae

Tacape

Tamusiga

Subus

Malva

Anatis

Ger

Oea

Leptis Magna

Darat

LIBYAE
INTERIORIS PARS

Sabratha

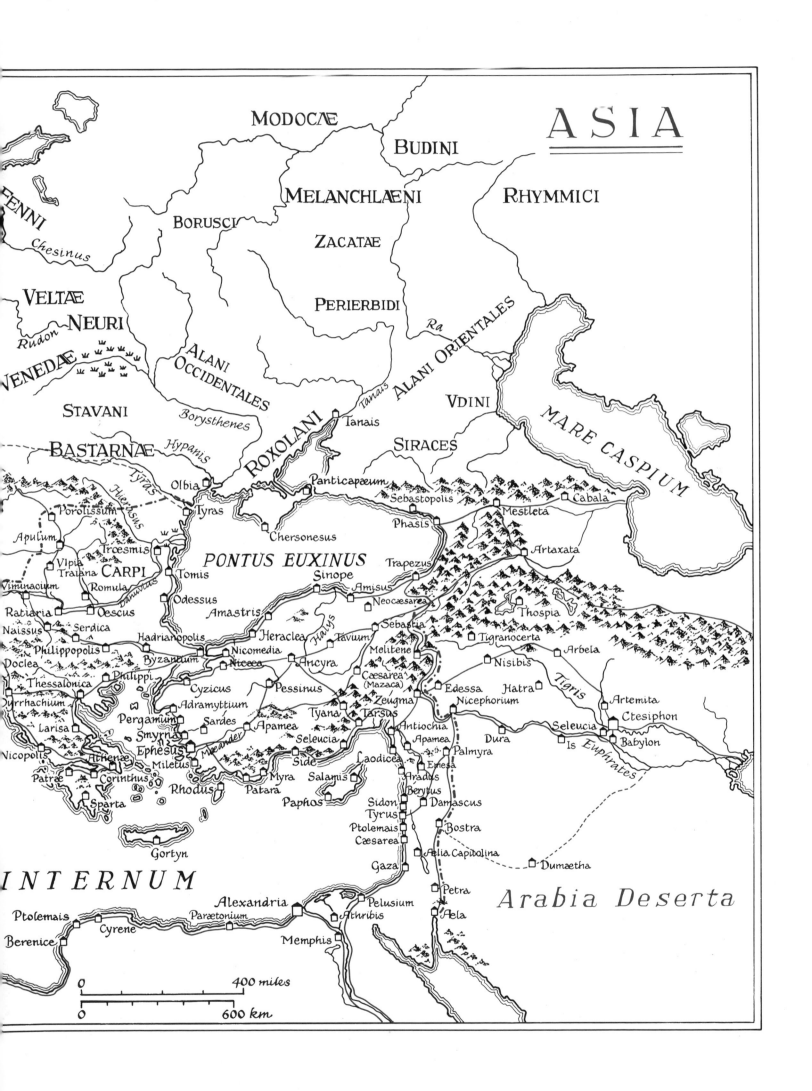

ASIA

MODOCÆ

BUDINI

RHYMMICI

MELANCHLÆNI

BORUSCI

ZACATÆ

FENNI

Chesinus

PERIERBIDI

Ra

VELTÆ

NEURI

ALANI ORIENTALES

VDINI

Rudon

VENEDÆ

ALANI
OCCIDENTALES

MARE CASPIUM

STAVANI

Borysthenes

ROXOLANI

Tanais

Tanais

BASTARNÆ

Hypanis

Cabala

Olbia

Panticapæum

Mestleta

Tyras

SIRACES

Sebastopolis

Porolissum

Huerhsus

Tyras

Phasis

Artaxata

Apulum

Troesmis

Chersonesus

PONTUS EUXINUS

Trapezus

Vlpia
Traiana

CARPI

Tomis

Sinope

Amisus

Vimiacium

Romula

Odessus

Neocæsarea

Thospia

Ratiaria

Danubius

Oescus

Amastris

Halys

Sebastia

Tigranocerta

Arbela

Naissus

Serdica

Hadrianopolis

Heraclea

Tavium

Melitene

Nisibis

Artemita

Philippopolis

Byzantium

Nicomedia

Ancyra

Cæsarea
(Mazaca)

Edessa

Hatra

Tigris

Doclea

Nicaea

Zeugma

Nicephorium

Ctesiphon

Thessalonica

Philippi

Cyzicus

Pessinus

Tarsus

Antiochia

Dura

Seleucia

Durrhachium

Pergamium

Adramyttium

Tyana

Apamea

Palmyra

Is

Babylon

Larisa

Smyrna

Sardes

Apamea

Seleucia

Emesa

Euphrates

Nicopolis

Ephesus

Meander

Side

Laodicea

Aradus

Athenae

Miletus

Myra

Salamis

Berytus

Damascus

Patrae

Corinthus

Rhodus

Patara

Paphos

Sidon
Tyrus

Bostra

Sparta

Gortyn

Ptolemais
Cæsarea

Ælia Capitolina

Dumætha

INTERNUM

Gaza

Arabia Deserta

Petra

Ptolemais

Alexandria

Paraetonium

Pelusium

Ælia

Berenice

Cyrene

Athribis

Memphis

0   400 miles

0   600 km

marvellous things for sale, but would accept nothing but gold in return, so that Roman Emperors worried continually about their balance of payments. Beyond India was China, from which came the silk that captivated Roman women and baffled Roman scientists—they could not even agree whether it was animal, vegetable or mineral. Few Romans ever realised it, but China was itself an Empire, larger, more populous and in many ways more sophisticated than their own.

This book is not a history of Rome. Rather it is a picture of the Roman world at the height of its wealth and power, in the middle of the second century AD—'the period in the history of the world', Gibbon called it, 'during which the condition of the human race was most happy and prosperous'. Sometimes we must look back, to see the steps by which Rome grew from a collection of huts to be the capital of a world power; sometimes the story must be carried forward, to show how, though the Roman Empire is no more, the ideas behind it have survived, to influence (among others) Charlemagne, Napoleon, Bismarck, the Hapsburgs, several British Prime Ministers and today's faceless bureaucrats of the EEC. However, many aspects of the Romans' history—their law, their art, their literature, their religion, their everyday life, their political problems and the causes of their final downfall—will hardly receive a mention at all. This is a book about communications: about how the Romans went from A to B and what they did at B when they arrived, about the towns that they built, the forts that they garrisoned, the resources that they discovered and exploited and the roads that linked all these into one coherent network.

Tradition has it that Rome was founded in 753 BC. The first few centuries of her history, however, need not concern us here. Many of the events ascribed to this early period are probably imaginary, and those that did occur had only local importance. It was not until the fourth century BC that the Romans, like an improved missile, extended their range from tens of miles to hundreds of miles and took their first steps towards becoming a world power. In 390 BC Rome was at the lowest point of her fortunes: most of the city was in ruins, sacked by the fierce Celtic tribesmen of the north, and there was even talk of abandoning the site altogether and making a fresh start somewhere else. Little more than a century later Rome had become the undisputed ruler of all the part of Italy that juts out into the sea, from Pisa and Rimini in the north to Reggio in the south.

The same period saw the building of the first Roman roads. These, like most of Rome's greatest achievements, were far from being a totally new idea. There had been routes of a kind in Italy—as, indeed, in most of Europe—well before the beginning of recorded history; more recently the Greeks had built an elaborate road system in southern Italy, as had the Etruscans in northern Italy. It was probably the Etruscans, indeed, who taught the Romans how to build roads (also drains, fortifications, temples and the first Roman houses built of stone instead of wattle and daub). The Romans, however, had a genius not for producing new ideas but for making the best of old ones; they carried on where the Greeks and Etruscans had left off, and ultimately produced a road system such as had never been known before and was not to be rivalled till many centuries afterwards.

Of the twenty-odd roads that eventually came to radiate from Rome, the oldest is the Via Salaria—the 'Salt Way'—following the river Tiber up into the mountainous interior of Italy: the second oldest may well be the Via Latina, running south through the rich land of Latium. Perhaps, indeed, these two are older than Rome itself, the city being founded at the point where they crossed. This would certainly explain the fact that from its very beginnings Rome, though a small town, was an important one, which all kinds of foreigners—Etruscans, Sabines, Gauls—wanted to seize and hold. But these early roads had nothing to distinguish them from thousands of others that wandered through all parts of the known world. The first road of the sort that we regard as characteristically 'Roman'—straight, paved and giving the impression throughout that Man, not Nature, was in charge of it—was the Via Appia, the famous Appian Way, begun in 312 BC by Appius Claudius the Blind. It linked Rome with the important city of Capua (modern Capua Vetere, not far from Naples), and was later extended south to Brindisi in the heel of the Italian boot, from which ships sailed regularly to Greece.

For some time the Appian Way was the only road of its kind; but gradually, over a century or so, more and more others were built in the same fashion. Some, like the Via Latina, were old routes now paved and reorganized *à la romaine*: some were new. The Via Aurelia, already mentioned at the beginning of this chapter, ran north from Rome up the Italian coast as far as Pisa. The even more important Via Flaminia went north-east, through the mountains, to emerge on the Adriatic seaboard; it terminated at Rimini, on the northern frontier of Rome's territory. The country beyond—what we now call northern Italy—was not then reckoned as a part of Italy at all: it was Gallia Cisalpina, 'Gaul on this side of the Alps', and its fierce inhabitants had long been a terror to the Italians of Italy proper.

Meanwhile Roman power was expanding overseas, largely at the expense of the great city of Carthage in what is now Tunisia. The first war between these two communities—the First Punic War, as it is technically called—was mostly fought in and around Sicily. In the course of

A Roman paved road

Above: Arch of Augustus at Rimini marking the junction of the Flaminian and Aemilian Ways

Opposite: Column at Brindisi marking the end of the Appian Way

Left: Two coins: coin of Caesar and coin of Pompey

18

it the Romans, usually regarded as a stiff-necked and inflexible people, performed an enterprising feat of adaptation. Starting almost from nothing (tradition has it that they used a wrecked Carthaginian ship as their first model) they made themselves into a sea-power. Enormous numbers of ships were lost in bad weather, but in battle the Romans nearly always gained the victory: by 241 BC Carthage, for all her centuries of sailing experience, had been driven off the sea by a nation of landlubbers. Sicily became the first province of Rome's overseas empire, and soon afterwards Sardinia, with Corsica, the second. Their inhabitants became not *allies* of Rome like the Italians, but *subjects*, ruled by a Roman governor and paying a regular tribute.

In the Second Punic War Rome had the misfortune to encounter a military genius, the great Hannibal, and came very close to disaster. Starting from Spain, Hannibal made his famous crossing of the Alps, entered Italy and defeated the Romans in four battles each more terrible than the last. Rome was saved largely by her network of roads and strongholds in central Italy, which Hannibal was unable to break. At length Roman successes outside Italy forced him to retire and defend Africa itself—where he was at last defeated. Rome gained two new provinces, along the south and east coasts of Spain, and soon afterwards was able to acquire yet another one in northern Italy. The Roman outpost at Piacenza on the river Po, whose founding had been interrupted by the arrival of Hannibal, was restored; and soon afterwards a new road, the Via Aemilia, linked it with the earlier outpost of Rimini. Though now paralleled by a railway and a motorway, this road is still in use today, one of the straightest and most obviously Roman of all Roman roads: it has even given its name—Emilia in modern Italian—to the whole district through which it runs.

One side-effect of the war with Hannibal was to have far-reaching consequences. Philip V of Macedon, for no very satisfactory reason, had joined in the war on Hannibal's side, thereby gaining the lasting hostility of Rome. Four 'Macedonian Wars' resulted, ending with the annexation of the kingdom to form yet another Roman province. A new military road was built across it, the Via Egnatia, first road of its kind outside Italy. But Roman expansion did not long stop at Macedonia: what Americans call the 'domino effect' came into play among the weak kingdoms of the East, and willy-nilly Rome found herself bringing more and more of them first under indirect influence and then under direct rule.

146 BC, the year after Macedonia became a province, was an important turning-point for Rome. It saw the destruction by Roman armies of two of the largest trading centres on the Mediterranean, Corinth and Carthage. (The fall of the latter city rang down the curtain on the Third—and very much Last—Punic War, and gave Rome yet another new province, called with simple grandeur Africa.) The wealth and power, the sophistication and vice, of these two great commercial cities poured into Rome.

The ensuing years were full of confusion and violence, as the Romans—like the Americans in more recent times—struggled to adapt a tradition of simple living, rugged heroism and small-town politics to the realities of running a world-wide empire. The wealth pouring in from Spain and Greece had made some Romans very rich, richer than their ancestors would have thought possible. But on the other hand, Rome's Italian allies were beginning to feel that they had done more than their share of fighting in Rome's battles and received less than their share of the rewards of victory; the government of the provinces was often shockingly rapacious; the class of *proletarii*—citizens with no property at all—was larger than ever before; and so too was the class at the very bottom of Roman society, the slaves. All these groups maintained a constant background of discontent, erupting on occasion into open warfare.

Rome's rulers faced opposition not only from their inferiors but from each other, and the amount of armed force involved in these disputes also increased alarmingly. In the last years of the second century BC the great general Marius reformed the Roman army, so that instead of being essentially a citizen levy it became a professional force—recruited largely from the *proletarii*. This, while greatly improving the army's quality, made it more dangerous not only to Rome's enemies but also to Rome herself. Henceforth a soldier's loyalty was not to the city of Rome, a place which he might never have seen nor have any cause to love, but to the commander who led him to victory, booty and a pension. A man with a strong army at his back could override the whole Roman constitution, and nothing could check his ambition save another man with an equally strong army. This particular problem was never wholly solved; the Army's influence, like Sherlock Holmes's 'scarlet thread of murder running through the colourless skein of life', pervades all the rest of Rome's history.

Marius himself became the first of Rome's 'warlords', maintaining himself in power, in defiance of the constitution, through his control of the Army. After him came Sulla, then Pompey the Great, then Julius Caesar. Caesar's murderers, Brutus and Cassius, fought his former supporters, Mark Antony and Octavian. Finally these last two fought each other. Octavian won, and in 30 BC was left in sole control of the Roman world—'the only man left on his feet', in Robert Graves' words, 'after an all-against-all sword-fight in the universal amphitheatre'. Three years later he took the title Augustus. He was the first Emperor of Rome, the most powerful man in the world.

Though he has never caught the layman's imagination as Julius Caesar has, Augustus' contribution to Rome and the world was more lasting and in many ways more important. In his long reign (forty-four years) he laid down guide-lines for the Empire which his successors were to follow for three centuries. The world depicted in the maps in this book is the world outlined by Augustus: later emperors filled in details which he, for the time being, had left blank.

The civil strife of the preceding years had done nothing to slow the growth of Rome's power; if anything, it had accelerated it, since a successful campaign against Rome's enemies was the surest way to supremacy in the city itself. In Asia, Pompey the Great had conquered Syria, Palestine and most of Asia Minor; all the land up to the river Euphrates was under direct or indirect Roman rule. At the other end of the Roman world Caesar had brought Roman rule to all Gaul, advancing Rome's frontier to the Rhine. Most recently, the fall of Cleopatra had brought Egypt into the Empire to become the largest, most populous and richest province of them all. In the early years of his rule, Octavian ran all Rome's far-flung territories himself; in 27 BC, however, he handed over some of the more peaceful and civilized ones to the Senate, while keeping direct control over the more backward ones (which, of course, contained most of Rome's armed forces). Thus arose the distinction between 'senatorial' and 'imperial' provinces, which we shall meet again several times in the course of this book.

Augustus himself carried on the tradition of his predecessors; he annexed much territory for Rome—northern Spain, the Alpine lands and all the country along the south side of the Danube. He also, however, gave much thought to frontiers. He was, in fact, the first ruler of Rome to propose that the Empire should have a fixed frontier at all; hitherto most Romans had pictured their country's power somewhat as we picture the Earth's gravity—radiating, though with diminishing force, to infinity. The Euphrates, the Danube and the Rhine became the limits of Roman rule, and in the years after Augustus' death only two significant advances were made

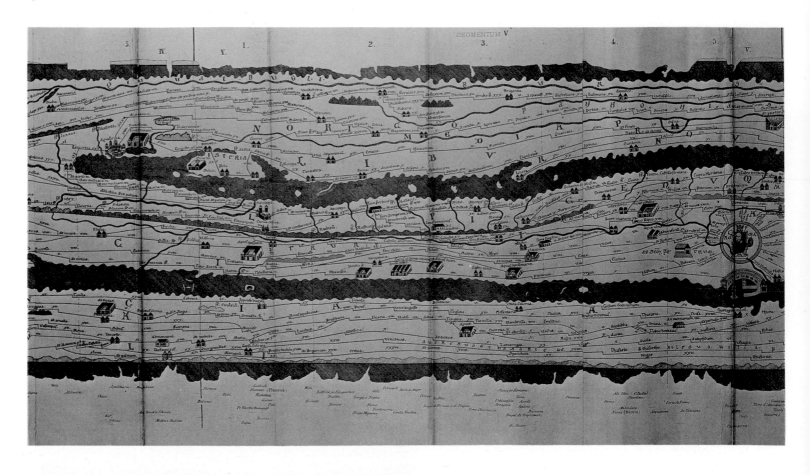

*Above: Part of the Peutinger table (see page 219).
The Danube lands are at the top, Italy in the
centre, with Rome near the right-hand edge, and
Africa at the bottom*

*Left: The city of Rome in the Middle Ages, only
about a quarter as large as it had been under the
Empire*

Opposite: Arch of Constantine at Rome

beyond them: Claudius' invasion of Britain in AD 43, and Trajan's conquest of Dacia (modern Romania) probably in AD 106, to form a salient province beyond the lower Danube.

Behind the frontiers grew up a network of towns with roads to link them, and in the building of these the army played a very large part. Indeed almost all Roman roads, from the Appian Way onward, had in their time been of military use, though many became purely civilian when the region they traversed was pacified and the armed forces moved on. But even in peacetime the soldiers were frequently called upon for building and engineering works. The Imperial Roman army could construct almost anything—roads, bridges, tunnels, forts, walls, canals and even buildings for purely peaceful use such as markets and bath-houses. It had its own potters, its own blacksmiths, its own carpenters and its own masons—a vast reserve of skilled labour, and in many of the Empire's outer provinces the only supply of skilled labour available. In peace as in war, for good as for evil, the army's influence was all-pervading.

Against this background, let us watch in imagination the actual building of a Roman road. The emperor, supreme head of everything, has called for one, and if it is a major road will honour it on completion with his own name—Via Claudia Augusta, Via Traiana, Via Hadriana. The provincial governor undertakes the administration. The army provides the skilled and some of the unskilled labour, supported in the latter by the local inhabitants—perhaps slaves, perhaps free citizens 'compelled to volunteer'. But there is still one link in the chain that we have not seen: who directs the actual work?

Enter, then, the Roman surveyor, the Roman architect and the Roman engineer—three modern professions often in those days combined in one man. His name is usually unknown to us; if any inscription about the building of the road survives, it will mention only the Emperor and perhaps the provincial governor. The 'Director of Works', however, was a very important and remarkable man, in whom Greek theory and Roman practice could be united with the happiest results. Vitruvius recommends that the ideal architect should know about arithmetic, geometry, astronomy, history, law, painting, music (regarded in the ancient world as a branch of mathematics, and useful for testing whether catapults and other siege-engines were properly strung) and philosophy, which made him 'high-minded and not arrogant but easy-going, fair, loyal and above all not greedy'. (Some modern architects and town-planners might benefit from an application of this last dictum.)

In addition, a first-class surveyor needed one further attribute not mentioned by Vitruvius— that mysterious quality, valued in our time by soldiers, archaeologists and fox-hunters, known as 'a good eye for country'. For though Roman roads are famous for straightness and on the whole *were* remarkably straight, they were not planned (as the Trans-Siberian Railway is said to have been planned) by the Emperor's drawing a ruled line on the map between two terminal points. The type of Roman road found in Britain, for example, is not dead straight from end to end, but more commonly consists of a series of straight sections, each joining the next at a slight angle. The surveyor's instruments were simple, the two principal ones being a portable sundial for fixing directions (the magnetic compass was as yet unknown) and a kind of cross-staff, called a *groma*, for determining straight lines. A much more elaborate and accurate device called a *dioptra*, akin to the modern surveyor's theodolite, was available if needed, but does not seem to have been widely used.

The surveyor's 'eye for country' could thus be more useful than his instruments. Suppose, for instance, that his road has to cross a river; where, precisely, should this be done? The narrowest

A Roman surveyor's staff (groma)

part of the river, which at first sight seems obviously the best place, has the drawback that where the stream is narrowest it will also be fastest and deepest. Better, perhaps, to choose a place where the water has spread itself a little and become shallower; but then the banks may be marshy, bringing new problems to the fore. Best of all, if it can be managed, is a place where gravel terraces fringe the river—so much better-drained, less boggy and soggy, than ordinary North European mud. The City of London, to name but one example, gained its first importance as the lowest convenient crossing place of a thoroughly awkward river. And for the crossing itself, would a ford (paved if necessary) be sufficient, or must there be a bridge? and should the bridge be of timber, brick or stone? Perhaps, if the army has urgent need of this particular line of communication, one might start with a bridge of boats, to be replaced in due course with something more permanent.

Suppose, instead, that the road is not crossing a river but following one—up into the mountainous lands of Switzerland, or Montenegro, or Wales, or Scotland. How, precisely, should it run? Not, certainly, right down along the river bank, where the ground will surely be unstable and enemies may come pouring down from the hilltops on both sides. Many a modern road, following such a low course, is overlooked by a Roman road much higher up on one side of the valley. But just how high should the road be? how can the basic principle, that a Roman road should be as straight as possible, be reconciled with the physical fact that contour-lines are usually not straight but curved, while cuttings and embankments, though buildable, will be costly in manpower, time and money? The surveyor must produce an answer; some of the answers he produced impress us even today.

Now the road approaches a mountain. (We shall assume for the moment that it is not a British road. Great Britain, by the standards of the world, is a remarkably flat country; its highest mountains, transported to the Mediterranean lands, would be accounted hills of very slight importance.) This mountain before us, suppose, is an Alp, and not even a Roman road will run straight up one face of an Alp and down the other. But the Roman surveyor can make a surprisingly close approximation to this ideal; steep gradients have no terrors for him. The users for which his road is built are not railway engines, nor motor-cars, nor even horses and carts, but the cavalry and infantry of the Roman army. (The army's heavy siege-engines are normally built on the spot, as near as possible to the place being besieged; no one will try to move *them* an inch further than is necessary.) So the road up to the pass-head can climb with an astonishing slope, using perhaps only three zigzags to reach the summit where a modern road may require twenty.

Then on the other side of the mountains comes a town. (Though on occasion important settlements grew up along Roman roads, the converse happened more often: roads were built to join towns that already existed.) It might be a famous town of the ancient world, as old as Rome or even older; it might be a tribal settlement, granted urban status by the Emperor and slowly developing from a huddle of huts into a city that the Empire might be proud of; or it might be an entirely new community, founded (like the road) by imperial decree—in which case our friend the Roman architect-surveyor would certainly have had a hand in building it. The great Augustus had set a tradition for emperors by planting new towns all over the Empire— more than any other ruler of Rome before or since; about 120,000 citizens, it is calculated, received land and new homes from him. Most of them were ex-soldiers, for on coming to power Augustus had found himself with far more fighting men than he needed. A succession of famous cities was built *for* the army and *by* the army, and often served a triple purpose. New towns under the Empire gave land to ex-soldiers—for to keep the army content had become even more important than before; they were often useful, as the early outposts of the Roman Republic

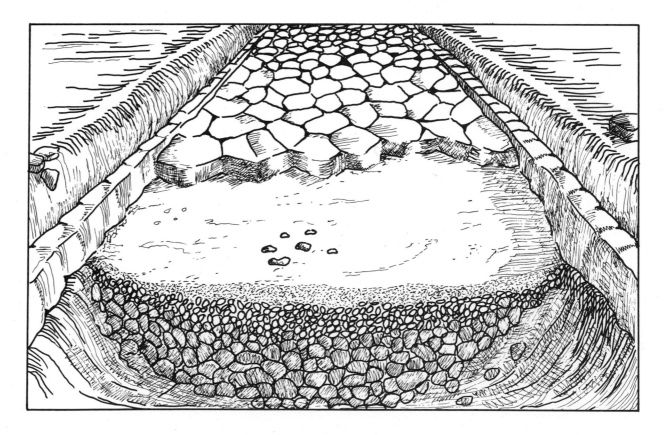

A detail of a Roman paved road

had been, in keeping a watch on newly-conquered and potentially hostile tribesmen; and they served as a model to these same tribesmen of what a properly organized Roman town should be like. The great city of Lyons was set up as an example to the Gauls; Cologne, to the Rhine-landers; Colchester, to the Britons (though these last learned the wrong lesson from their 'free sample', and began their revolt in AD 60 by burning it to the ground). Each time the Emperor's edict went out to found such a town the Roman surveyor would be there with his staff and sundial, ready to lay out its plan in accordance with the highest mathematical and religious principles.

Road-travel in the ancient world was tiring, building a new road even more so; let us say farewell to our imaginary surveyor as he returns home by the Empire's other communications system—a watery one, improved by Romans though laid out by Nature, and in many ways more important to the Empire than the much more famous land-based system.

For though the Roman road-builder's enterprise sometimes reminds us of his spiritual descendant, the nineteenth-century railway-builder, Roman roads were not railways and could never be as useful. The ancient world's top speed was that of a horse at full gallop, and at such a speed nothing could be carried save the horse's rider and a few light parcels. Goods on a slightly heavier scale could be carried by horse and cart; but this was not as easy as it might seem. Though the horse had been in use for some two thousand years and the cart for even longer, the ancient system for linking the two together left much to be desired. Roman harness was developed from an arrangement originally designed for oxen, with which it had worked excellently: but applied to horses this harness had an awkward habit of pressing on their windpipes and nullifying half their potential tractive effort—especially when a Roman horse and cart was trying to climb one of the slopes that a Roman engineer had thought not too steep for military traffic. If goods had to be transported by land, pack-animals were the normal means of doing so; but whenever it was physically possible, the wise trader replaced a hundred pack-animals by one smallish boat, to achieve the same result at a fraction of the cost.

Water transport on its largest scale, of course, involved braving the deep seas: but though the Romans had begun their rise to power by defeating Carthage at sea, they always regarded the 'blue water' with profound suspicion. Romans of the old school were not gamblers, and seafaring in the ancient world was a gambler's choice. With a fair wind, the traveller might reach

Left: Coin in honour of Agrippina the Elder, showing Roman cart

Alexandria from Rome in ten days; with a consistently unfair wind, he might need ten weeks. It is not for nothing that Europe's second oldest poem deals with the adventures of a man who tried to sail from Troy to Ithaca (some 500 miles by the shortest sea-route) and took ten years to do it. Ancient ships were not good sailers, and on a sea voyage the most alarming things could happen: the Greeks managed to tolerate and even enjoy the problems of the sea, the Romans never did. *Inland* water-transport, however, could combine the carrying capacity of water with the safety of the road; almost every town of any consequence in the Empire was built on some kind of watercourse, accessible if not to great ships at least to small boats.

Farewell, then, for the moment, to our anonymous Roman surveyor-architect-engineer, as he floats away down the river (the Rhine, the Rhône or the Thames, or perhaps a canal which he himself has helped to build). Away he goes. Behind him stand on one side Augustus, Caesar, Sulla, the Gracchi and all the eminent Romans who thought that new cities should be founded; on the other side Archimedes, Hippodamus, Aristotle, Plato and all eminent Greeks who discussed what a city, once founded, should be like. In front of him come the anonymous cathedral-planners of the Middle Ages, then a long row of architects whose name and fame are known to all. Let this be his epitaph, written some two thousand years after his death yet conveying the same spirit:

> If you had seen the country before the roads were made,
> You would lift up your hands and bless General Wade.

But in our book this great, though part-imaginary, Roman is not yet dead; more of what he did we shall presently see.

II

BRITANNIA

. . . And I was told by Doctor Lowe,
Whom Mr Wimpole's aunt would know,
Who lives in Oxford writing books,
And ain't so stupid as he looks,
The Romans did that little bit
And we did all the rest of it.
By which we hardly seem to score . . .

G. K. Chesterton, *The Flying Inn*

GEOGRAPHERS SOMETIMES DIVIDE Great Britain into a lowland and a highland zone, the former taking in southern and eastern England, while the latter is in three separate parts—Devon with Cornwall, Wales and the north. The lowland zone has a comparatively dry climate and, on the whole, rich heavy soil; the highlands have much more rainfall and a poorer soil. In Roman times there was a social distinction matching this physical one: the remains we find in the lowlands are mostly civilian, those from the highlands mostly military.

This distinction, though useful, can be and sometimes has been emphasised too much. 'Highland Britain' is not a solid mass of mountains; indeed the very highest peaks have always for obvious reasons been inhabited very thinly or not at all. Settlement concentrates, rather, in the river-valleys and coastal plains. In the past there was often seasonal migration, tribes moving with their livestock up to high pastures in summer and down again to more sheltered regions in winter. Several of the tribes which caused Rome the greatest trouble were of this sort—not 'mountainy men' pure and simple, but groups who controlled *some* low ground, enough to support a large and formidable population, yet at the same time had hill-country to which they could retreat when pressed by Roman armies. Such were the Silures, on the coastal plain of South Wales; the Brigantes, who spread all over northern England but had their heartland in the plain of York; and the Caledonians, who controlled the east coast plain of Scotland and had in addition all the Grampian Hills in which to wage guerrilla warfare.

'Lowland Britain', conversely, is not a dead level plain. In early times, indeed, many of its flatter parts were avoided, because they supported a dense growth of forest and the soil was too stiff to work with the tools available. Early settlement was most abundant where the soil was lightest and best drained—on the gravel terraces of the rivers, for example, on the chalk uplands of southern England, or on the limestone belt which runs diagonally across the Midlands. Important prehistoric routes—the Harroway, the Icknield Way, the Jurassic Way—followed these lines of high ground, the centre from which they radiated being Salisbury Plain, where we find Britain's most famous prehistoric monument. One of the Romans' greatest contributions to English history is their replacement of this road pattern by a new one of their own creation, much less affected by the nature of the ground it crossed, and centred not on the Stonehenge region but on London.

BRITANNIA

OCEANUS
HYPERBOREUS

Orcades
Insulae

OCEANUS
GERMANICUS

CORNOVII

LUGI

DECANTAE

Varar

Tuesis

VACOMAGI

Deva

TAEXALI

CALEDONES

Inchtuthil

Tava

VENICONES

Bodotria

Vallum
Antonini

Clota

Trimontium

SELGOVAE

Bremenium

Blatobulgium

Vallum Hadriani

Luguvalium

Corstopitum

Vedra

Vinovia

ROBOGDII

Vidua

Logia

Regia

VOLUNTII

ERDINI

BRIGANTES

Cataractonium

Isurium

Eburacum

OCEANUS

HIVERNICUS

Bremetennacum

NAGNATAE

Binvinda

Belisama

Petuaria

Abus

AUTINI

Eblana

Mona

Mamucium

Lindum

GANGANI

Senus

Buvius

CAUCI

Segontium

Deva
Deva

Aquae
Arnemetiae

CORNOVII

Trisantona

Mediolanam

Cetocetum

VSDIAE

Viroconium

Ratae

Venta I.

ICENI

IVERNI

Manapia

ALBION

Durobrivae

VELLABORI

Do-Bunni

Duroliponte

Dabrona

Magnis

Lactodurum

Moridunum

Isca

CATUVELLAUNI

Camulodunum

SILURES

Glevum

Corinium

Verulamium

Isca

Venta
S.

Tamesis

Londinium

Aquae
Sulis

Durobrivae

Rutupiae

Calleva

Durovernum

Castellum

BELGAE

Venta B.

CANTIACI

Dubris

Lindinis

Clausentium

Isca

DUROTRIGES

Noviomagus

Gesoriacum

Tarvenn

Tamarus

Durnovaria

Vectis

OCEANUS
VERGIONIUS

OCEANUS
BRITANNICUS

Samarobri

Coriallum

Juliobona

Caesaromagu

Rotomagus

OCEANUS OCCIDENTALIS

HIVERNIA

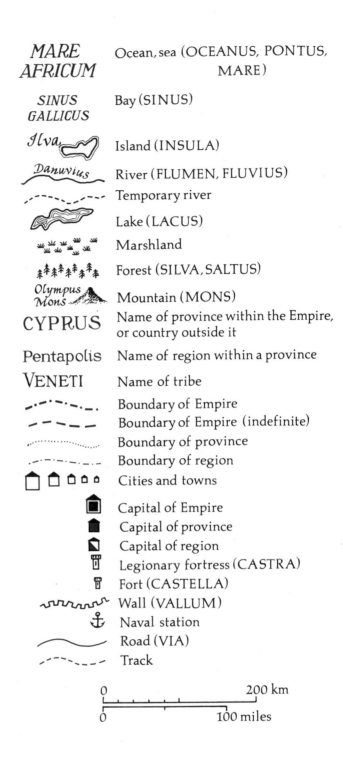

When the Romans first reached Britain, they found its inhabitants possessing a certain unity—all, except perhaps in the far north of the island, spoke the same language, and all had some knowledge of the use of iron—but varying widely in their general way of life. British prehistory is a story of new peoples, new techniques and new ideas entering the land from the Continent, spreading fairly rapidly through the lowland zone, but penetrating the highlands only slowly, so that the latter region long retains practices abandoned everywhere else. The most technically advanced tribes of pre-Roman Britain lived in the south-east: historians call them the Belgae, while archaeologists call their way of life 'Iron Age C'. They had introduced to Britain the first coins, the first pottery to be turned on a wheel instead of hand-made, and perhaps (though this is disputed) a new and heavier type of plough with which to work the heavy soils of the Midlands. North and west of the Belgic heartland were other tribes with a more old-fashioned way of life, 'Iron Age B'; further north and west still, in the highlands, lived tribes of even simpler habits, pastoral more than agricultural, whose basic pattern of existence—'Iron Age A'—had changed little for many centuries.

Though Julius Caesar's expeditions of 55 and 54 BC have the honour of being the first accurately dated events in British history, and brought him great kudos at Rome, they must, considered in their own right, rank among the least successful events in his career. On both occasions he failed to find a suitable harbour, and had to draw up his ships on an open beach, where many were wrecked by storms. In the first expedition the transports with the cavalry never reached Britain at all, and Caesar was left virtually marooned in east Kent, unable with his heavy infantry to make any impression on the fast-moving Britons. The second expedition, with a larger force, achieved more; it advanced through north Kent, forced the crossing of the

A reconstruction of a British chariot

Thames and captured an important Belgic stronghold (probably Wheathampstead, near St Albans). The tribe to whom this place belonged, the Catuvellauni, were forced to come to terms with Caesar; but they did not respect these terms for any length of time after he had gone away again.

The permanent conquest of Britain now became, so to speak, an item on Rome's military agenda, but for the time being there were far more urgent things to do nearer home. Not until AD 43—the second standard date in school history-books—was 'Operation Britannia' transferred, by the Emperor Claudius, from paper to practice.

The century between Caesar and Claudius had seen various political changes in Britain, but the same tribe, the Catuvellauni, was still the leader of anti-Roman feeling. They had expanded their power east to Colchester (which became their new capital), north to Northampton, west as far as Oxford or even further, and south into Kent, Surrey and Hampshire. An invasion of Sussex, however, proved to be one step too far; the deposed ruler of that region appealed to Rome, and the Claudian invasion was got under way.

Here, perhaps, while the invading army musters at the port of Boulogne, we may say a little about how it was composed. Altogether some forty thousand men were used, half of them legionaries and the other half auxiliaries—an important distinction to make in any account of the Empire's military history. Legions formed the backbone of a Roman fighting force. Each contained some five thousand men, nearly all infantry in heavy armour, slow-moving, liable to suffer in any kind of long-range combat, but almost invincible when hand-to-hand fighting began. Originally each legion had been distinguished only by a number (Caesar's crack legion, whose eagle-bearer was first ashore in the invasion of 55 BC, was called simply the Tenth), but during Rome's civil wars the numbering system had become confused, and legions of the Empire had both a number and a name. The four that embarked from Boulogne in AD 43 were called II Augusta ('the Emperor's Own'), IX Hispana ('the Spanish', after a country where it gained distinction), XIV Gemina ('the Twin', formed like some British regiments of today by amalgamating two older units) and XX Valeria (named after some member of the great Valerius family—possibly Claudius' wife, the Empress Valeria Messalina).

The auxiliaries, as their name implies, were originally intended to support the legions in battle, particularly in situations where rapid movement was required. Their fighting units were much smaller than legions (five hundred men was the usual size, one thousand occasional) and varied much more widely in appearance. Some consisted entirely of cavalry, others were all infantry, while others again had a combination of both. Many were originally recruited from a particular country or even a particular tribe (like the Gurkha regiments in the British Army today) and long preserved a traditional tribal dress and mode of fighting. Syrians, for instance, made the best archers; Africans, the best light cavalry; Gauls, the best heavy cavalry. A tribe called the Batavi, from the mouth of the Rhine, were particularly valuable in any operation that involved swimming or boating.

Claudius' intelligence service, more effective than Caesar's, had discovered an excellent harbour on the Kentish coast at Richborough, later to become Roman Britain's chief port. From here the Roman troops followed a course similar to Caesar's; moving through north Kent, they forced first the crossing of the river Medway (probably near Rochester) then that of the Thames (probably near London). Claudius himself supervised the capture of Colchester, the enemy's capital, now to be the headquarters of Rome's newest province, Britannia.

Working out the military history of Roman Britain is a laborious and thankless task. The

Above: Tombstone of a Thracian cavalry trooper

Left: Bronze figure of a Roman legionary, second century AD

Above: Aerial view of the fort at Richborough. The cross-shaped structure in the centre is all that remains of a monument set up by the Romans in honour of their landing in AD 43. The channel behind the fort used to be much wider than it is now

Right: Aerial view of the Fosse Way

written sources are very sketchy, and every time historians draw up a likely-seeming account, archaeologists make some new discovery that forces them to think again. In outline, however, what seems to have happened is as follows. The Twentieth Legion at first remained at Colchester —Base Camp One, so to speak—while the other three spread out in a three-pronged attack on the north and west of England. The Second Legion, under the future Emperor Vespasian, formed the left prong of the trident; it advanced into south-west England, storming many hill-forts, and at length established itself at Exeter, ready for an advance into the highlands of Devon and Cornwall. The Fourteenth Legion, in the centre of the advance, moved up the line later taken by Watling Street—north-westward, past St Albans and through the Midland forests to a base at or near Leicester—exactly where is uncertain. The Ninth Legion moved north along the line of Ermine Street: at first it seems to have been divided into several parts (as, indeed, the Second and Fourteenth may well have been, though the evidence in their case is less compelling) before concentrating into a single base at Lincoln. The two termini of this first Roman advance, Exeter and Lincoln, were joined by an important transverse route, the Fosse Way, proposed as the first frontier of the Roman province; it gave Rome control of nearly all lowland Britain, and any advance beyond it was likely to cost Rome ever more time and manpower for ever-decreasing returns.

The problem was, however, to persuade or compel the tribes of highland Britain to accept the Fosse Way as the frontier of an alien power's territory. On Rome's left wing, the Dumnonii of Devon seem not to have been a serious danger—written sources tell us nothing about wars against them, archaeological discoveries as yet very little. At the other end of the frontier line the Brigantes of northern England were for the time being well-disposed to Rome. The Welsh tribes confronting the middle of the Fosse Way, however, were persistently hostile, and troops had to be brought forward to deal with them. Legio XIV moved forward from the Leicester region, beyond the Fosse Way, to a new base at Wroxeter (near Shrewsbury) on the river Severn, well placed for an advance into the valleys of central Wales. Legio XX left Colchester, traversed the province and invaded south Wales; it established itself at Usk, ready for an advance up the river Usk into the heartland of the Silures, Rome's most powerful and dangerous enemies in Britain.

Just when the Roman conquest of Wales seemed to have reached completion (Suetonius Paullinus, governor of the province, had culminated it in AD 60 by capturing the Druid stronghold of Anglesey) a revolt on the other side of Britain brought the Romans back to where they had started, and very nearly threw them out of the island altogether. This famous revolt of Boudica (popularly, but wrongly, known as Boadicea) might, described by a historian of the right turn of mind, have given us an interesting exercise in the strategic use of Roman roads. Unfortunately Tacitus, our chief source for the period, has quite the wrong turn of mind from the geographer's point of view; preoccupied with high moral questions, he gives only the broadest outline of what happened, leaving many gaps that can be filled in only by guesswork. Boudica, queen of the Iceni in what is now Norfolk, launched her rebellion at a very favourable time, with the provincial governor and half the Roman army far away in North Wales. The Ninth Legion, stationed somewhere in the east Midlands, was the nearest to the uprising: its commander, Petillius Cerealis, led a force against the rebels—only to see it almost completely wiped out. The Second Legion, somewhere in the West Country, refused to leave its base, and it was left to Paullinus himself, with the Fourteenth Legion and part of the Twentieth, to meet and destroy the Boudican army (precisely where this happened is unknown). But by this time

Colchester, London and St Albans, the three largest towns in the province, had all gone up in flames.

After the suppression of Boudica's revolt came a period of peace and consolidation (scornfully dismissed by Tacitus as a period of idleness and ineptitude). No new territory was conquered, and in AD 66 the Fourteenth Legion (now called *Legio XIV Gemina Martia Victrix*, 'Martial' and 'Conquering' in honour of its British victory) was withdrawn from the province. This opened an awkward gap in Rome's frontier system. With four legions to hand, one could confront northern England, one north Wales, one south Wales and another the south-west; but with only three available, one legion would have to do the work previously done by two. It was probably at this time, therefore, that the fortresses at Exeter and Usk were abandoned; the Second Legion took up a new base at Gloucester, on the lowest crossing of the Severn, where (with good fortune) it could watch south Wales and Devonshire at the same time.

The seventies AD saw renewed Roman advance in Britain, under three successive governors of the highest military distinction. The first of these was Petillius Cerealis—the same man who had led the Ninth Legion to disaster against Boudica; since then he had atoned for this blunder with a brilliant campaign on the lower Rhine. He brought with him to Britain a new legion, II Adiutrix ('the Assistant Legion': it had been formed, hurriedly, from marines of the Roman fleet during the great civil war of AD 69). This legion moved into the fortress of Lincoln, whose previous occupier—the Ninth Legion—advanced to an entirely new base at York. The powerful Brigantes, rulers of all northern England, were defeated, and Rome gained a new foothold in the highland zone of Britain.

Cerealis was succeeded by Julius Frontinus, who set about a task that had been troubling Rome for nearly thirty years, the permanent conquest of Wales. The far south-west of Britain, it seems, was now reasonably peaceful, so with four legions once more in the province, three could be used against Wales, leaving only one to cover the northern frontier. Legio II Augusta pushed forward from Gloucester to a new base at Caerleon, on the Usk river, and harried the Silures of South Wales. Legio XX advanced up the Severn valley from Wroxeter. Legio II Adiutrix operated in north Wales, from a new headquarters at Chester—a port in those days, suitable for amphibious operations and well-placed for a fresh advance into northern England once the conquest of Wales was complete.

Frontinus left Britain in AD 78. He was something of a *rara avis* among the Roman nobility, in not considering the technical details of engineering as beneath his notice: his last official post was supervisor of Rome's water-supply, where he startled his subordinates by personally inspecting all the Roman aqueducts, and wrote a book on his findings. In the absence of any evidence one way or the other, it is pleasant to imagine that this interest in engineering may have come to him years earlier, while watching his soldiers build a road through Wales or lay water-pipes at Chester.

After Frontinus came the most famous of all Britain's Roman governors, Julius Agricola. Though this man has a whole biography to himself (written by his son-in-law, the historian Tacitus) we know remarkably little about what he did or what he was like. Sitting at dinner next to the martinet Paullinus, the dashing Cerealis or the technically-minded Frontinus, one could at least think of a remark to set the conversation going. Julius Agricola, as presented to us by Tacitus, has the depressing characteristic of appearing to tell us everything while in fact telling us virtually nothing. Still, he may have been a man as fierce in character as in his military achievements, and Tacitus may have censored his terser and more circumstantial remarks—

Roman road at Blackstone Edge, Yorkshire

Cuddie's crag on Hadrian's Wall in Cumberland

we, today, have no means of telling.

With his usual leaning towards generalities, Tacitus omits to tell us how Agricola actually began his campaign. In all probability, however, he launched it with a two-pronged attack on northern Britain –one force (probably the Twentieth Legion) moving up along the west side of the Pennines, and another (probably the Ninth) going up the east side, each building forts and roads to link them as it advanced. Wherever the ground permitted, a cross-link joined the two lines. One such ran over the Stainmore Pass, to link Catterick with Carlisle; another, now called the Stanegate, joined Carlisle to Newcastle; a third, not yet traced from end to end, followed the river Tweed; a fourth ran from somewhere near Edinburgh to somewhere near Glasgow, cutting across Britain at its narrowest part and forming a temporary frontier of the Roman province. Such a 'ladder pattern'—two main roads to form the shafts of the ladder, and cross-links forming the rungs—had been used by Rome many centuries earlier to maintain a grip on central Italy; it was to be used again, with equal effect, to hold much of North Africa in about AD 200.

In AD 83 Agricola pressed on beyond the Edinburgh–Glasgow line—the 'Highland Line' as it was later to be called—to attack the Caledonians of the far north. Here the 'ladder pattern' could no longer be used. Beyond the Clyde river the Scots mountains come right down to the sea, forming many capes and firths; two places may be a mile or two apart by boat, yet ten or twenty times that distance by road, and to build a route direct across the mountains, avoiding the promontories, was beyond the skill of even Roman engineers. Fortunately, however, the tribes of western Scotland seem to have been either friendly, or else too few to be a serious threat to Rome; at all events, hardly any Roman remains have yet been found in their territory. It was on

39

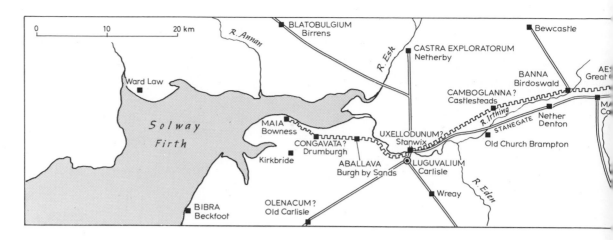

the east coast of Scotland, where the mountains leave a coastal plain between themselves and the sea, that the chief anti-Roman tribes mustered; and it was up the east coast that Agricola directed his next advance.

Here, again, he used a tactic well known to the Romans of the Republic centuries earlier. A single military road advanced up the east coast plain of Scotland, and wherever it crossed a large river, a Roman base was built to block the passage where the river emerged from the hills. The 'wild Highlandmen' could no longer pour down from their glens to ravage the eastern lowlands, and, even more important, should they be so unwise as to do so, could not return to the Highlands without confronting a powerful Roman force. Of all the rivers that come down to the sea on this coast, the longest and largest is the river Tay; and (though ancient geographers are somewhat vague on this subject) it seems to have been Strath Tay that held the Caledonians proper—the last major centre of anti-Roman feeling in Britain. Certainly a very important stronghold of a somewhat later period, Dunkeld (*dun* means 'fort' and *keld* means 'Caledonian') stood on the river Tay, and equally certainly it was where the Tay emerges from the hills that the Romans built their chief base from which to control Scotland—Inchtuthil, the most northerly legionary fortress known in the world.

In AD 84 Agricola at last met the Caledonian tribes in a pitched battle (at a place called Mons Graupius—the precise location is, unfortunately, unknown) and utterly defeated them. For a time it seemed as if Roman rule might extend all over Britain, but this was not to be. Soon after Agricola's recall from Britain war broke out on the Danube; Legio II Adiutrix had to be withdrawn from the province (it eventually based itself at Budapest); and the Roman forces in Britain fell back, first to the Forth–Clyde line, then further south still to the Stanegate, Agricola's road linking the Tyne to the Solway.

Early in Hadrian's reign the Stanegate line was reinforced by a continuous barrier—Hadrian's Wall, the strongest and best preserved of all Rome's frontier works. In its final form it was eighty Roman miles (rather over seventy English miles) long. Its eastern terminus was at the place now called Wallsend-on-Tyne, near Newcastle; its western end was at Bowness, on the Solway Firth west of Carlisle, with a line of forts and towers running further west still down the Cumbrian coast. Every third of a mile along the Wall there was a tower; every mile, a fortlet; every five miles or so, a full-sized fort. The garrison of the whole system was some 10,000 men.

Despite numerous books to the contrary, there is still (I suspect) an idea floating about in the layman's mind that Hadrian's Wall was built 'to keep the Picts and Scots out'—a kind of ancient Maginot Line, purely defensive, and like all purely defensive works doomed to failure. This

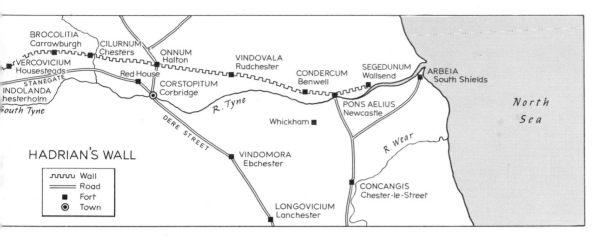

idea is totally wrong. Apart from the obvious error in the dates (neither Picts nor Scots are mentioned till some centuries later) the Wall as originally planned was not purely defensive; Roman armies of the time did not wait in their forts to be attacked, but frequently carried the war into their enemies' country. Besides, the Wall was a barrier that faced both ways; the tribes immediately to the south of it were quite as violent and anti-Roman as those to the north of it. It was only a part, though the most impressive part, of a military network that reached right down to York and Chester, and at times right up to Edinburgh and Glasgow. And finally, Hadrian's Wall cannot be called a failure. It protected Roman Britain for nearly three centuries, becoming useless in the end not because its defenders had acquired a 'Maginot mentality' but because they had been withdrawn to an entirely different part of Europe.

The map early in this chapter shows a short-lived situation dating from the reign of Hadrian's successor Antoninus Pius, when for a few years Rome reasserted control over the south of Scotland. Hadrian's Wall for a while ceased to be the frontier, and a new barrier was built following Agricola's old frontier line between the Forth and the Clyde. This 'Antonine Wall' was only about half as long as Hadrian's, some thirty-five miles in all; it was much less substantial, and built throughout of turf instead of stone. It had forts along it—but considerably smaller ones. Its exact date is controversial, but it would seem to have been built in about AD 140, abandoned in 155, held again from about 160 to 165, then abandoned once more, this time for good. Thereafter Hadrian's Wall formed the frontier of the Roman province.

Rome's military history has taken up a large part of this chapter, but appropriately so; throughout its existence Britain was very much a military province. Garrisoned by three or four legions with a large number of auxiliary troops, it was one of the highest commands to which a Roman officer could aspire, rivalled in importance only by Pannonia and Syria. Large tracts of the province—Wales and northern England—were dominated entirely by military constructions, the native tribes never developing settlements of any consequence; and even in the south and east, where a flourishing civil life did spring up, the Roman army exerted much influence on it by choosing the sites of towns, laying out their buildings and causing them to grow.

Four towns—Colchester, Lincoln, Gloucester and York—had a special status as Roman *coloniae* or 'colonies', towns founded by official decree of the central government. All had strong military connections. Colchester, the oldest, had been first an important pre-Roman centre and then the headquarters of the Twentieth Legion; the emperor Claudius inaugurated the civil settlement when the troops moved out. Lincoln and Gloucester were similarly founded on the sites of

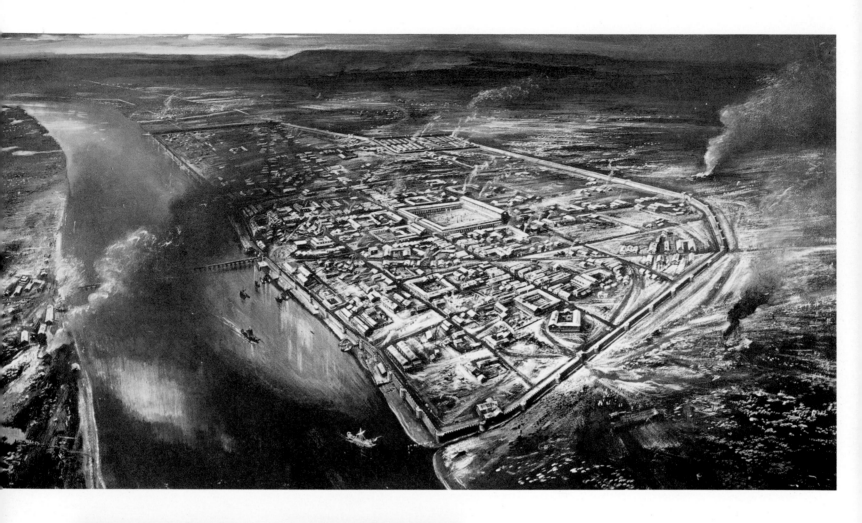

Above: Reconstruction by Alan Sorrell of Roman London in the fourth century AD

Left: Roman lighthouse at Dover

Opposite: Roman baths at Bath (since the photograph was taken, the baths have been drained and interesting material found underneath)

disused legionary bases, one by Domitian and the other by Nerva, in the late nineties AD. At York the pattern was a little different, the civil settlement being not on top of an abandoned military base, but alongside one still in use. When it received the title of *colonia* is not known.

Though not of outstanding size (many native towns were much more extensive) the *coloniae* may have had an importance greater than one would deduce from surface area alone. Being built *by* Romans *for* Romans, they may well have had more closely-packed buildings, and perhaps taller buildings, than towns of other sorts. York became a provincial capital in about AD 200, as did Lincoln about a century later; all four towns were important in the Middle Ages, and all but Colchester are county towns today.

London, the capital and largest town of the province, was something of an anomaly. From its position at the lowest convenient crossing of the Thames, one might have expected it to be an important pre-Roman settlement, but no trace of such a thing has yet been found. It seems to have grown by itself, soon after the Roman conquest, as a mercantile town—grown so fast, indeed, that one might almost call it a boom town. At the time of Boudica's revolt, less than twenty years after the conquest, it already had some 30,000 inhabitants and was the seat of the province's financial administration. Soon rebuilt after the Boudican destruction, it flourished more than ever, eventually replacing Colchester as the headquarters of the provincial governor, but its exact status in the Roman hierarchy of cities is still something of a mystery.

The other type of large town found in Roman Britain was the tribal capital, for the Britons, like their kinsmen in Gaul, had the habit of forming large tribal groupings each with a single central meeting-place. Whereas in Gaul, however, the tribes had on the whole been allowed to develop their towns in their own way without intervention from outside, tribal capitals in Britain were often strongly influenced by the Roman military presence. Though some of them (St Albans, Canterbury, Silchester) had been places of consequence before the conquest, many had not. For example, the large town of Wroxeter began its existence as a Roman legionary fortress, turning into a civil settlement (and capital of a tribe called the Cornovii) only after the troops had moved on. The even larger town of Cirencester likewise had military beginnings, this time as a cavalry fort on the Fosse Way. The local tribe here, the Dobunni, had their headquarters a few miles away at a place called Bagendon, which gradually went out of use. Further south, similarly, Dorchester in Dorset replaced the great Iron Age hill-fort of Maiden Castle. The *Pax Romana* made hill-top settlements of this kind inconvenient and unnecessary, and round any Roman military base the natives would find jobs to be done, money to be earned and all kinds of useful contacts to be made.

Communications in some modern nations are centralized, in others decentralized. The great road and rail arteries of England, for example, radiate from London; one can travel towards the capital, or away from it, but to travel in any other direction can be remarkably difficult. French communications likewise centre on Paris. West Germany, by contrast, is decentralized; its towns are linked and cross-linked by many roads with no one outstanding nodal point.

Communications in the lowland zone of Roman Britain were—then as now—centred on London, which the Romans seem to have planned almost from the very beginning of their conquest as the chief nodal point of their road system. From London one road ran south-east, through north Kent past Rochester to Canterbury, along the line followed by the armies of Caesar and Claudius; at Canterbury the route split into three branches, to the three British Channel ports—Lympne, Dover and (most important of all) Richborough.

Another Roman road, now called Stane Street, left London in a south-westerly direction, to link it with the important town of Chichester in what is now West Sussex. Between the two ends of this road were no towns of any consequence whatever; it ran through the empty country that the Romans called *Anderida Silva*, the Saxons *Andraedeswald*, the modern Weald of Sussex, then a vast forest inhabited only by a few iron-workers and charcoal-burners.

A third road, forerunner of the Great West Road though not on exactly the same line, left London in a westerly direction to cross the Thames at Staines and eventually reach Silchester. This latter is one of the few towns of Roman Britain that has no modern settlement either on top of it or close by it. The site is fairly near Reading, fairly near Basingstoke and fairly near Newbury. As a road centre it was in some respects better placed than any of the towns that have replaced it in our own time, and Roman Silchester, after London, was perhaps the most important nodal point in all lowland Britain. It was linked to Chichester, to Winchester, across Salisbury Plain to Dorchester, from which one could travel along the Second Legion's military road to Exeter and eventually right down to Land's End, to the small but much-visited spa town of Bath, to Cirencester, second city of the province, and northward to the Thames valley and Watling Street.

This latter street, perhaps the most famous Roman road in Britain, is still partly in use today; the A5 follows it in places, and its line is closely paralleled by the M1 motorway and what used to be the London and North Western Railway. Having linked London with St Albans, it passed over the Chiltern hills and traversed the sparsely-peopled forests of the Midlands to reach the flourishing city of Wroxeter (near Shrewsbury, on the river Severn). The last stage of the road ran north from Wroxeter to Chester.

Ermine Street, like Watling Street, is still an important line of communication in our own time; the Great North Road (A1) runs very close to it, as does the old Great Northern Railway. For the first seventy miles of its course north from London the road served no place of any consequence. Where it crossed the river Nene, however, stood the important town of *Durobrivae*, 'the walled town by the bridges', modern Water Newton, near Peterborough. This region, from the third century onwards, was a great centre of pottery manufacture; in fact clay from the Peterborough area is still in use today, though now not for pots but for bricks. After Water Newton the next large town was Lincoln. To reach the terminus of the route, York, one had to diverge either to the east (crossing the Humber estuary by ferry) or to the west, via Doncaster and Tadcaster. A straight road would have become bogged in the marshes where many sluggish rivers enter the Humber.

The last of the great roads radiating from London was the eastern road, closely followed in more recent times by the Great Eastern Railway, via Chelmsford to Colchester and thence to a place called Caistor-by-Norwich, chief place of Rome's old enemy the Iceni. This part of England is potentially one of the most productive of all, as admirably suited to arable farming as the West Country is to stock-rearing. In Saxon and early Norman times East Anglia was one of the most populous parts of England, Thetford and Norwich two of its largest cities; the latter retained a place well up in the top ten of English towns right down to the Industrial Revolution. In Roman times, however, a curious blight seems to have hung over the whole area. Caistor, the predecessor of Norwich, was among the smallest tribal capitals in the province. Colchester, as we have seen, lost its status as provincial capital to London. Chelmsford may have been planned by the Romans as a major city in its own right (it bore a very grand name, Caesaromagus or 'Caesar's market', of a type otherwise unknown in Britain but given to many tribal capitals in Gaul) but if this was the Roman plan, it was not fulfilled by events; Chelmsford never became more than a modest town of the second rank. To some extent the depressed state of the area can be explained by the revolt of Boudica and Roman reprisals after it, but it still seems surprising that the effects of these should have lasted such a long time.

One part of eastern England with an unusual pattern of settlement was the Fenland. In the Iron Age, and again in Saxon times, much of this region was too marshy to have any inhabitants at all, but the Romans, partly through superior engineering skill, partly thanks to a temporary improvement in the climate, were able to drain some of the marshland and grow corn on it. It seems likely, from the systematic nature of the work, that it was directly organized by the central government, the drained land becoming the personal property of the emperor. An important canal, the Car Dyke, ran from near Cambridge up to Lincoln, whence another canal, the Foss Dyke, reached the river Trent. Bargeloads of Government grain, one may imagine, went up this water system to feed the legion at York and the auxiliary troops still further north—coming back, perhaps, laden with coal from the neighbourhood of the Wall.

London was not quite such an all-controlling road centre in Roman times as it is today. Though most roads in the lowland zone of Britain ran to or from it, the highland zone had a system of its own based on an entirely different principle, and the boundary between the two, the great road now called the Fosse Way, was not directed towards London at all; it ran diagonally across the country from Exeter in the south-west, via Ilchester, Bath, Cirencester and Leicester, to Lincoln in the north-east. Beyond the Fosse Way, roads tended to be decentralized, crisscrossing in a complex network with no obvious key points. Roads in these wild parts of Britain were barriers as well as highways, meant not only to help the movement of Roman armies but also to hinder the movement of Rome's enemies. Should the Silures or the Brigantes wish to muster their clans in revolt, they would find their gatherings watched by Roman patrols, blocked by Roman forts at key positions and broken up before they had time to form.

Wales was gripped in a rectangular framework of roads. The south-east corner of the frame was Gloucester; the south-west, Carmarthen (chief place of a tribe which unlike the others in Wales seems to have been pro-Roman); the north-west corner of the frame was Caernarvon; the north-east, the great fortress of Chester. Inside the frame many roads, some not yet located throughout their length, crossed in a complex network.

The road system of the north has already been described. It was built like a ladder, the shafts being the two great highways running north from Chester and York, while the rungs were roads cross-linking them wherever the form of the country permitted. Beyond the Antonine Wall the west coast route could go no farther. The eastern route, however, pressed on in a great loop right round the Grampian Highlands, perhaps reaching as far as Elgin or even Inverness. The northern part of this route was merely a track, probably never made into a paved road, but its course can be clearly seen from the line of Roman marching-camps that stand along it.

Further north still, beyond the Great Glen of Scotland, no Roman sites have been found. Yet even the tribes of these remote parts were not completely cut off from the rest of the world. One chief of the Orkney Isles sent an embassy to Claudius almost immediately after the conquest of Colchester, when the Roman forces were still some five hundred miles from his territory. In 84, the year of Agricola's last campaigns in the far north, a Roman fleet subdued the Orkneys and came within sight of the Shetlands—identified with the mysterious island of Thule, at the northernmost fringe of the known world. Though Roman direct rule never reached so far north, Roman trade and Roman political influence pressed on, far beyond the Empire's military frontier.

III

HISPANIA

Spain is a country where large armies starve and small ones are beaten.

The Duke of Wellington

ROM VERY EARLY TIMES the Iberian peninsula has been famous (or infamous) for the extreme badness of its communications. In complete contrast to neighbouring France, which as ancient geographers noted seems almost designed by Nature to make long-distance travel across it as easy as possible, Spain is shaped in such a way as to make any kind of communication as *hard* as possible. First, it is extremely mountainous. The average elevation of its surface is greater than that of any other European nation except Switzerland. Then, the river valleys that break up this mass of mountains do not fit together, as the rivers of France do; each forms a self-contained little box, and to cross from one box to another generally involves negotiating a high and difficult mountain pass, racked by bad weather and often infested with bandits.

A further difficulty of the land as seen by its early explorers (men from the Levant, from Greece and later from Italy, but all reaching Spain via the Mediterranean) is that it faces the wrong way. Most of its principal rivers—the Guadalquivir, the Guadiana, the Tagus and the Douro—rise on the eastern side of the peninsula and flow away westward to enter the Atlantic, an ocean with tides, prolonged storms and vast empty spaces, all very alarming to the mariner brought up on Mediterranean navigation. The 'Pillars of Hercules' (the Rock of Gibraltar on one side of its strait, and the hill of Ceuta on the other) long marked the boundary between the known world of the Mediterranean and the half-known or unknown world of great 'Oceanus'; a voyage beyond them was always something of an adventure. There was *one* large Spanish river, the Ebro, that flowed the right way from these early travellers' point of view, and this one gave its name (spelt Iberus in ancient times) to the whole country. Iberia, to the early Greeks, was the land of the river Iberus, just as India, at the opposite end of the world they knew, was the land of the river Indus. But to ascend the Ebro valley led one only into the mountainous wilderness of the Cantabri, in the far north of Spain, from which land it was extremely difficult to move in *any* direction. The Cantabri in their remote fastnesses remained virtually untouched by civilization until the Romans conquered them in the last years BC.

The early history of Spain involves four different groups of people—the Iberians, the Celts, the Phoenicians and the Greeks. The Iberians, a somewhat mysterious race, are thought to have entered Spain from Africa round about 2500 BC. Their language, the ancestor of modern Basque, is so far as we know unrelated to any other form of speech, ancient or modern. The

Celtic-speaking tribes entered the land from the opposite direction, over the Pyrenees, in a series of incursions between the eighth and sixth centuries BC. The Phoenicians, coming by sea from the Levant, are traditionally supposed to have set up their first and most important Spanish trading post (Gadeira or Gades, the modern Cadiz) as early as 1100 BC, though archaeological study would suggest a much later date. Besides Cadiz, the Phoenicians also founded outposts at Malaga, Almuñecar (anciently called Sexi) and Ibiza in the Balearic Isles. Finally, the Greeks appeared on the scene in the sixth century BC. Their foundations included a town called simply Emporion or 'The Market', now known as Ampurias and preserving an unusually complete collection of remains. The port of Alicante (called Akra Leuce or 'The White Cape' by the Greeks, Lucentum by the Romans) is also of Greek origin, but about its ancient appearance virtually nothing is known.

In about 535 BC the Phoenician colony of Carthage beat the Greeks decisively in a sea-battle off the town of Alalia in Corsica, and thereby gained a monopoly of trade in the western Mediterranean. This was to persist until the third century BC, when it was violently—and successfully—challenged by the rising power of Rome.

In 241 BC the Romans crowned their first great victory over Carthage by annexing most of Sicily. Three years later they went on to seize Sardinia and Corsica. Among the more eminent of Carthaginian generals at the time was one Hamilcar Barca. Passionate in opposition to the growing Roman Empire, he set out to Spain to 'bring in a new world to redress the balance of the old'. (At about the same time he had imposed on his son an oath of eternal hostility to Rome. This little boy's name was Hannibal; we shall hear more of him presently.)

Launching himself from the ancient Phoenician base of Cadiz, Hamilcar set about the conquest of southern Spain. The campaign cost him his life, but under his son-in-law Hasdrubal it continued. In 227 BC the small Iberian town of Mastia was taken over, enlarged and renamed New Carthage (*Carthago Nova* in Latin, Cartagena in modern Spanish). All the east coast of Spain as far as the river Ebro came under Carthaginian control, and a treaty officially established that river as the boundary between Roman and Punic spheres of influence.

On Hasdrubal's death the Carthaginian 'Army of Spain' was taken over by a man of still greater military ability, none other than the great Hannibal. He at once plunged deep into the interior of the country, crossing the Tagus river and reaching as far as Salamanca, over three hundred miles from the Mediterranean. He then turned back to the east coast, to attack the one town in these parts that still resisted him, Saguntum, now called Sagunto, near Valencia. But the Saguntines appealed to Rome, and the Romans intervened. (How they reconciled this in their own minds with the earlier treaty, whereby Saguntum, being far to the south of the Ebro, should have been closed to Roman interference, remains something of a mystery.) Be that as it may, the clash over Saguntum led to open war between Rome and Carthage.

Though the most famous battles of this 'Second Punic War' were fought in Italy, the Spanish theatre of war was quite as important as the Italian. Two important lines of communication were involved. One was the route down the east coast, from Ampurias near the Pyrenees down past the Ebro, past Saguntum where the conflict had begun, past Alicante, to the great Punic headquarters at New Carthage. The second route branches off this first one, climbing into the interior and passing through difficult country before descending again into the valley of the Guadalquivir, which it then follows down to Cadiz. It was along these two routes that the armies marched and countermarched, each side trying to push the other back.

The Roman forces, under the brothers Scipio, at first did well. After winning an important battle near Tortosa, on the lower Ebro, they were able to advance beyond it and at length recapture Saguntum. But an attempt to advance up the 'Road to the Interior' ended in disaster: deserted by their Spanish allies, the two brothers were separately surrounded and killed on the barren uplands of south-east Spain.

Rome's response was to send out a fresh army under yet another member of the Scipio family—the future conqueror of Hannibal, later to be dignified with the title *Africanus*. Soon after his arrival in Spain this energetic young man scored a notable success by storming the great Punic base at New Carthage, thereby bringing the whole of the east coast under Roman control. He then led his forces into the interior, as his father and uncle had done, but managed to avoid the fate that had befallen them. He reached the valley of the Guadalquivir safely, and there broke the remaining Carthaginian armies in two great battles, Baecula (Bailen), on the upper course of the river and Ilipa (Alcala del Rio), further downstream near Seville.

Rome's final victory in the war gave her two new provinces. The east coast formed the province of *Hispania Citerior* or 'Nearer Spain'; the south coast, with the rich valley of the Guadalquivir, made up *Ulterior* or 'Further' Spain. The governors of both provinces soon found themselves in difficulties. Beyond the frontier of Further Spain lived the powerful tribe of the Lusitani, who repeatedly invaded Roman territory and responded to Roman counter-attacks with guerrilla warfare (at which all Spanish tribes, even in those early times, were highly adept.) The most formidable of their leaders, Viriathus, launched a 'war of movement' that spread itself right across the centre of the peninsula; his operations reached from Segovia in the north to Cordoba in the south, and from the Atlantic Ocean in the west to the headwaters of the Tagus in the east, covering an area about the size of England. They ended only when the Romans contrived to have him murdered.

The province of Nearer Spain faced equal threats. The Roman forces succeeded in advancing fairly steadily up the river Ebro; but the valley of this river is shut in, as already mentioned, like the Light Brigade, 'mountains to right of them, mountains to left of them, mountains in front of them'. The tribesmen to the right, in the Pyrenees, seem to have been too few to be a danger; at all events we hear little of their military activity. The tribesmen ahead, the Cantabri, remained for the time being remote from Roman affairs. But the mountains on the left of the valley very soon attracted Roman attention. They were known in ancient times as Mons Idubeda; today some of them are called the Montes Universales, the 'All-Embracing Mountains'. Many a Roman soldier, desperately fighting his way through them, might have thought the modern name of this range an all-too-appropriate description, for the local inhabitants, collectively known by the rather indefinite name of 'Celtiberians', were among the most formidable fighting men in guerrilla warfare *and* in pitched battle to be found in all Spain.

The Romans, confined in their box of the Ebro valley, had two ways of breaking out and establishing their presence in different boxes. If one ascended the Ebro as far as the Iberian town of Salduba (later renamed Caesaraugusta, now called Saragossa and still an important natural crossroads) it was possible, soon afterwards, to turn left and ascend a river called the Jalon, a tributary of the Ebro, up as far as its source. (Not far from the summit of this pass, at a place called Medinaceli, stands a large and well-preserved Roman triumphal arch. And the anonymous Roman soldiers in whose honour it was built well deserved it.) Soon after Medinaceli one meets a river called the Henares, which flows into the Tagus, which flows all the way to the sea. Its valley broadens out, enabling Roman forces from Nearer Spain, descending the river, to join

Above: Roman bridge at Espot in the Pyrenees
Below: Roman arch at Medinaceli

Above: Roman bridge over the Tormes at Salamanca
Below: Aqueduct at Tarragona

hands with the army of Further Spain that had discovered the lower course of the river by working northwards from Cadiz.

This line of communication is still important today; it is followed by a railway and a major road. The Romans had another route, however, which today is followed only by a minor road, but which in its time had greater military importance than the 'Road to the Tagus'. This one worked its way through the 'All-Embracing Mountains' a little further north than the Tagus road, to strike another river almost as long as the Tagus, and with an equally broad and potentially prosperous valley—the great river called Durius by the Romans, Duero by the Spaniards and Douro by the Portuguese—the name, apparently Celtic, meaning something like 'hard' or 'tough'. To reach the valley of the Douro, at all events, proved a very hard and tough task for the Roman armies. Near the source of the river stood a town called Numantia, whose inhabitants were passionately hostile to Rome and resisted overwhelmingly numerous Roman armies for ten years. Scipio Aemilianus (the grandson of Hannibal's conqueror) at length starved the town into submission, but only after a siege that lasted eight months, with 60,000 Romans confronting a mere 4,000 Numantines.

The destruction of Numantia (in 133 BC) gave the Romans control of about two-thirds of the peninsula, with which they remained content for about another century. These years were occupied more with civil than with foreign war, as Rome's great men began to realise the tremendous power that lay at their feet if they could only pick it up before their rivals did. Spain was involved in civil war in the seventies BC, when a general named Sertorius set himself up there as a sort of uncrowned king, resisting repeated attempts by the Roman central government to dislodge him, till at length he was murdered by his own men; and the great war between Caesar and Pompey involved two Spanish campaigns, one culminating in the battle of Ilerda (Lérida) in 49 BC, the second in the battle of Munda (Montilla) in 45. On both occasions Caesar won; the latter battle destroyed the last remnants of the Pompeian armies and left him supreme ruler of the Roman world. (He was to live in this high position for just two days short of a whole year.)

The final conquest of all Spain was due to that remarkable and often underrated military operator, the emperor Augustus. The unconquered part of the peninsula, though small, contained some very difficult country, with mountains reaching above 8000 feet, and two extremely warlike tribes—the Cantabri, who have given their name to the whole mountain-range, and the Astures who are commemorated in the present-day Spanish province of Asturias. Augustus' attack on these two tribes began in 26 BC, and seven years later all resistance had ceased. The entire Iberian peninsula lay under the rule of a single government, something never achieved before and only on one occasion since (in the late sixteenth and early seventeenth centuries when the kings of Spain also ruled Portugal). The task had cost the Romans two centuries of almost continuous fighting.

Augustus also made an important change in the political organization of the land. The two original provinces of 'Nearer' and 'Further' Spain, confined at first to the Mediterranean coast, had spread themselves inland with roughly equal speed, so that the frontier between them ran diagonally across the peninsula from near Corunna in the north-west to near Cartagena in the south-east. Augustus split 'Further Spain' in two: the rich, populous and civilized southern half became a province in its own right, called Baetica after the river Baetis (Guadalquivir) that flowed through the middle of it. This province was reckoned peaceful enough to be handed over to the control of the Senate. Its capital was Corduba, now called Córdoba. The region immediately north of Baetica became the province of Lusitania, named after the largest of the tribes that inhabited it. A new city was set up as its capital, on the site of the town now called Mérida; its ancient name was Emerita Augusta, 'City of the Emperor's Veterans'. The old province of 'Nearer Spain' continued to exist, and was indeed enlarged somewhat, so as to take in all the regions where a military force might be required and leave the other two provinces as purely civilian. Under the Empire, however, it was no longer called 'Nearer Spain' but 'Tarraconensian Spain', after its capital Tarraco, the modern Tarragona.

Though many English words are derived from Latin originals, often there has been a change of meaning in the course of their evolution. Those who had large quantities of Latin inflicted upon them at an early age may perhaps remember, for example, that odd pair of words *obtineo*, which means 'I occupy', and *occupo*, which means 'I obtain'. Similarly, although the Latin word *civitas* has given rise to the English word 'city', there is an important difference between a city and a *civitas* which anyone wishing to understand the Roman (or the Greek) world should bear in mind.

A modern dictionary defines *city* as 'a town incorporated by charter; a large and important town; a cathedral town'—but at any rate some kind of *town*, some kind of built-up area. *Civitas* in Latin (and its equivalent in Greek, *polis*) could mean this, but often it meant something much larger—not only the town itself, but also the whole territory administered from, and controlled by, the town. It would really be better, on many occasions, to translate the word by 'borough', 'canton', 'county' or even 'nation'. Two cities of classical Greece could be as wholly independent of each other as two nations of the modern world; Athens and Sparta, for example, had views on the nature of man and society quite as divergent as today are those of the USA and the USSR. Under Roman rule the independence of cities was curtailed—they were no longer allowed to make war on each other, for instance, though on some occasions they still did—but the idea of the *civitas* as a unit of government persisted. One of the first things done by the Romans on taking over a new province was to subdivide it into *civitates*, blocks of territory, each one preferably having a town as its headquarters. In some remote parts of the Empire—in some parts of Spain, indeed—there were no suitable towns available, but the Romans could, and did, still establish *civitates*, cantons that for the time being lacked capitals pending the development by the natives of a higher level of civilization. We should say today that Exeter was a city, and Devon the county of which it was capital. The Romans would put this the other way round; to them Devon (or Dumnonia) was a *civitas*, and Exeter (Isca) the place from which it was governed. And Dumnonia certainly could have had, and perhaps in actual fact did have, the status of a *civitas* even before it was decided that Exeter was to be its capital.

So, when Pliny the Elder informs us that the province of Baetica contains 175 cities, he is stating not an opinion but a fact, culled from the pages of some Roman official list. The information does not stop here, for he goes on to say that of these 175, nine are *coloniae*, ten *municipia*, twenty-seven possess 'Latin rights', six are 'free', three 'federate' and the remaining 120 'tributary'. For in the Roman Empire there was a hierarchy of cities as there was of people, some possessing greater privileges than others. At the bottom came the simple 'tributary' or tax-paying city, without any special rights or immunities. Then, some cities could be 'free', immune from some (though not all) kinds of Roman taxation, or 'free and federate' meaning that not only were they free, but there was a written treaty (*foedus* in Latin) stating the fact and confirming them as allies of Rome. The other grades were largely concerned with Roman citizenship. In

HISPANIA ET MAURETANIA

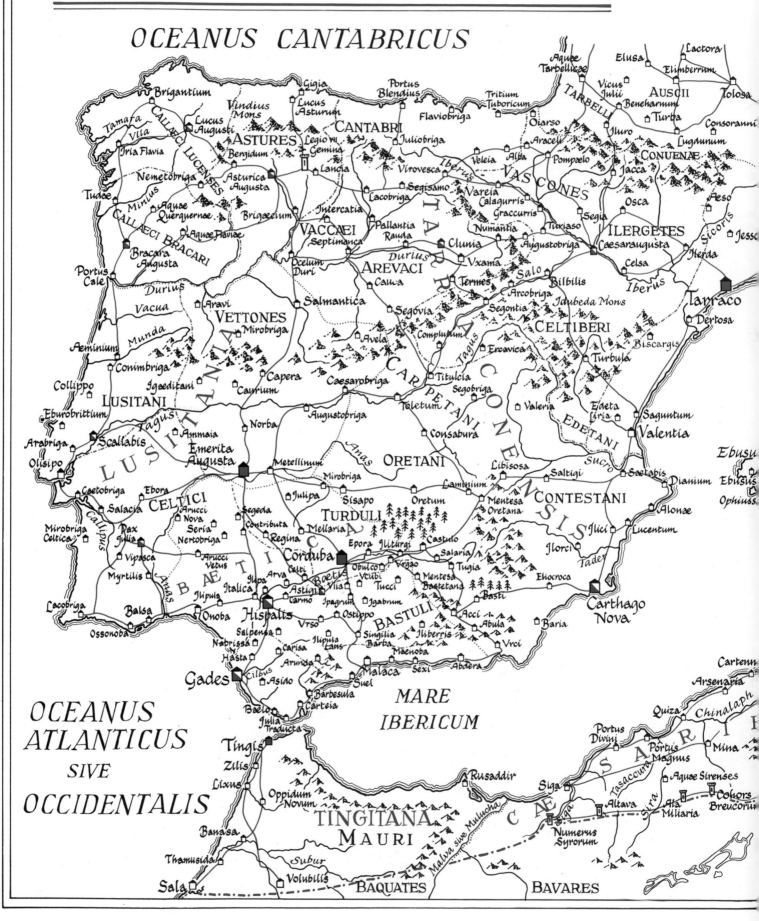

OCEANUS CANTABRICUS

OCEANUS
ATLANTICUS
SIVE
OCCIDENTALIS

MARE
IBERICUM

GALLIÆ PARS

Albiga
Nemausus
Luteva
Arelate
Baeterræ
Aquæ
Sextiæ
Antipolis
Carcaso
Maritima
Massilia
Forum
Julii
Agatha
Olbia
Narbo Martius
Tauroentum
Atax
SINUS GALLICUS
Julia
Libyca
Ruscino
Illiberris
Ausae
Rhodae
Emporiae
Aquae
Calidae
Gerunda
Blandæ
Iluro
Baetulo
Barcino

MARE
BALEARICUM

Jamo
Mago
Palma
Pollentia
Nura
(Minor)
Columba (Major)
Capraria
**Baleares
Insulæ**

MARE SARDOUM

(Jol)
Caesarea
Rusuccuru
Rusguniae
Rusazus
Saldæ
Igilgili
Iomnium
Choba
Tipasa
Icosium
Bida
Tubusuctu
Cuicul
Serbes
Navasath
Gunugu
Aquae Calidae
Auzia
Sitifis
NUMIDIAE
Zucchabar
PARS
Tigava
Oppidum
Novum
Thamallula
Zabi
Lamasba
Columnata
Vsinaza
Lambaesis
MASAE
GAETULI
Salinae
Tubunenses
Tubunae
Ausum
Vescera
MELANOGAETULI
Gemellae
**LIBYAE
INTERIORIS
PARS**
Nigris
Castellum
Dimmidi
NIGRITAE
Thasuni

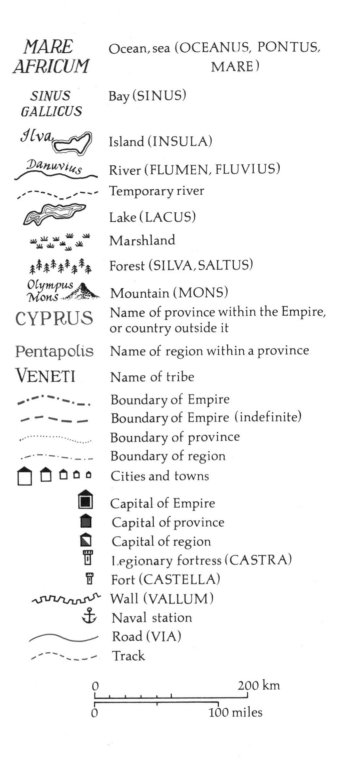

MARE AFRICUM	Ocean, sea (OCEANUS, PONTUS, MARE)
SINUS GALLICUS	Bay (SINUS)
Ilva	Island (INSULA)
Danuvius	River (FLUMEN, FLUVIUS)
	Temporary river
	Lake (LACUS)
	Marshland
	Forest (SILVA, SALTUS)
Olympus Mons	Mountain (MONS)
CYPRUS	Name of province within the Empire, or country outside it
Pentapolis	Name of region within a province
VENETI	Name of tribe
	Boundary of Empire
	Boundary of Empire (indefinite)
	Boundary of province
	Boundary of region
	Cities and towns
	Capital of Empire
	Capital of province
	Capital of region
	Legionary fortress (CASTRA)
	Fort (CASTELLA)
	Wall (VALLUM)
	Naval station
	Road (VIA)
	Track

0   200 km
0   100 miles

towns with 'Latin rights', the chief magistrates were awarded the status of Roman citizens; in the more highly-privileged *municipia* and *coloniae*, all citizens possessed it. At least under the Early Empire, it was a valuable status to have, carrying with it exemption from several taxes and the right to appeal to the emperor himself against a judgement of a provincial governor. ('Hast thou appealed unto Caesar? Unto Caesar thou shalt go.')

Many of Baetica's 175 cities have not yet been located at all, and about those that have been fixed on the map we often know remarkably little. The largest town in the province under the early Empire was the capital, Cordoba (a *colonia*); the second largest was Cadiz (a *municipium*, the chief port of the province, and famous for the number of remarkably rich men who dwelt there); the third largest was Seville (another *colonia*; in the later Empire it outgrew the other cities and was made the administrative head-quarters for all Spain). But at all three cities so much building and rebuilding has gone on since those days that we know little or nothing about their ancient appearance. Indeed, only one town in the whole of Baetica can be called well-preserved. This is a place anciently called Italica, now called Santiponce, not far from Seville. It was a *municipium* in Pliny's time, but the emperor Hadrian (who was born there) raised it to the rank of *colonia*. The Roman hierarchy of cities was not an immutable one; promotion from one class to another was far from impossible, in fact, fairly frequent.

Though the smallest of the three Spanish provinces, Baetica was without doubt the richest. The fertile valley of the Guadalquivir was well-suited to all types of agriculture, and above all to the growing of olives (whose oil was used not only for eating and cooking, but also for lighting

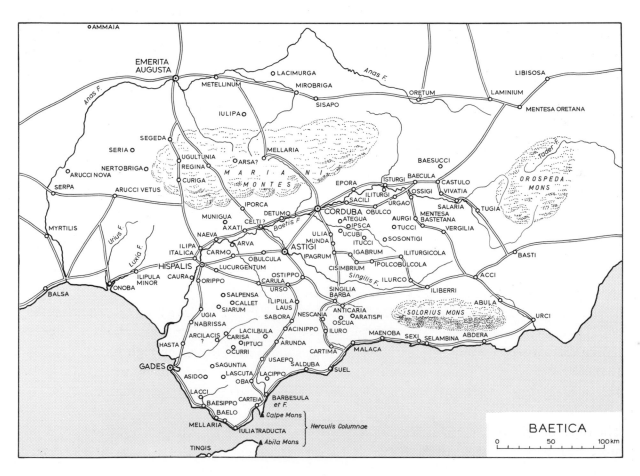

and as a substitute for soap). Baetic olive oil was esteemed as the finest in the ancient world; North Africa at length came to produce a greater quantity, but for quality the oil of Spain remained unrivalled. On the outskirts of Rome there is a large mound, practically an artificial hill, called the Monte Testaccio; it is composed entirely of broken pottery, and analysis of the pieces has shown that most of the pots came from Spain and very probably contained oil—every jar of which helped to enrich the ancient Rockefellers of Cordoba and Cadiz.

Spanish influence spread beyond Spain itself. As the Roman Empire grew in power and wealth, persons from ever-remoter provinces were able to aspire to high positions within it. (The Romans were singularly free from any kind of 'master-race' habit of thought.) Spaniards and men of Baetica especially, appeared very early on the Roman scene. The first non-Italian consul at Rome was from Cadiz, as was the first non-Italian to be awarded a triumph (these two men were uncle and nephew, and both had the same name, Cornelius Balbus). The first-century writers Seneca and Lucan both came from Cordoba. Trajan, the first non-Italian emperor, was born in Italica, as was his cousin Hadrian. The ancestors of Marcus Aurelius had come to Rome from a place called Ucubi (modern Espejo).

Lusitania, lying as it does further from the Mediterranean sources of civilization than Baetica, was correspondingly poorer and less developed. Though larger in area, it contained only 45 recognized 'cities' as against Baetica's 175 (although even this, compared with some provinces remoter still from the centre of affairs, was quite substantial; Roman Britain never had more than half as many). The provincial capital, and also its largest city, was Augustus' new foundation of Emerita Augusta (modern Mérida) built on the banks of the river which the Romans called Anas. (The Arab conquerors of Spain added their own word for 'river'—usually spelt *wadi* in English—to the front of the Roman name, to give the river its modern name, Guadiana). If, as seems plausible, Augustus founded the city of Merida partly in the hope of boosting trade along the Guadiana valley and making it into a second Baetica, he was disappointed; this particular valley-box in the Spanish Lucky Dip remained, even after some centuries of Roman rule, a box with very little in it.

Lusitania had no one overwhelming source of wealth, such as olive oil provided for Baetica. It was suited to a more mixed type of farming: corn could be grown, some vines and some olives, and much land was suited to the rearing of livestock. For though Spain, like all the lands round the Mediterranean, had a much greater expanse of forest and woodland in Roman times than it has now, still even in those days Lusitania had some broad treeless expanses, well suited to the breeding of cattle and horses—the latter in particular; Lusitanian horses were so swift that a legend arose that the West Wind himself was their sire. As any Argentinian or Mexican will tell you, the cowboy with all his traditional trappings was known in Spanish America long before he appeared in the USA, and many of the Spanish conquistadors of America came from those barren highlands that had once belonged to Roman Lusitania. Perhaps a kind of 'proto-cowboy' could have been found on those same highlands in Roman times. But the *rancheros* of Lusitania, unlike the *olivadores* of Baetica, stayed at home and did not engage in high Roman affairs: a Roman 'Who's Who' could be highly comprehensive without mentioning a single Lusitanian except the guerrilla leader Viriathus, who was not really part of the Roman world at all.

The third province of Roman Spain, Hispania Tarraconensis, was remarkably large. It covered more than half the modern nation of Spain, plus a fair-sized slice of what is now Portugal; of

Above: Amphitheatre at Italica near Seville
Below: Theatre at Merida
Opposite: Roman bridge over the Tagus at Alcantara

all provinces in the early Roman Empire, only Egypt covered a greater area. It was also remarkably heterogeneous. Some towns in it, like Ampurias and Alicante, were almost as old as Rome; others were brand new. According to the Elder Pliny, it possessed 179 true and authentic cities, plus 114 communities that still persisted in the tribal way of life. (A Latin *civitas*, as we have already explained, did not necessarily imply the existence of any settlement that we, today, would call a city.)

The oldest and largest settlements were nearly all to be found either on the eastern seaboard or else in the Ebro valley. Along the coast was a string of substantial towns: New Carthage (Cartagena) in the far south, then Alicante, then Valencia and Sagunto, then Tortosa near the mouth of the Ebro, then the provincial capital Tarragona, then Barcelona (which began to grow, at Tarragona's expense, under the late Empire, eventually to become the second largest city in Spain) and finally the old Greek city of Ampurias under the Pyrenees.

From Tarragona a fairly easy route led over a range of hills and down to Lérida (the ancient Ilerda) from which the rest of the Ebro valley could be reached. This, indeed, was probably one reason why the Romans put the provincial capital at Tarragona in the first place: all along the east coast of Spain communications with the interior are poor, but at Tarragona they are a little better than in most other places. With just a casual glance at the map, one might have supposed that Tortosa would be a better centre for communications; after all, Tortosa stands actually *on* the Ebro, so surely it would be a simple matter to run a Roman road straight up alongside the river. Unfortunately, however, in order to reach Tortosa the Ebro river has to work its way through a range of hills by means of a very narrow and awkward defile. This particular box in the Chinese box-puzzle that forms Spain happens to be closed off in front as well as at the back and on both sides. For this reason Tortosa has never been in the past, nor is now, a great communication centre.

Despite the difficulties of entering it in the first place, however, Roman interest in the Ebro valley developed early on. The Iberian town of Salduba was a key-point in several early campaigns. Under the Empire it took a new name (Caesaraugusta, now corrupted to Saragossa or Zaragoza) and became the administrative headquarters of the entire valley. The city of Graccurris (modern Alfaro, some miles further up the river) takes its name from Sempronius Gracchus, father of those two famous but ill-fated brothers who tried to reform the Roman constitution in the late second century BC. Still further north, on a tributary of the Ebro, an important city still preserves the name of Pompey the Great, who was also active in these parts; he named it after himself, Pompaelo, and its modern name is Pamplona.

Beyond the Ebro valley, 'cities' in the Roman sense of recognized political units remained as numerous as ever, but 'cities' in the *modern* sense of 'large towns' were few and far between. In contrast to the tribes of Gaul and Britain, which tended on the whole to be large and each have one substantial settlement as a capital, Spanish tribal organization was dauntingly intricate; each tribe was a kind of Chinese puzzle of its own, within the greater puzzle that was Spain itself. Tribes were divided into clans, and these into septs, and these again sometimes into still smaller subunits, each with its own diminutive village-capital. The original Roman plan on taking over the country was to set up nearly every one of these tiny units as a 'civitas' in its own right—so that a political map of early Roman Spain would have looked like a patchwork quilt. Even Pliny, usually fond of lists, runs out of enthusiasm when dealing with this multitude of insignificant places. 'The Varduli have fourteen nations . . . the Pelendones have four, among which Numantia is especially famous . . . the Vaccaei have seventeen states, among them Intercatia,

Pallantia, Lacobriga, and Cauca . . . but among the seven states of the Cantabri, Juliobriga is the only place worth mentioning.' By the time he has reached the region of Lugo, in the far north-west of Spain, he can say only that the territory includes 'sixteen different nations, but little known and with barbarous names'.

One Roman arrangement that may have helped to unite these scattered Spanish settlements was the system of what are called *conventūs*. A *conventus* was a subdivision of a province, somewhat analogous to a modern judicial circuit, the idea being that litigants, instead of having to travel all the way to the provincial capital, could have their cases heard in some smaller town more close at hand. All three of the Spanish provinces were subdivided in this way. Baetica had four *conventūs*, with capitals at Cordoba, Seville, Cadiz and Ecija: Lusitania had three, based on Merida, Beja and Santarem. But it was in Tarraconensis, the largest and most diverse of the three provinces, that the *conventus* system found its greatest importance. Though it has sometimes been suggested that the object of the system was to break up the Spanish tribal organization, the truth is more likely to have been the opposite. The problem of Spain, from a Roman governor's point of view, was not excessive union but excessive division; the tribes did not provide *enough* of a unifying force, and the *conventūs* were used to help the Spaniards to pull themselves more closely together.

Three of the *conventus*-capitals in Tarraconensis we have already met: they were Cartagena, Tarragona and Saragossa. The fourth, which administered much of the Douro valley, is no longer inhabited; the Romans called it Clunia, and its Spanish name is Coruña del Conde. Beyond the *conventus* of Clunia lay that of Asturica, closely corresponding to the territory of the tribe called Astures. Asturica itself (modern Astorga) bore the honorary title of *Augusta* after the emperor who founded it; it would seem to have been planned, from the very beginning, as an artificial tribal capital. Pliny calls it *urbs magnifica*, a 'magnificent city'; either he was exaggerating, or else much of ancient Astorga has not yet revealed itself to modern investigators. So far as we know, the city was never very large—and in mediaeval and modern times it has been somewhat eclipsed by another town, also of Roman origin, but deriving from the military rather than the civil authority. After Augustus' final conquest of all Spain it became possible to reduce the army of occupation, and several legions were sent away to reinforce the Rhine or Danube; *one* legion, however, was still thought necessary to keep the peace in Spain, and from the seventies AD onward this one was Legio VII Gemina. The camp-site of this force seems not to have had a name of its own—at all events, no ancient writer ever calls it anything but simply Legio. In due course it became a city and took the name of Leon (which thus has the same origin as Caerleon in Wales and Lejjun in Palestine).

Beyond the conventus of Astorga lay two smaller ones, both of whose capitals, like Astorga, bore the Emperor's name. They were Lucus Augusti (modern Lugo) and Bracara Augusta (modern Braga). Note in passing, that although Roman Lusitania was in a sense the ancestor of modern Portugal, the two territories do not very closely correspond. Braga did *not* belong to Lusitania, but *does* now belong to Portugal; conversely several important cities of Roman Lusitania (Merida, Salamanca, Avila) are not Portuguese today, but Spanish.

Spain, like France, has undergone an important change between Roman times and the present day: then its system of communications was decentralized, now it is at least to some extent centralized. Madrid, like Paris, has become the centre from which most roads radiate.

This change occurred only fairly recently. Madrid, by the standards of southern Europe, is a

Above: Aqueduct at Segovia

Opposite: Temple of Diana at Evora

very modern town: it does not appear to have existed at all until the ninth century AD, and it was made the national capital (by Philip II) only in the sixteenth. Even today, it still does not have the official status of a *civitas* (in Spanish, a *ciudad*) but only the lower rank of a *villa* (what the French call a *ville*, and the Romans usually described as a *vicus* or 'village'). Toledo, which in a way can be regarded as the predecessor of Madrid, is a far older settlement, well known to the Romans under the name of Toletum. But though Pliny calls it *caput Carpetanorum*, the 'capital of Carpetania', it does not seem to have been of any great size. Only in the sixth century, when the Visigoths made it their capital, did it acquire more than local importance.

In fact, all central Spain under Roman rule was something of a backwater. It was neither rich enough to forge ahead by itself, nor backward enough to attract the government's attention. The basic pattern of Roman communications ran round the edges of the peninsula: from Cadiz to Cordoba to Cartagena, then up the east coast to Tarragona, then across to Astorga, down to Merida and back via Seville to Cadiz again. Even in our own day, Spain is nothing like as highly-centralized as France; it never has been, and in all probability never will be—the facts of geography prevent it. Philip II had a centralizing turn of mind—his plan to make Madrid the Spanish capital was only part of a much greater scheme—but died, largely of overwork caused by trying to centralize everything on himself, and his work found no successor. Spain has never had a king like Louis XIV or a great central court like Versailles. Perhaps because of this she never had a single great revolution, starting at the capital and working outward, but instead had a prolonged and bloody civil war which neither side can really be said to have won. Spanish communications, or the lack of them, make *total* victory extremely difficult.

Under the later Roman Empire one receives the impression that all Spain, not only the centre, declined in importance. To Romans of the Republic Spain had been a very news-worthy place: not only was it often the scene of important battles, but also, more excitingly, it was the source of unbelievably large supplies of precious metal. It was the loot of Spain which, more than anything else, transformed Republican Rome from a fairly poor city into a very rich one. Romans of this time regarded the country as a kind of Eldorado, an incredible, unlimited source of mineral wealth, just as the Spaniards themselves were later to regard their own discoveries in the New World. And how appropriate it is that one of the gateways to this world should be called Cartagena, 'Newer New Carthage'.

Spain certainly was remarkably rich in minerals: nearly every metal known to ancient science could be found there. Gold was found particularly in the north-west, in the land of the Astures, where some Roman mines are still well preserved today. There were silver mines near Cartagena (their presence greatly influenced the Carthaginians in their decision to found Cartagena in the first place) and also further north near Huesca (the *argentum Oscense*, which gave the Roman rebel Sertorius an advantage denied to most secessionists, a stable and inflation-proof currency). Copper was abundant in the south-west of the country, particularly along the Rio Tinto where it is still worked to this day. Tin could be found in the north-west, good iron in several places, and mercury near a town in the Sierra Morena called Sisapo (modern Almaden, which is Arabic for 'The Mines').

But perhaps the importance of all these has been exaggerated. In the first place, mines under the Empire were automatically the property of the emperor; they brought no riches directly to those in whose territory they lay. Secondly, mines are 'wasting assets'—they get used up. Spain still produces iron and copper but her supplies of silver and gold vanished long ago. On the whole things like corn and olives, horses and cattle, were a better source of wealth.

Also, as far as we can see (and in the present state of Spanish archaeology we cannot see very far), Roman Spain was always a producer of raw materials; she never took the step taken by her neighbour Gaul to become a centre of manufacture. Under the later Empire the centre of gravity of European affairs shifted northward; the Rhineland, France and northern Italy became the industrial powerhouse of Europe, the Danube her principal military zone and breeding-ground for emperors. Spain, removed from the clash of great events, entered a state in which it has remained for long periods (though with some famous exceptions) ever since—a self-contained land, cut off from the rest of the world by physical barriers, and attending strictly to its own business.

Bridge on the Via Domitia, southern France

IV

GALLIA

De brique en marbre seront les murs reduicts,
Sept et cinquante années pacifique,
Ioye aux humains, renoué l'aqueduct,
Santé, grands fruicts, ioye et temps melifique.

Prophecies of Nostradamus

THE BOUNDARIES OF ANCIENT GAUL were the Pyrenees, the Alps and the river Rhine. It thus took in not only all modern France, but Belgium and Luxembourg too, plus parts of Holland, Germany and Switzerland. To enlarge their country to its ancient size has been the ambition, never achieved for any length of time, of some of France's greatest rulers.

The geographer Strabo noted how beautifully easy the communications of Gaul were, in complete contrast to those of Spain, where all nature seemed to conspire to make travel as difficult as possible. The rivers of the country fitted neatly together in such a way that the traveller could go up one and down another without ever having to cross passes of any height. From very early times, for instance, there had been an important route across the south-west corner of France, up the Aude river and down the Garonne, giving direct access to the Atlantic and avoiding the long sea voyage around Spain. In Roman times the towns on this route (Narbonne at one end, Bordeaux at the other and Toulouse halfway between) were among the largest and most important in all Gaul.

The valley of the Rhône was an even more important natural route. This river caught the imagination of the Greeks as soon as they discovered it: like the Po, the Danube, and the Nile, but unlike the vast majority of rivers in the Greek world, it carries water all the year round instead of drying up in summer. It was not, however, easy to navigate. Its mouths tend to block themselves with sandbanks, making it hard for ships of any size to enter it, and even when this is overcome the sailor's troubles are by no means over. The river's current is extremely powerful, and is often supported by a strong wind funnelled down the valley—the notorious *mistral*. Travellers usually followed the river bank rather than venture on the water itself.

At Lyons, however, a Roman foundation and one of the largest cities in Roman Europe, travel becomes easier. Westward there is a fairly easy route from the Rhône valley to that of the Loire, which can be descended to the Atlantic; eastward the upper Rhône provides a way into the Alps; northward its tributary the Saône is very much easier to navigate than the main river. (The contrast between Rhône and Saône, the one so swift and the other so sluggish, was a curiosity of nature frequently pointed out by ancient geographers.) After ascending the Saône, a traveller could bear a little to the west and descend the Seine, past Paris, to reach the Channel;

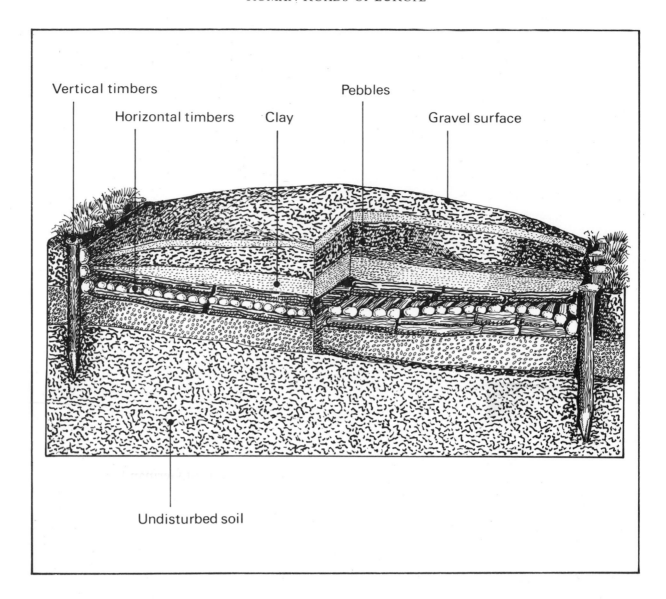

Vertical timbers   Horizontal timbers   Clay   Pebbles   Gravel surface

Undisturbed soil

A cross-section of a Roman bog road

or, bearing a little to the east, he could come down into the valley of the Moselle, which flows into the Rhine, which flows into the North Sea. One Roman official even proposed, in the emperor Nero's reign, to link the Saône to the Moselle by a canal and make a fresh-water route from one side of Gaul to the other, but his plan was brought to nothing by the jealousy of a rival official.

Some parts of the land were avoided by these natural lines of communication. One such region off the beaten track was the mountainous land of the Arverni (modern Auvergne, in the Massif Central); another was the north-west of the country, modern Brittany; a third was the territory now occupied by Belgium, most of which was either forest or swamp. It was regions such as these which put up the greatest resistance to the Roman conquest. On the whole, however, Gallic communications were excellent. Many roads of the Roman period followed tracks dating from much earlier; and the Roman route-books often measure distances along them not only in Roman miles (as is usual elsewhere in the Empire) but in units called leagues (*leugae*) which must go back to before the conquest.

The city of Marseille (called Massalia by the Greeks, Massilia by the Romans) has an undisputed claim to be the oldest in France. Founded by Greeks in about 600 BC it quickly established trading contacts in the Gallic hinterland, all round the western Mediterranean and sometimes even in the Atlantic. These, however, brought the city into conflict with the even more powerful trading community of Carthage, and as a result the Marseillais entered into friendly relationship with Rome. In 124 BC a Roman consul, Sextius Calvinus, was called into Gaul to defend Marseille against some tribesmen who had been attacking it; he defeated them, and set up in their territory a fort which he named after himself—Aquae Sextiae, the modern Aix-en-Provence. Three years later, Domitius Ahenobarbus (an ancestor of the emperor Nero) intervened still more decisively, annexing all southern France to form the new province of Gallia Transalpina or 'Gaul beyond the Alps'. Narbonne was the provincial capital, linked with Italy by a new road called the Via Domitia after its builder. Marseille, though officially still independent and recognized as an ally of Rome, was now wholly surrounded by territory under direct Roman rule.

'All Gaul is divided into three parts', the opening sentence of Caesar's *Gallic War*, used to be drummed into the head of every schoolboy. Just what the three parts were, however, is something not so widely remembered. The first and smallest was Aquitania, in the far south-west of the country between the Pyrenees and the river Garonne; its inhabitants differed in custom (and perhaps also in language) from other Gauls, having close affinities with the tribes of Spain. Everything from the Garonne up to the river Seine formed 'Celtic Gaul', the largest of the three parts. Beyond the Seine, extending east to the Rhine, was the third part, Belgic Gaul. The Belgae were basically Celtic, but claimed to have a certain amount of German blood in them, which (they said) made them braver than their pure Celtic neighbours to the south and west. These, then, were the three parts to which Caesar refers. He would have been more correct, in a sense, to speak of four or even five parts: southern France was also Gallic, as was northern Italy. But these areas were already under Roman rule in Caesar's day; his attention was directed to the lands that lay beyond the Roman frontier—a position that he proposed to change as soon as possible.

In 58 BC Caesar led his armies northward, ostensibly to protect a pro-Roman tribe (the Aedui, in what is now Burgundy on the easiest route to inner Gaul) against their enemies (Helvetii in what is now Switzerland, Sequani in the Jura region, and Germans further to the east). All three of these groups were defeated, and he gained a firm hold on central France.

The next phase of conquest entailed an advance still further north into the country of the Belgic tribes. One of these, the Remi of Reims, surrendered unconditionally; most, however, refused to give up without a fight. Most formidable of all were the Nervii, who on one occasion, on the river Sambre, took a large Roman army completely by surprise and very nearly wiped it out. Only Caesar's own genius managed to snatch victory from defeat. The incident is mentioned by Shakespeare in Mark Antony's famous speech:

> If you have tears, prepare to shed them now.
> You all do know this mantle: I remember
> The first time ever Caesar put it on;
> 'Twas on a summer's evening, in his tent,
> That day he overcame the Nervii: . . .

Above: The 'Maison Carrée' at Nîmes

Opposite: Julius Caesar, conqueror of Gaul

Roman force of arms had thus opened a way right across Gaul, from the Mediterranean to the North Sea. The next stage was to turn about and come back again, subduing the tribes in what is now western France. This, on the whole, proved easier than the conquest of the east, the western tribes being less populous and to some extent less warlike than their eastern neighbours—the Belgic tribes' boast that they were the most deadly in Gaul was not altogether an idle one. However, there were exceptions. One such was the tribe of the Veneti, in what is now Brittany (the town of Vannes preserves their name). Here Caesar had his first experience of Atlantic seamanship, and found himself in an awkward situation; the Venetic ships, built to withstand the gales of the Bay of Biscay, were taller and more solid than the Roman ones, and could not be damaged by ramming in the usual Mediterranean fashion. The Romans at length gained the victory only by tearing down the enemy ships' rigging with grapples, then boarding and (in typical Roman manner) treating the whole affair as if it were a land battle that happened to be fought on floating platforms. By the end of 56 BC Caesar had gained control of all Gaul.

In the next few years he was able to turn his attention further afield. He twice crossed the Channel to visit Britain, and twice crossed the Rhine to visit Germany; but these expeditions, though bringing him great glory at Rome, had little lasting effect. Meanwhile discontent with Roman rule was building up in Gaul itself. In 52 BC the anti-Roman parties in the land at last found a leader: his name was Vercingetorix, and appropriately he was a prince of the Arverni (the men of Auvergne) who from their mountain fastness in the Massif Central had consistently opposed the Romans for the past hundred years. At last, some ten years too late, all the tribes of Gaul joined in a final desperate attempt to expel the Roman invader. Even the Aedui, for all their pro-Roman tradition, changed sides and joined the revolt.

Caesar, however, was equal to the occasion. He was in Italy when the revolt broke out, but returned at once to France and made a spectacular crossing of the Cevennes in mid-winter—a famous example of what the Romans called *Caesariana celeritas*, 'Caesar's High Speed'. After prolonged fighting he at length trapped Vercingetorix in a hill-top stronghold called Alesia, beat off a large Gallic relieving army and forced the chief to surrender. With the capture of its leader, Gallic resistance died away.

Thus conquered by Caesar and organized by his heir Augustus, Gaul became an important part of the Roman world. In social and economic life it can be divided into three parts, though not the same three that Caesar describes. The first part was southern France, with a special character of its own; then there was the main body of the country, the 'Three Gauls' conquered by Caesar; and finally there was the Rhineland, where military influence produced special features not found in the rest of Gaul.

Southern France—Gallia Narbonensis as it was called under the Empire—had a long start over its inland neighbours in the race to civilization. It had been under Roman rule the longest of the Gallic provinces, since 121 BC, and exposed to Greek influence from Marseille for nearly five centuries before that. In the early days of Roman rule the province was nicknamed Gallia Braccata, 'Gaul in Trousers', while northern Italy was called Gallia Togata or 'Gaul in Togas'—trousers, regarded in more recent empires as a first step to civilization, were to the ancients always a symbol of barbarism. But the southern Gauls took to Roman ways very rapidly; by the seventies AD the elder Pliny could describe the land as 'more like a part of Italy than a province'.

The road system of Narbonensis was a straightforward one, taking advantage of obvious natural routes. The chief axis of communication was the Via Domitia, crossing the province from the Rhône to the Pyrenees; two other important roads branched off from it, one running north up the Rhône to Lyons, the other north-west from Narbonne, via Toulouse, to reach the Atlantic at Bordeaux.

The cities of the province had very diverse origins. Some, like Marseille, were Greek foundations. Others, like Narbonne and Aix, developed under the Republic. Many were established by Caesar and Augustus to house retired soldiers. Men from the Second Legion were settled at Orange, on the Rhône; men from the Sixth, at Arles further down the same river; the Eighth Legion sent its veterans to Fréjus; and the famous Tenth, Caesar's crack legion, helped to enlarge the already important city of Narbonne.

Arles and Fréjus may have been founded with a special economic motive. Marseille, halfway between them, had made the mistake of supporting Pompey against Caesar, and yielded only to a prolonged siege (during which every tree for miles around was felled to build engines of war). The new foundations, together perhaps with Narbonne, may have been intended to punish the recalcitrant city by taking away its trade; and for some time in the Empire Marseille was, so to speak, under a cloud. Time, however, has restored the status quo. Marseille with its splendid harbour is once again the principal port of southern France, while Fréjus, Arles and Narbonne are not ports at all. It is difficult, indeed, to visualize how the last two could *ever* have been ports for ships of any size. Written sources, however, assure us that they were.

Besides these cities founded by official authority, Gallia Narbonensis had its fair share of those that had grown spontaneously from native settlements. Some of these, such as Nîmes, Vienne and Toulouse, were outstandingly large—in area, considerably bigger than Narbonne and the other 'official' foundations. Here, as on several other occasions, written records and archaeology tell conflicting stories.

East of Narbonensis, and closely associated with it, were the three diminutive Alpine provinces —the Maritime, the Cottian and the Graian Alps. This region had resisted Caesar's attacks, and was not conquered until the time of Augustus. The Cottian Alps, indeed, kept a semi-independent status, under two successive kings called Cottius, right down to Nero's reign. Though insignificant in themselves, all three provinces were traversed by important roads. In the south the Via Julia Augusta, established by Augustus, ran close to the coast, skirting the Maritime Alps. It was not as easy on the ground as it looks on a small-scale map; in many places the hills leave no gap between themselves and the sea, and the road has to climb and loop very abruptly. A much more popular route from Italy to Gaul was that over the Mont-Genèvre pass: from Susa, the capital of the Cottian Alps province, one could easily reach either the lower, the middle or the upper Rhône valley. Travellers aiming for the Rhineland from Italy would go still further north, and use either the pass of the Graian Alps (the Little St Bernard, as it is called now) or that of the Poenine Alps (the Great St Bernard).

North of Gallia Narbonensis lay the block of land known as the 'Three Gauls', derived from the famous 'three parts' into which Caesar divided the country he conquered. Augustus had preserved the division, though with some alterations, and made three provinces of the new territory— Gallia Aquitania, Gallia Lugdunensis and Gallia Belgica. Aquitania took in the south-west of Gaul, from the Pyrenees to the Loire; its first capital was at Saintes, but later the seat of government was shifted to the flourishing commercial city of Bordeaux, on one of the best natural harbours of all the French coast. Lugdunensis was a long narrow province, shaped like a banana

Above: The trophy at La Turbie near Nice set up by the emperor Augustus to celebrate his victories in the Alps

Opposite above: The Pont du Gard, bringing water to Nîmes

Opposite: The amphitheatre at Arles

or a boomerang; at one end of it were the remote capes and bays of what is now Brittany, at the other end stood the provincial capital—Lugdunum, the modern Lyons. This city was planned by Augustus and his lieutenant Agrippa to be in some sense the metropolis of all Three Gauls, the religious centre where all the tribes of the three provinces met, and a nodal point from which radiated a number of important roads. Gallia Belgica covered the lands east of the river Seine. Its first capital was the city of Reims, chief place of the Remi, who (like the Santones of Saintes) had supported Caesar in his Gallic campaigns. Later, however, the administration was shifted to Trier, notwithstanding that the owners of this city, the Treveri, had long been fiercely opposed to Rome. Whether the men of Reims were pleased or sad at this fall in their city's status is not recorded; there are indications from other provinces (notably Britain) that to have one's home town made into a provincial capital was by no means an unmixed blessing.

The roads of the 'Three Gauls' differed from those of modern France in one outstanding way; in ancient times they were decentralized, now they are centralized. Today, all France's principal lines of communication radiate from Paris. The Roman system, by contrast, formed a fairly uniform network spreading all over the country. There were more important roads in the eastern half of Gaul than in the west (probably because there were more inhabitants in the eastern half) and the system had two points, Lyons and Reims, at which an exceptionally large number of routes met, but neither Lyons nor Reims was anything like the all-embracing nexus that is modern Paris. This last city was already in existence when the Romans reached Gaul (it is mentioned in Caesar's commentaries) and under the name of Lutetia Parisiorum received official recognition from the Roman government as a tribal capital. But for a long time it was a place of no great consequence: the Parisii, to whom it belonged, were one of the smallest independent tribes in Gaul, and surrounded by larger and more powerful neighbours. To the east were the Remi of Reims, whose city had become a provincial capital; westward lived the Carnutes of Chartres, whose territory (before the Roman conquest) had been the scene of a great annual meeting of all the Druids in Gaul; to the south were the Senones of Sens, whose kinsmen long ago had overrun Italy, given their name to the town of Senigallia and sacked Rome itself. These Senones indeed had at times exercised a kind of overlordship over the Parisii, and this arrangement was long preserved in the organization of the Church: until the seventeenth century the *Bishop* of Paris was subordinate to the *Archbishop* of Sens.

Unlike Narbonensis, or the Rhineland, or Britain, or the Danube provinces—that is to say, unlike most of the Celtic-speaking world—the 'Three Gauls' were left by Rome to develop towns mostly on their own initiative. Having planted one large city, Lyons, at the centre of the territory, to serve as a kind of sample of what a civilized Roman town should be like, the Romans planted no more. A few other towns later came to be called *coloniae*, 'colonies', but such titles were merely honorary; no Roman citizens were transferred *en masse* to the cities of northern Gaul.

Before the Roman conquest there had been two main patterns of settlement in Gaul, the Celtic and the Aquitanian. Aquitania proper, the land between the Garonne and the Pyrenees, had close affinities with Spain, and, like the Spaniards, the Aquitani were divided into a multitude of small tribes each with its own diminutive settlement. The Romans at first gave nearly every one of these official recognition as a city in its own right; under the early Empire this small area contained more than twenty officially recognized cities. As time went on, however, more and more small states were amalgamated to form larger ones. Pompey the Great, Caesar's rival, had begun the process in 72 BC by founding a new city and peopleing it with men who had fought against him in Spain. The town's name was Lugdunum, the same as that of Lyons, and it came to be regarded as the capital of an *artificial* tribe—the Convenae, meaning 'the men who came together'. Its modern name is St Bertrand-des-Comminges.

The Celts, unlike the Aquitani, formed tribes of considerable size, each with one substantial settlement as its headquarters. The Romans found this arrangement convenient, and carried it on under their own administration; each tribe became a recognized political unit or *civitas*, and its chief place gradually took on the appearance of a Roman town. The only substantial change was that some Gallic towns, built more for defence than convenience, were shifted to more accessible sites when the Roman presence made defence no longer important. Rome's old allies the Aedui, for example, gave up their hill-top headquarters on Mont Beuvray and established a new capital on lower ground a few miles away at Autun. Their western neighbours the Arverni similarly abandoned their pre-Roman capital (a hill-fort called Gergovia, where Caesar met with a serious reverse in 52 BC) and replaced it with the more accessible site of Clermont-Ferrand. But many pre-Roman towns—Paris, Amiens, Reims, Bourges, Besançon— retained their importance all through the Roman period and on into mediaeval and modern times. Often they have preserved to this day the names of the tribes to which they belonged. Paris was the capital of the Parisii, Reims of the Remi, Amiens of the Ambiani, Bourges of the Bituriges, and so on. (In England, by contrast, it is usually the town's name, not the tribal name, that survives today if either does: Corinium of the Dobunni is now called Cirencester not Dobuncester, and Venta of the Belgae is Winchester, not Belchester.) There is probably more continuity between ancient and modern patterns of settlement in France than in any other country of the Roman world, Italy itself not excepted. Nearly every *civitas*-capital in the Three Gauls has survived to be a place of consequence today, and conversely nearly every large city of present-day France can boast a Roman origin. This last is *not* true of Britain: with the notable exception of London, most of that country's largest towns today—Birmingham, Manchester, Liverpool, Leeds, Newcastle, Bristol—were small or non-existent in Roman times.

An odd feature of Gaul, noticeable in the 'Three Gauls' particularly, is the way in which many towns shrank under the later Roman Empire. In the first two centuries AD most Gallic towns were undefended, and it is often hard to tell just how large they were at this time, but when we can estimate their early size, we nearly always find that the late Roman town (enclosed by walls usually dating from the third century) covers only a fraction of the earlier settlement. The area of Autun, for example, shrank from 200 hectares to 11; Bordeaux, from 125 to 31; Paris, from 53 to 9. What, one wonders, happened to the citizens when the change occurred— had they all died off, or left the city for the countryside, or did they somehow manage to squeeze into a much smaller area, or did some of them normally live outside the walled enclosure and use it only as a refuge when the city came under attack? So far, unfortunately, the question has no satisfactory answer.

The third part of Gaul with a special character of its own was the Rhine frontier district. Julius Caesar, not altogether accurately, had called the Rhine the cultural boundary between 'Gauls' and 'Germans', and had failed to achieve anything against the latter. Augustus' invasions of Germany were equally unsuccessful. Thereafter, save for minor changes, the Rhine remained the frontier of the Roman Empire.

Along the river, accordingly, grew up a number of military and semi-military settlements. Not far from Basle, a village called Augst preserves the name of Augustus himself; on its site

GALLIA

OCEANUS VERGIVIUS

OCEANUS BRITANNICUS

OCEANUS AQUITANICUS

OCEANUS CANTABRICUS

ALB·IONIS PARS

Ratae
Moridunum · Magni
Gleyum · Salinae · Duroliponte
Isca · Venta · Corinium · Lactodurum
Verulamium · Camulodunum
Calleva · Londinium
Aquae Sulis · Rutupiae
Lindinis · Venta · Durovernum · Dubris
Clausentum · Noviomagus
Durnovaria · Vectis · Gesoriacum

MENAPII · Scaldis
Castellum
BELGICA · Tarvenna · Turnacum
Bagacum
Namnetacum · Camaracum
Samarobriva · Augusta V.
CALETES · Isara · Augusta
Juliobona · Caesaromagus
Crociatonum · Rotomagus · Augustomagus · Durocortorum
Augustodurum · Aregenuae · Noviomagus · Matrona · Jatinum
Cosedia · Mediolanum · Lutetia · TRICASSES
Ingena · Olina · Nudionum · Metiosedum · Augustobona
Gesocribate · OSISMII · Fanum Martis · LUGDUN · Autricum · Agedincum
Vorgium · Conate · Noviodunum · CARNUTES · SENONES
VENETI · REDONES · Meduana · Vindinum · Cenabum · Autessiodurum · Icauna
Darioritum · TURONES · Liger · DUI
NAMNETES · Juliomagus · Caesarodunum · ENSIS
Condevincum · Avaricum
PICTONES · Caris · Decetia
Limonum · Argentomagus · Elaver · Liger
SANTONES · Vigenna · Crosa · Aquae Neri · Aquae Calidae
LEMOVICES · Rodumna
Mediolanum · Carantonus · Augustoritum · Augustonemetum · Forum Segusiavo
Iculisna · ARVERNI
AQUI · TANIA · Ruessium
Vesunna
PETROCORII · Duranius · CADURCI · Anderitu
Burdigala · Divona · Oltis
Boii · Sirmatius · Garumna · Segodunum · Vardo · Condatomagu
Cossio · Aginnum · RUTENI · Luteva
VASATES · Tarnis · Albiga
Aquae · Aturus · Elusa · Lactora · Baeterae
Tarbellicae · Vicus Julii · Elimberrum · NARBONENSIS · Agatha
AUSCII · Tolosa · Garumna
Noega · Beneharnum · Carcaso · Atax · Narbo Martius
Lucus Asturum · Oiarso · Orbis
Minius · Lucus Augusti · Juliobriga · Tritium Tuboricum · Iluro · Lugdunum · Ruscino
Legio VII Gemina · Alba · Pompaelo · Jacca · Julia Libyca
Lancia · Veleia · Iberus · Segia · Osca · Ruscino
Asturica Augusta · Astura · Lacobriga · Virovesca · Varela · PYRENAEI MONTES
Brigaecium · Pallantia · Pisoraca · Segisamo · Calagurris · Caesaraugusta
Graccurris

HISPANIAE PARS

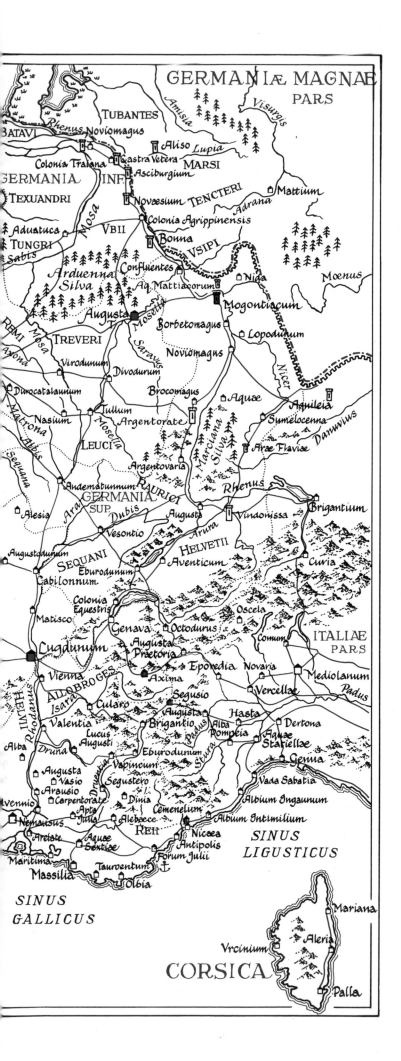
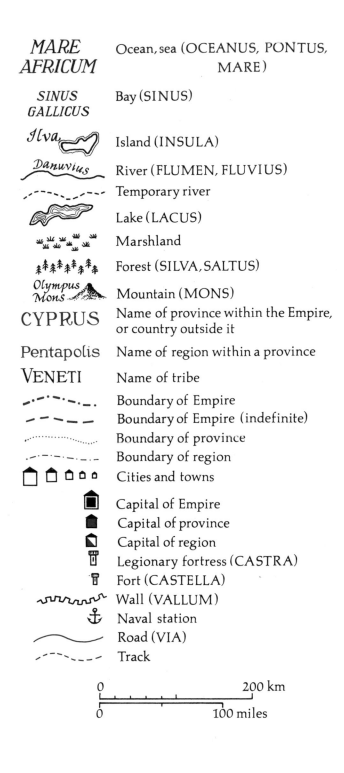

A detail of a Roman bridge

once stood the military colony of Augusta Raurica. Further downstream, Strasbourg was a Roman legionary base; further down still, Mainz was an even more important one. The valley of the Main, which joins the Rhine here, offered one of the easiest ways for a Roman army to invade the wilds of 'Greater Germany', and, conversely, for a German force to attack Roman territory. Mainz was thus a vital point in both attack and defence; it was the capital of Roman Upper Germany, and under the early Empire was garrisoned by not one but two legions—some ten thousand fighting men. Later emperors, however, gave up the habit of putting two legions in one camp since it seemed to breed quarrels and mutinies.

Not far below Koblenz (which still preserves its Latin name of Confluentes, 'the confluence' of the Moselle river with the Rhine) the province of Upper Germany ended and that of Lower Germany began. The provincial capital was Cologne, founded by Augustus and further developed by Claudius. Its full name was *Colonia Claudia Ara Agrippinensium*—Claudia after the emperor, Agrippinensium after his wife Agrippina. Military bases in the province included Bonn, Neuss and, most important, a place called Vetera, near Xanten. This last, like Mainz, covered an important route into hostile territory (up the valley of the river Lippe) and for a time required a garrison of two legions.

Below Vetera the river enters the marshy country of the Batavi, where its course has changed repeatedly over the years. In Roman times it had three branches. The most southerly was the channel now called the Vaal, on which stood the Batavian capital, Nijmegen. The middle channel, now called the Old Rhine, reached the sea near Leiden; though it formed the frontier of the Empire, it then as now carried comparatively little water. The third branch flowed through a fresh-water lake called Flevo, the predecessor of the Zuider Zee.

Through most of the first century AD the Rhine was the most important and eventful of Rome's frontiers, incidents on it being frequently of the sort that would have made front-page news if the Romans had had newspapers. In the early part of the century the river was garrisoned by no fewer than eight legions—two at Vetera, two at Cologne, two at Mainz, one at Strasbourg and one at a place called Windisch in what is now Switzerland. Thereafter, however, the force on the river gradually decreased. In the second century the garrison was down to four legions—XXX Ulpia Victrix at Vetera, I Minervia at Bonn, XXII Primigenia at Mainz and VIII Augusta at Strasbourg. It was the Danube frontier, not the Rhine, that in these years presented the greatest threat to Rome.

Roman Gaul was a rich land, rich enough to stand out as an example of wealth among all the lands of the Empire. The Jewish historian Josephus records a speech made by king Herod Agrippa II, trying (without success) to stop a Jewish revolt. 'Look at the far-flung empire of Rome,' he says, 'and contrast your own impotence . . . Are you richer than the Gauls, stronger than the Germans, cleverer than the Greeks, more numerous than all the nations of the world?' And later, again speaking of the Gauls, he mentions 'the prosperity that wells up from their soil and enables them to flood the whole world with their goods'.

This last remark points out an important fact. Gaul, alone among the provinces of the western Empire, was industrial; Gaul alone produced manufactured goods and not exclusively raw materials. Already in Augustus' reign, the old-established potters of Arezzo in Tuscany were going out of business; they were being undercut by a similar but cheaper ware made mostly at a place called La Graufesenque, near Millau in the Cevennes. This was the famous 'Samian ware', examples of which turn up on nearly every Roman site in Europe.

La Graufesenque did not keep its predominance for very long. By the second century AD the centre of production had shifted to Lezoux, near Clermont-Ferrand, and later it shifted further north still, to be concentrated at Rheinzabern on the Rhine and Trier on its tributary the Moselle. The glass industry followed a similar northward course, eventually settling down at Cologne. There were obvious advantages in producing these goods as near to the customer as possible; and the biggest customer was the Roman army in its stations along the Rhine.

So, as the military importance of the Rhineland decreased, its social and economic importance grew. It became the power-house, the industrial heartland, of Europe (as of course, to a very large extent, it still is today). It even managed to maintain much of its prosperity through the unpleasant civil wars of the third century. The odd shrinkage that affected so many towns in the interior of Gaul at about this time is much less noticeable among Rhenish towns: late Roman Mainz and Worms, Cologne and Tongres, were all extremely substantial cities, while Trier was positively outstanding. With its walls enclosing 285 hectares (about 700 acres) it was by far the largest city in Gaul, and probably, until the founding of Constantinople, the second largest in

Above: The Porta Nigra at Trier

Opposite: Glass jugs manufactured at Cologne

Left: Example of Samian ware made in central Gaul

Europe. From it, in the fourth century, was administered a quarter of the Empire, covering Britain and Spain as well as the whole of Gaul.

The fall of the Rhineland to Germanic peoples at the beginning of the fifth century was thus a deadly blow, economic as well as military, from which the Roman Empire in the West never recovered. At the same time it marked the birth of the German nation as we now know it. For many centuries Germany virtually *was* the Rhineland, its principal cities the three former Roman capitals of Trier, Mainz and Cologne; the tribes beyond the river long remained little more civilized than they had been in Julius Caesar's day. To reunite the 'Three Gauls' and the 'Two Germanies' of Rome has been the ambition of some of Europe's most famous—and infamous—rulers.

V

GERMANIA

Von der Maas bis an der Memel, von der Etsch bis an dem
Belt,
Deutschland, Deutschland über alles, über alles in der
Welt!

German National Anthem

MOST NATIONAL ANTHEMS deal either with the ruler of a group of people ('God save our gracious Queen!') or else with the people considered as a whole ('Allons, enfants de la patrie!'). The national anthem of Germany is unusual in that it deals with neither of these, but with the *land* itself. The territory in question is even defined geographically—'from the Maas to the Memel, from the Etsch to the Belt'—a generous definition, seldom realized in actual fact.

Ancient Germania was considerably larger than the modern nation. It still did not reach 'from the Maas to the Memel' (the Maas, or Meuse, river flowed entirely through possessions of Rome, while the Memel river, far to the east, belonged not to Germans but to Balts), but it did at least reach from Rome's frontier on the Rhine as far east as the Vistula. On the southern side it came nowhere near the Etsch (this river, better known perhaps as the Adige, today belongs entirely to Italy, and did likewise in Roman times); ancient Germania stopped at Rome's other great military frontier, on the Danube. But in the far north it did indeed reach the Belts, which are straits separating various Danish islands. All that we now call Denmark undoubtedly belonged to this ancient Germanic world; so did the greater part of Holland, all of Czechoslovakia and about half of Poland.

The land impressed Roman writers as a grim and gloomy place. All the non-Mediterranean parts of Europe, from their point of view—France, Britain, northern Italy, even some of Spain—suffered from a cold, damp, miserable climate in which far more trees grew than any civilized human being could find necessary, but the coldness, wetness and tree-iness of Germany were unsurpassed. Right across the southern half of the country, all through what now forms Bavaria and Czechoslovakia, stretched Western Europe's largest belt of continuous woodland, the vast Hercynia Silva or 'Oak Forest', and similar though smaller blocks of forest occupied much of the northern half. The woodland was interspersed, too, with marshes, swamps and quagmires, where the great perennial rivers—Rhine, Weser, Elbe, Oder and Vistula—overflowed their banks. On the north-west shores of Germany great Oceanus himself added to the flooding. It is thought that in the third century AD the water-level in these parts began to rise, forcing the Friesians, Saxons, Angles, Jutes and other local tribes first to take up a kind of duckboard existence (they built their settlements on ever-higher artificial mounds, which survive to this day and are called *terpen*) and at length to leave the country altogether.

Above: The Black Forest. A type of country much commoner in northern Europe then than it is now

Opposite: The 'Grand Camée'. The crowned figure at the top, floating in the 'Upper Air', is Augustus; to his left is his stepson Drusus. His other stepson, the emperor Tiberius, is shown enthroned at the centre, flanked by Germanicus and Drusus the Younger. The boy on the far left is the future emperor Caligula. All these fought the Germans, with limited success

Concentrated settlement was possible only in a few favoured parts of the country, above all along the great rivers. For although in some places these spread out into lagoons of impassable mud, in other places they were bordered by gravel terraces, raised above the worst of the flooding, reasonably well-drained and easy to cultivate. The size of the rivers, too, brought an advantage as well as a disadvantage; unlike most watercourses of the Mediterranean world, they could be navigated as easily in summer as in winter. As in North America when the Europeans first discovered it, or in Amazonia to this day, travel by water was very much easier than travel by land. Yet it would be wrong to see the land (as some Roman writers apparently did see it) as an *utterly* pathless wilderness. Though never permanently conquered by the Romans or adorned with their roads, Germany did have some well-defined natural lines of communication of its own.

The first entry of the German-speaking peoples into history was a violent one, and shows that even in ancient times they had a large measure of that quality which modern Germans call *Wanderlust*. Two tribes called the Cimbri and Teutones, originating from the extreme north of Denmark, traversed the whole of Germany to emerge from the Alps in 113 BC, defeat a Roman army and vanish into the mountains again as suddenly as they had come. Eight years later they reappeared—some hundreds of miles further west, on the river Rhône. At the battle of Orange they inflicted a disastrous defeat on two combined Roman armies, and went on to threaten Italy itself. Only the skill of Gaius Marius, Rome's premier general at the time, saved the situation.

About fifty years later, another body of Germans tried a manoeuvre of the same sort. It likewise failed, however, through coming up against a Roman of military ability still greater than Marius'—none other than Julius Caesar himself. This time the German force was more diverse than before. Instead of two tribes, Caesar mentions seven—the Harudes, the Marcomanni, the Triboci, the Vangiones, the Nemetes, the Eudusii (whose kinsmen were later to appear in English history under the name of Jutes), and above all, the Suebi. Precisely who the Suebi were is not altogether clear. Caesar himself portrays them as a single tribe, though one of unusual size, power and bellicosity, and responsible directly or indirectly for every breach of the peace that occurs in the Rhineland. Tacitus, however, takes a different view; while agreeing with Caesar about the warlike prowess of the Suebi, he maintains that they were not a tribe so much as a way of life. Some German tribes were Suebic, while others were not; those who *were* had certain manners and customs in common, the most notable being their habit of fastening their hair into a knot. Caesar's own particular Suebi, the Suebi *par excellence*, so to speak, may well have been the tribe known to later writers as the Quadi, who were to persist as one of Rome's most formidable enemies.

In 58 BC Caesar encountered the Suebic confederation in the valley that is now called the Belfort Gap. (From that day to this, the valley has kept its importance as a possible line of invasion of France by Germany, or *vice versa*; Belfort itself remains one of France's principal strongholds.) The Romans won a crushing victory. The great Suebic alliance thereupon broke up. Some of Caesar's enemies remained in the Rhine valley, made their peace with Rome, and in due course became useful and fairly well-behaved citizens of the Roman Empire. The city of Worms was developed by the Vangiones, that of Speyer by the Nemetes; both became important places of mediaeval and modern Germany. Some tribes of the confederation, however, refused to stay anywhere near the land of their conqueror; like one of Caesar's later enemies (Commius of Belgica, who at length hid himself in the remote island of Britain) they may well have thought that, even if they never saw another Roman face again, that would still be too soon. Two tribes at least, the Quadi and Marcomanni, certainly seem to have taken this point of view; frustrated by Caesar in their original plan to swing westward into Gaul, they instead turned away to the east, ascending the river Main.

The land they thus reached was occupied by Celtic-speaking tribes; it was in fact the original centre, the *Urheimat*, from which the Celts had spread out in so many directions. The tribes remaining there, however, were unable to withstand the German attack. Some were forced to leave the region altogether, some lingered on as vassals of the Marcomanni and Quadi, who now ruled the land themselves.

The stage is now set for the most dramatic episode in all the *splendeurs et misères* of early German history—the great German War of the emperor Augustus. This man, determined as his great-uncle Julius Caesar had been to make Rome into a Central European rather than a purely Mediterranean power, decided that the imperial frontier should follow the rivers Elbe and Danube; this would give a single line, fairly easy to defend, in place of the previous hotchpotch of provinces and 'spheres of influence', some of them lacking any definite size or shape. The first stage in translating this plan into actuality—the advance of Roman forces, under the emperor's stepsons, Tiberius and Drusus Caesar, to the Danube—was a huge success. The second stage entailed an advance from Julius Caesar's frontier line on the Rhine eastward as far as the Elbe, thus taking in about half of 'Greater Germany'. The task was entrusted to Drusus, who set about it with considerable success—until 9 BC, when in a campaign along the river Saale his horse fell on him, the resulting wounds turned gangrenous and he died.

Rome at this time seemed to be suffering from a shortage of capable generals, or, to be more precise, of capable generals whom the Emperor could trust. Having raised himself to power through a violent and bloody civil war, Augustus throughout his life was reluctant to give large-scale military powers to anyone but himself and his closest friends and relations. For some years his lieutenants had been his son-in-law Agrippa and his stepsons Tiberius and Drusus. Now Agrippa and Drusus were dead, and Tiberius could not be everywhere at once. After his brother's death he was sent to complete the conquest of Germany, which he did; then, however, he had to be hastily transferred back to the Danube, where a large-scale revolt had broken out. In AD 9 news of his final victory over the rebels was quickly followed at Rome by news of terrible disaster in the province he had been forced to leave.

Augustus, by a rare error of judgement, had thought the German province much more pacified than it really was; after the departure of Tiberius, he had chosen as its governor one Quinctilius Varus, a considerable lawyer but no kind of soldier. In AD 9 Varus, with three legions, was ambushed in the Teutoburger Forest; hardly a man on the Roman side survived. Germany was lost, and only dissension among the German tribesmen stopped them from overrunning Gaul too. Augustus, it is said, was never quite the same man again.

Thus broken, Rome's grip on Germany was never restored. In later years there were several attempts; under Tiberius, Germanicus Caesar (the son of that Drusus Caesar who had contributed so much to the original Roman conquest) launched two expeditions into the country and gained some success. Both times, however, he lost large numbers of men, some in battle and others by shipwreck (for these were amphibious operations, making use of a Roman fleet on the North Sea). Finally Tiberius recalled him. Tacitus, our chief source for the events of this time, puts this down to pure jealous spite on the emperor's part, but then Tacitus was always convinced that Tiberius was the archetype of a Bad Man. In fact on this occasion Tiberius may

Above: A light cart in use, found on a monument near Frankfurt

Left: Eighth century AD carving of a Scandinavian boat

Opposite: Marcus Aurelius, the last Roman emperor to practise an offensive policy against the Germans

AVGVSTINVS TRINCIVS IACOBVS BVCCA BELLA
CAESAR DE MAGISTRIS CONSERVATORES CVR

well have been right; certainly his own policy, of using diplomacy rather than force against the Germans, produced as good results as his nephew's at much less cost.

In the late first century AD the Flavian emperors launched a new attack on Germany, though on a more modest scale than before. A glance at the map will show that the Roman frontier, following the upper Rhine and upper Danube, takes an extremely roundabout route; by driving a straight line from Mainz on the one river to Regensburg on the other, much manpower could be saved. The emperor Vespasian began this task, by bringing most of the Black Forest area under Roman control. He bounded it with a new road, linking Strasbourg with the Danube via a fort called Arae Flaviae, 'the Flavian Altars' after his family name. The site is now called Rottweil.

His younger son, the emperor Domitian, was also active on the Rhine. Ancient writers are hostile to this emperor, and play down his campaigns as minor incidents magnified by propaganda to appear as large-scale wars. More recent studies, however, show that Domitian's Rhine war was a more serious affair than his enemies pretended. He attacked the Chatti, one of the most powerful and well-disciplined of all German tribes, and utterly defeated them; a new system of roads and forts was set up, giving Rome some of the most fertile parts of Chattian territory. Hadrian, determined in Germany as in Britain to maintain Rome's existing possessions rather than add new ones, reinforced the frontier of the conquered land with a wooden palisade; and his successor, Antoninus Pius, made some further changes to give the frontier its final form. The region thus enclosed was called the Agri Decumates, meaning 'Lands of Ten', though we do not know precisely why. One of the last Roman territories to be conquered, it was also one of the first to be abandoned.

The last important Roman attack on German territory was made, rather surprisingly, by that

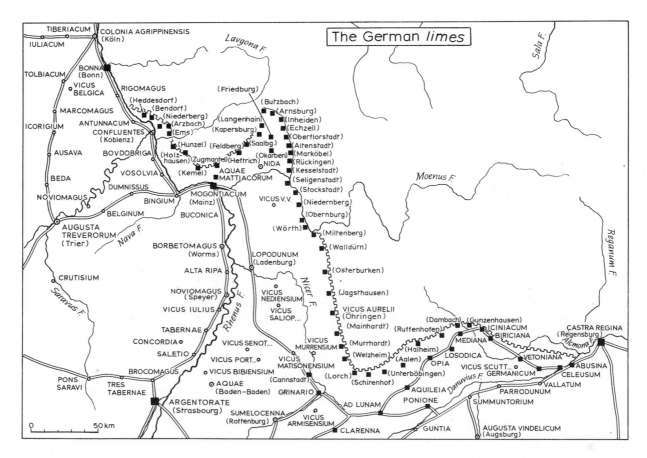

most unwarlike of rulers, the philosopher-emperor Marcus Aurelius. Despite his lack of enthusiasm for the subject, he met with very fair success. Having flung the Danube Germans back from an invasion of his own empire, he carried on with a pursuit into their territory, and by AD 180 he was proposing to annex a substantial piece of this and make from it the Roman province of Marcomannia. But in that year he died, and his unworthy son Commodus let the Germans off lightly. Thereafter Roman attacks on Germany ceased, and in future it was the Germans who took the offensive.

Ancient Germany, like ancient Gaul, can be divided into three parts. The North Germans inhabited Scandinavia; the East Germans, what is now Poland; the West Germans, all the rest of the land.

The North Germanic peoples in Scandinavia were far removed from the Roman world, and in classical times very little was ever found out about them. Even the existence of the land was not known until about the time of Christ, and all ancient writers without exception pictured it as an island somewhere near the edge of the world. So, apparently, did its inhabitants—the *avia* part of the name Scandinavia is Old German for 'island'. But one or two remarks by ancient writers strike a chord. Tacitus, for instance, mentions a people called the Suiones, who are very probably the early Swedes living round Lake Mälar—where we find Sweden's earliest capital, Uppsala, and her modern capital, Stockholm. He also remarks in passing that 'the shape of their ships differs from the normal in having a prow at both ends'. Here is the earliest description of the famous Viking longship, later destined to spread terror throughout northern Europe. The geographer Ptolemy, writing about fifty years after Tacitus in the middle of the second century AD, mentions another tribe in Scandinavia called the Dauciones; and these may well be the early Danes. For it is well agreed that the Danes originated in what is now Sweden, and only later crossed into Denmark—as the name of that country implies; it began as Den-*mark*, the Danish March or frontier-land of the Holy Roman Empire *against* the Danes.

The West German tribes, being closest to the Roman world, were naturally the best known. All claimed descent from a common ancestor Mannus, the first man. From his three sons, so tradition ran, descended three groups of tribes—one on the Rhine, one on the sea-coast of Germany, and one in the interior.

The tribes on the Rhine, known as Istaevones, lived under the watchful eyes of a considerable Roman army, and were never allowed to amount to anything very important. Julius Caesar had noted of the Germans that each tribe liked to surround itself with a belt of uninhabited land, if necessary preventing its neighbours by force from settling therein. By an odd irony, or perhaps by deliberate imitation, the Roman Empire took up exactly the same policy along its German frontier, and sought to produce a kind of *cordon sanitaire*, or what modern military jargon might call a 'depersonnellized zone' between itself and its enemies. Several small but brisk skirmishes occurred as first one tribe then another tried to settle on lands that Rome wished to have left empty. (There is a terribly persistent tendency to see, in one's mind's eye, a Roman frontier—the Rhine, the Danube or Hadrian's Wall—as a static barrier, with lines of Roman soldiers on one side and hordes of howling barbarians on the other. But, as the example just given shows, Roman forces must frequently have penetrated some way beyond the frontier. The Romans sometimes found themselves shut up inside forts; but most of the time they preferred to organize a 'war of movement' against an enemy who was himself highly mobile.) So the Istaevonian tribes (Chamavi, Tubantes, Usipetes, Tencteri and others) led a shaky existence, closely watched

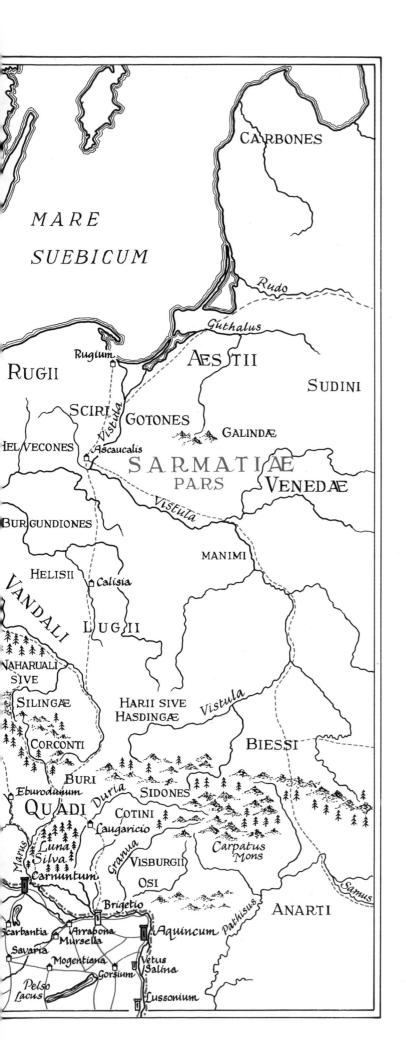

MARE
SUEBICUM

CARBONES

RUGII
Rugium
SCIRI   GOTONES
ÆSTII
SUDINI
Rudo
Guthalus
HELVECONES
Ascaucalis
GALINDÆ
SARMATIÆ
PARS   VENEDÆ
BURGUNDIONES
Vistula
HELISII   Calisia
MANIMI
VANDALI
LUGII
NAHARVALI
SIVE
SILINGÆ
HARII SIVE
HASDINGÆ
Vistula
CORCONTI
BIESSI
BURI
Eburodunum   SIDONES
Duria
QUADI   COTINI
Laugaricio
Luna
Silva   VISBURGII   Carpatus
Mons
Marus
Carnuntum   Granua
OSI
Brigetio
Pathisus
ANARTI
Scarbantia   Arrabona   Aquincum
Savaria   Mursella
Mogentiana
Gorsium   Vetus
Salina
Pelso
Lacus   Lussonium
Samus

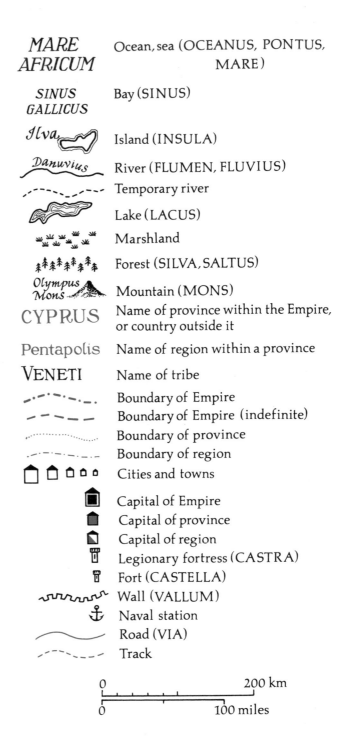

MARE AFRICUM	Ocean, sea (OCEANUS, PONTUS, MARE)
SINUS GALLICUS	Bay (SINUS)
Ilva	Island (INSULA)
Danuvius	River (FLUMEN, FLUVIUS)
	Temporary river
	Lake (LACUS)
	Marshland
	Forest (SILVA, SALTUS)
Olympus Mons	Mountain (MONS)
CYPRUS	Name of province within the Empire, or country outside it
Pentapolis	Name of region within a province
VENETI	Name of tribe
	Boundary of Empire
	Boundary of Empire (indefinite)
	Boundary of province
	Boundary of region
	Cities and towns
	Capital of Empire
	Capital of province
	Capital of region
	Legionary fortress (CASTRA)
	Fort (CASTELLA)
	Wall (VALLUM)
⚓	Naval station
	Road (VIA)
	Track

0   200 km
0   100 miles

by a Power greater than all of them put together. In the third century, however, disunity within the Roman world was matched by growing unity beyond its frontiers, and these hitherto unimportant tribes came together to form the powerful coalition known as the Franks.

Along the North Sea coast lived the Ingaevonian tribes. The country from Lake Flevo (the Zuider Zee) to the mouth of the Ems river was occupied by the large tribe of the Frisii, formidable both in alliance and in enmity with Rome. The Dutch province of Friesland preserves their name to this day. Further east, between the Ems river and the Elbe, dwelt the even larger tribe of the Chauci, who met with a mysterious fate; after the mid-second century ancient writers simply cease to mention them, putting in their place another group better known to Englishmen, the Saxones. What exactly happened—whether the Saxons conquered and overran the Chauci, or whether for some unknown reason the whole tribe changed its name—we do not know.

Beyond the Chauci, in what is now Jutland, lived a number of smaller tribes, two of which— the Anglii or Angles, and the Eudoses or Jutes—were later also to make a contribution to English history. It should be noted, however, that the traditional view that 'Angles, Saxons, and Jutes' *alone* made the English invasion is certainly wrong. There were numerous Friesians among the invaders, and probably lesser tribes as well. Moreover, the rise in water-level along this coast had produced a general shifting to and fro, and a blurring of the old tribal boundaries, even before the sea-crossings began. If you asked an Early Englishman, as he stepped from his long-boat on to the beaches of Kent or Essex, whether he was an Angle, a Saxon or a Jute, I doubt if you would have received any coherent answer.

The third branch of the West Germanic peoples, known as the Herminones, lived in the interior of the country. Since most of it was covered by dense belts of forest, such tribes were constrained about where they could live, and most of them dwelt on the banks of the great German rivers, which as well as being less tree-bound than other regions offered an easy means of communication. Going eastward from Rome's frontier on the Rhine, one next comes to a river called the Ems; but none of the tribes there were of any great importance. Beyond the Ems flows a more considerable river, the Weser, on whose banks lived three large tribes. Near the river mouth were the Chauci whom we have already met. Further upstream lived the Cherusci, a tribe which for a time controlled many of its neighbours; it was a chief of this tribe, Arminius by name, who smashed the Roman forces in the battle of the Teutoburger Forest. Later, however, through the machinations of their neighbours and of the Roman Empire, the Cherusci were forced down into a state of nonentity. 'On the flank of the Chauci and Chatti' remarks Tacitus, 'the Cherusci have been left free to enjoy a peace . . . once the good and true, they now hear themselves called the slovenly and slack'.

The decline of the Cherusci had been matched by an increase in the power of their neighbours, the Chatti of the upper Weser. Living as they did fairly close to the Roman frontier, these people had learned more of Roman discipline than their neighbours: Tacitus pays them a considerable compliment—'Other Germans may be seen going to battle, only the Chatti to war'.

Beyond the Weser runs a still larger river, the Elbe. Along this river and its tributaries lived the people collectively known as Suebi—the gentlemen with the peculiar hairstyle, Julius Caesar's enemies, who have already been mentioned. Tacitus tells us about some of their tribes. The largest group was called the Semnones; they lived in the region where the city of Berlin stands today. Later, however, they moved closer to the Roman frontier, as the leading lights of a confederation called the Allemanni or 'All-men'. This group continually threatened Rome's possessions on the upper Rhine from the third century onward, and finally took them over for themselves;

the French name for Germany, *Allemagne*, preserves their name to this day. Another Suebian tribe worthy of special mention is the group called Langobardi, the Lombards. They were a small tribe, says Tacitus—not surprisingly, since they lived in the particularly bleak and barren part of Germany now called the Lüneburg Heath—but what they lacked in numbers they made up in militancy. At a time when all their neighbours were off to seek their fortunes in the crumbling Roman Empire, the Lombards almost alone remained in Germany; then in the sixth century, like the last shot from a locker that all had supposed empty, they burst forth from their homeland and overran most of Italy. The northern part of that country still bears their name.

The Semnones and Lombards, however, made little impact on the affairs of the early Empire. More urgently relevant were the southern members of the Suebic group, who confronted Roman forces along the Danube. Here lived three large tribes, one well disposed towards Rome, the other two bitterly hostile.

On the upper course of the Danube, bordering the Roman province of Raetia, lived the Hermunduri, whose name may be preserved in the modern district of Thuringia. Almost alone among German tribes they were consistently friendly with Rome. Tacitus tells us that they were even allowed to cross the Danube and penetrate Roman Raetia as far as its capital, Augsburg, in order to trade—though he omits to tell us, unfortunately, what goods they brought with them to sell.

Further down the river, the Marcomanni and Quadi, in close alliance with each other, were usually anti-Roman. The Marcomanni, under a king with the odd name of Maroboduus (which means 'Seabottom') were the very last tribe whom the Romans planned to conquer in Augustus' great advance to the Elbe; they were saved at the last minute, first by the revolt further down the Danube and then by the battle in the Teutoburger Forest. Indeed, had it not been for the rivalry between Maroboduus and Arminius (the victor in the forest battle) things might have gone much harder for Rome than they did go. For whereas Arminius, despite frequent contact with the Roman world, was conservative—believing that Rome could teach the Germans nothing—Maroboduus was more liberal. He was quite willing to accept some Roman ideas; he even built a capital city for his tribe, named after himself and more like a true town than anything previously known in those parts. Many Roman businessmen came there to trade. But at length the Tories in the tribe objected to this policy and flung their leader out; he died in exile at Ravenna. Thereafter the Marcomanni grew more and more anti-Roman. By AD 200 they and their allies the Quadi were being watched by six Roman legions—one-fifth of the entire Roman Army confronting a mere two tribes.

Beyond these 'West German' tribes, a long way from the Roman world and therefore at first little known, were the 'East Germans'. By accidents of history, however, these tribes at length became better known—and more feared—than their neighbours to the west. The three principal East German groups were the Goths, the Burgundians and the Vandals. (Note in passing that, though the simpler history books still speak of 'Goths, *Huns* and Vandals' as if these were all much of a muchness, the Huns were entirely different from the other two groups. They were not Germanic or indeed European at all, their kinship being rather with the Mongols and Tartars of Central Asia. Their presence terrified the German peoples almost as much as it did those of Rome. Note also, Gentle Reader, that the Burgundians *were* originally German—not, as I suspect you may have supposed, always an integral part of France.)

Goths, Burgundians and Vandals had all originated in the far north of Europe. To this day there are two provinces of Sweden called East and West Götland; there is an island in the Baltic called

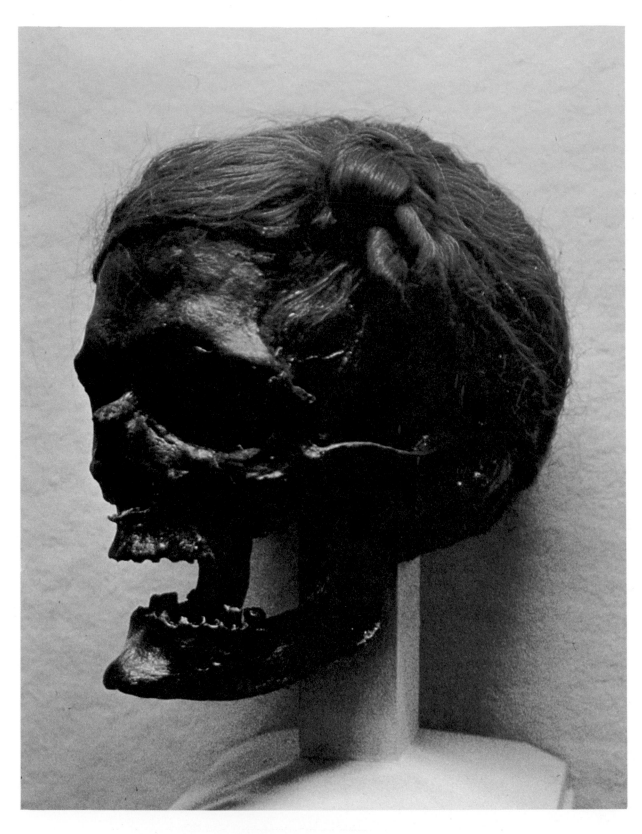

Above: Head of a man found at Österby, showing the characteristic Suebic hairstyle

Opposite: Marcus Aurelius's Column at Rome, recording his German victories

Bornholm, originally Burgundarholm; there is a region of Denmark called Vendsyssel, the 'settlement of Vandals'. But one by one these tribes had crossed the Baltic to settle in the land now called Poland.

The fierce *wanderlust* that afflicts all Germanic-speaking peoples descended on the Goths again in about AD 200. They left their previous home, in what is now north Poland, and moved south-eastward, up the Vistula and down the Dniester, and so to the shores of the Black Sea. There they made an ever-increasing nuisance of themselves. In AD 251 a Roman emperor, Decius, lost his life in battle with them; twenty years later another emperor, Aurelian, was forced to give up to them the rich province of Dacia (modern Romania). It was thus, probably, that the distinction grew up between Visigoths or 'West Goths', who moved into the new territory, and Ostrogoths or 'East Goths' who remained in their earlier home by the Black Sea.

Late in the fourth century the Huns arrived in Europe from central Asia, and like a well-thrown bowling-ball flung the German tribes in all directions. There followed a period of confused movement and battle, both inside and outside the Empire: at the end of it we find Vandals in North Africa, Visigoths in Spain, Ostrogoths in Italy, Franks and Burgundians in France and Anglo-Saxons in England. The entire western half of the Roman Empire had disintegrated into an assemblage of Germanic kingdoms.

Study of the East German peoples has led us to a point some centuries later than the date of the maps in this book, which refer to the mid-second century AD—a time at which the Germanic world was comparatively quiet and stable. Having seen the tribes who dwelt there, let us now look at their patterns of settlement and communication.

Tacitus tells us that the Germans had no towns, but lived in isolated villages. In his numerous writings about them he mentions only two settlements—Mattium, which was the chief place of the Chatti, and a town founded by king Maroboduus of the Marcomanni. Both tribes lived near the Roman frontier, and may have taken Roman frontier cities as their example. But most German settlements were insignificant not only by Roman standards but even by those of the Celtic world with its great hill-forts.

The geographer Ptolemy, about half a century later than Tacitus, contradicts him by naming no fewer than ninety-four cities in Germany—at least, the word he uses, *polis*, is the standard Greek word for 'city', but throughout his writings he uses it to mean very little more than 'place'. Where these places were is usually unknown. Some were probably Roman forts; some may have stood within the Roman Empire and not in 'Germany' proper. At least one, with the fine Teutonic-sounding name of Siatutanda, probably never existed at all. A passage of Tacitus mentions a skirmish between Romans and Friesians, in which the tribesmen fled 'to protect their possessions' (in Latin, *ad sua tutanda*). Ptolemy has taken this and invented the *city* of 'Protect-their-Possessions' complete with spurious latitude and longitude!

But a few of Ptolemy's 'cities' may be genuine German settlements. I have put some on the map, mainly to remind the reader that settlements of a kind did exist. Ancient Germany was not the trackless waste that it is sometimes made out to be.

The routes linking these settlements followed well-defined natural lines. One particularly important one, known today as the Hellweg, was especially favoured by Roman armies. From the important military base at Vetera on the Rhine, it ran up a tributary of that river called the Lippe almost as far as its source near Paderborn, then worked its way through the ill-omened Teutoburger Forest to reach the Weser near Minden. Tiberius, Drusus and Germanicus Caesar all made much use of this line, and several Roman military sites have been found along it. Beyond the Weser the road carried on past Hildesheim (an early mediaeval German town and bishopric) and struck the Elbe somewhere near Magdeburg. Another useful east-west route, also much used by Roman armies, left the Rhine further south, at Mainz, and followed the valley of the river Main. Thence, after passing through the great 'Hercynian Forest' that then occupied most of southern Germany, one could enter Bohemia, watered by the upper course of the Elbe and its tributaries. Routes such as these, with others further east that are less well-known, provided as it were the 'weft' of German communications, for crossing the land in an east-west direction; the 'warp' of communication in a north-south direction was provided, more easily, by the valleys of the great rivers themselves.

A note by Pliny the Elder shows the interesting results that could be achieved by use of these simple routes. In the reign of Nero, he tells us, a Roman businessman made his way from Carnuntum (Rome's principal military base on the Danube, not far from Vienna) all the way to the shores of the northern sea, and returned with an enormous amount of amber—enough to decorate all the equipment for a large gladiatorial display. This amber must have come from the Baltic peninsula now known as the Samland, near the city of Königsberg, which today produces nearly all the world's supply. In ancient times amber was also found in quantity along the North Sea coast, but this is so no longer. We can trace, at least roughly, the route which the Roman explorer must have followed; up the Morava river from Carnuntum, then across the Carpathians into the country of the Vandals. He could either have taken a boat down the Vistula river, past the site of Warsaw, to its mouth; or he could have chosen a shorter route directly north. This would have taken him past a settlement called Calisia, which is almost the only one of Ptolemy's eighty-four 'cities' that can be identified, as the lawyers say, beyond all reasonable doubt; it is the town now called Kalisz, which has yielded some interesting early remains. Further north still he would meet the Vistula again further downstream and descend it; from its mouth near Danzig it was not far to the Land of Amber.

This particular businessman is one of the very few about whose career we know anything at all, and even so, we do not know his name. But other similar men, not mentioned in even a paragraph of the writings that have survived for us, carried the products of Rome deep into Germanic territory. Archaeologists have discovered Roman objects—coins, pottery, metalware and glass—all over Germany, on the Baltic islands, and even in remote Scandinavia. Many such objects may have been the product of plunder rather than trade; many may have been passed from one tribe to another, not bought from a Roman trader on the spot; but some at least must mark the passage of other enterprising Romans like Pliny's anonymous gentleman.

At the height of Great Britain's Imperial power, people used to say that 'Trade follows the Flag'. It was G. K. Chesterton, I believe, who first said that just the opposite was nearer the truth, 'The Flag follows Trade'. As with the British, so it was with the Roman Empire. Armies and campaigns and wars and battles have always made news: business adventures (in an age without professional economists) hardly ever. Yet these quiet tradesmen of Rome, working their way across Germany by routes that Drusus and Germanicus never knew, had their own part to play in the slow development of that huge amorphous land called 'Germania Magna' into the Germanic society that we know today. The boundaries of the Roman Empire never exactly marked the limit of human civilization: still less did they ever mark the limit of human knowledge.

VI
ITALIA

'I am pointing at the Appian Way,' I replied solemnly. 'It was begun in the Censorship of my great ancestor, Appius Claudius the Blind. The Roman Road is the greatest monument ever raised to human liberty by a noble and generous people. It runs across mountain, marsh and river. It is built broad, straight and firm. It joins city with city and nation with nation. It is tens of thousands of miles long, and always thronged with grateful travellers. And while the Great Pyramid, a few hundred feet high and wide, awes sight-seers to silence—though it is only the rifled tomb of an ignoble corpse and a monument of oppression and misery, so that no doubt in viewing it you may still seem to hear the crack of the taskmaster's whip and the squeals and groans of the poor workmen struggling to set a huge block of stone into position—' But in this unpremeditated gush of eloquence I had forgotten the beginning of my sentence.

Robert Graves, *Claudius the God*

AS EVERY SCHOOLBOY KNOWS, Italy is shaped like a boot. Less well known is that, like all well-cared-for boots, it has a boot-tree inside it to preserve its shape—in the form of the Appennine range of mountains. These start in the north-west of the country, where they join the Maritime Alps above Genoa; they swing across to the east side of the peninsula, reaching their greatest height in the region now called the Abruzzi; then they cross over to the west side again to fill the 'toe' of the boot. From them Italy receives its basic shape.

A long-standing tradition in Europe decrees that maps shall be drawn with north at the top, and to conform with this countries are usually described starting in the north and working down to the south. A description of ancient Italy, however, might do better to work in the opposite direction (as favoured by Chinese geographers and map-makers) for it was the south of Italy that first made contact with the civilized world. For many centuries Italy's largest cities and most prosperous countryside were to be found in the southern half of the peninsula—just the reverse of the present-day state of affairs.

A numerical ordering on this principle was used by the emperor Augustus, when he divided Italy into eleven regions for the purpose of collecting his new tax, the *vicesima hereditatum* or five per cent death duty. (Hitherto, free citizens of Italy had been in the happy position of paying no tax of any kind at all.) Southern Italy comprised the second and third regions of the system, and it is here that I propose to begin.

All southern Italy, together with the neighbouring island of Sicily, had been exposed to Greek influence ever since about 700 BC. Naples, Paestum, Reggio di Calabria, Locri, Croton, Sybaris and Taranto were all of Greek origin; so too, on the island, were Messina, Catania and above all Syracuse. The rulers of this last city made it the most powerful of them all, dominating all Sicily except the extreme west and at times having influence on the Italian mainland as well. Until overtaken by Rome under the late Republic, it could claim to be the largest city in Europe. But the prosperity of Syracuse and the other Greek cities of the south was destroyed by a

Opposite: The Appian Way

prolonged series of wars, each more violent and devastating than the one before—Greeks against Greeks, Greeks against Carthaginians, Greeks against Romans, and finally the tremendous duel between the two super-powers Rome and Carthage, with the Greeks reduced to the role of helpless onlookers.

The final victory of Rome brought peace, but not prosperity—or at best, prosperity of a very one-sided kind. Southern Italy under Greek rule had been a land of many small holdings of the self-employed: under Roman rule it became a land of vast estates (*latifundia* in Latin) run and managed by slaves. (It was in southern Italy that Spartacus the ex-gladiator obtained the greatest support for his famous slave-revolt in 73 BC). The landlord of the *latifundia* was usually a great man at Rome—and an absentee from his lands. Here, for example, speaks the slave-turned-millionaire Trimalchio, in the *Satyricon* of Petronius:

> This wine comes from an estate of mine that I haven't seen yet, it's said to join my estates at Tarracina and Tarentum. [These two places, by the way, are over two hundred miles apart!] What I want to do now is add Sicily to my little bit of land—then when I want to go to Africa I could sail there without leaving my own property.

Plunged in gloom though it might be, southern Italy under the Romans was at least a part of Italy—with all the privileges that that entailed. Sicily was worse off still. In 241 BC the Romans had taken it over and made it the first province of their overseas Empire: Sicilians paid tribute to Rome and were governed by a Roman governor—who might well be a remarkably wicked and avaricious man. Perhaps the greatest of all Roman speech-makers was Cicero, and among the best-known of his speeches is that with which he led the prosecution of Gaius Verres, ex-governor of Sicily, for gross over-exploitation of his province. All Roman governors of the Republic exploited their provinces to a greater or less extent; Verres, however, was at length found guilty of going to an extent beyond what even the Romans themselves could tolerate. Whom shall we blame in the end? Hannibal smashed the economy of 'Greater Greece' with war; Verres and other Roman governors squashed the remains with their rapacity; the great Roman landlords—Trimalchio, who was imaginary, and others who, though nameless, really existed—ground up the pieces to plunge the whole land into a state of depression which (despite prolonged efforts by the Italian government) persists to this day.

The First Region of Augustus' system was an exception to the general ordering; naturally enough, the honour of being first was given to the territory that included Rome itself. This was a long narrow block of land, running down the west side of Italy from the river Tiber to the river Silarus—fairly low-lying on the whole, but interrupted by the craters of numerous extinct volcanoes, one of which—Vesuvius—surprised everyone in AD 79 by proving itself not extinct at all. The ash from these volcanoes gave remarkable richness to the soil, and Campania (the land round the Bay of Naples) was reckoned to be the very garden of Europe. Three or even four crops a year could be grown without exhausting the soil, and almost any type of plant would flourish. Corn, however, was unpopular, so Roman agricultural writers tell us, because it brought relatively little profit; much more money could be made from a small area by planting vines, olives, fruit-trees or even flowers—for Campania was a great centre of scent-manufacture.

The metropolis of Campania was Capua, then one of the largest cities in Italy. The very first Roman paved road, the Via Appia, had been built to link this important centre of trade with Rome itself. Capua also had a reputation for debauchery; Roman historians liked to claim that

Hannibal's army was ruined by the dissipation of wintering there after its great Italian victories. Under the Empire Campania was still a 'holiday-land'. Naples, which had kept much of its Greek culture, was popular with Romans who wanted to see 'a little bit of Greece' without going all the way to Greece itself. Baiae, further west, was also a popular resort—the Brighton of the Roman Empire, its sea-front lined with the villas of rich and fashionable Romans. Puteoli, halfway between the two, was a more workaday town—the chief port of Campania, and for a time the principal port for Rome. In Augustus' time the spices of India, the incense of Arabia, the silk of China were all unshipped at Puteoli to make the last stage of their long journey to Rome by land.

Immediately to the north of Campania lay Latium, the land from which the Roman Empire had its beginning, and the land from which the Romans' language took its name. 'Latium' originally seems to have meant 'the broad land'—here the Appennine mountains left a comparatively broad space between themselves and the sea, so that the word 'Latin' is related to the word 'latitude'.

The Latin-speaking peoples had originally had many cities of roughly equal size—Rome, Tivoli, Palestrina, Anzio and many others—but gradually Rome rose to a predominancy that quite overwhelmed all the rest. At first merely a member of what was called the 'Latin League', she rose in due course to dominate it, and in 338 BC (an important date for those interested in Roman political history) suppressed it altogether, emerging thereby from *leading member* to undisputed *ruler* of a confederation. Under the Empire Latium contained many towns of quiet consequence, but Rome outshone them all as the sun outshines the stars.

Imperial Rome was a remarkable city. Its population, at the height of its importance in the

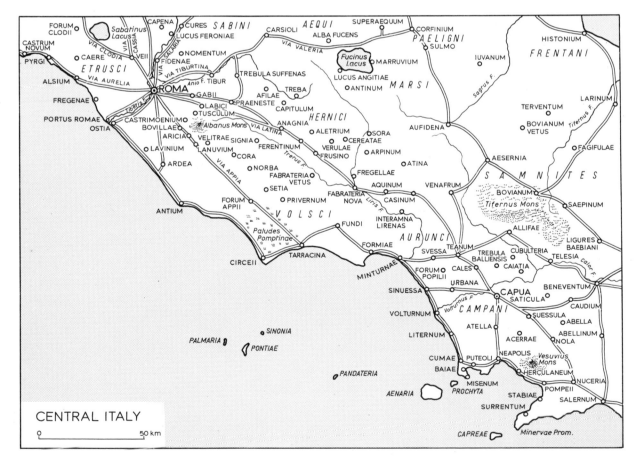

Above: General view of Pompeii

Opposite: Greek theatre at Syracuse with the harbour visible in the distance

Below: Coastal scene—wall painting from Pompeii

second century AD, was something like a million—not large by modern standards, but colossal by those of the ancient world. The city's growth brought with it a considerable traffic problem; there was no kind of regular street plan, and the narrow roads found themselves constantly choked with vehicles. Julius Caesar, as Dictator, tried to solve the problem with an edict forbidding all wheeled traffic from within the walls during the hours of daylight; but this draconian solution can hardly have won the thanks of the general public. Here is Juvenal on the subject:

> Insomnia causes more deaths among Roman invalids
> Than any other factor (the most common *complaints*, of course,
> Are heartburn and ulcers, brought on by over-eating.)
> How much sleep, I ask you, can one get in lodgings here?
> Unbroken nights—and this is the root of the trouble—
> Are a rich man's privilege . . .

> Here's the great trunk of a fir-tree
> Swaying along on its waggon, and look, another dray
> Behind it, stacked high with pine-logs, a nodding threat
> Over the heads of the crowd. If that axle snapped, and a
> Cartload of marble avalanched down on them, what
> Would be left of their bodies? . . .

It was London in the nineteenth century, not Rome in the first, that received the title of 'The Great Wen', but many a Roman would have agreed that Cobbett's phrase applied to his own city as well. The war-lords of the late Republic had developed the practice of keeping the people quiet with free corn-doles and free entertainment. The Emperors carried this 'Bread-and-Circuses' policy to even greater lengths. At times, indeed, one receives the impression that no Roman of Rome ever did a stroke of actual work. The city seems like a great sink, consuming the wealth of the world and in return producing nothing whatever. But this picture is almost certainly false. Among those million inhabitants there were many idlers, both rich and poor, and it is they who attract the attention of the satirists; but there were also numerous quiet, hard-working and unspectacular people who would have deeply resented the modern popular picture of Roman life. 'No news is good news'—and conversely, good news is no news.

For a better view of Romans at work, one must leave Rome itself and look at Ostia. This was the port of Rome, some twelve miles downstream at the mouth of the Tiber—or rather, at what used to be the mouth of the Tiber in those days; the river since Roman times has pushed the coastline some way further out. The city was an old one (it is supposed to have been founded by Ancus Macius, fourth of the semi-legendary 'Seven Kings of Rome') but for a long time it had only modest importance, because its harbour was so appallingly bad. The Tiber mouth was blocked by sand-bars, and in bad weather ships might hang about outside these for days or even weeks, unable to discharge their cargo. As we have already seen, the silks and spices from the Far East were often unshipped at Puteoli, over a hundred miles further south. But silks and spices arrived in comparatively small quantities. Even on Roman roads, carts and waggons could not possibly carry enough food to supply a million Roman citizens. The bulk of the food, corn especially, *had* to arrive by sea; and any delay could bring financial crises, panic buying and even actual deaths from starvation. It was the emperor Claudius who put a stop to this state of affairs by building a new, artificial harbour in which ships could unload with greater safety. Trajan built a second basin, smaller but still more secure. The settlement that grew up round these was called Portus Augusti, and a new road, the Via Portuensis, linked it to the capital. Ostia itself also grew, quite eclipsing Puteoli as a port, to become one of the most considerable cities in Italy. Its remains are impressive even today.

Immediately east of the First Region lay the Fourth Region. It consisted mostly of high ground, including indeed the highest peaks of peninsular Italy, and its inhabitants lived in small valleys and pockets of low ground tucked in among the hills. They were a very mixed group: two large and well-known tribes, the Sabines and Samnites, plus a number of smaller ones such as the Aequi, Marsi, Paeligni and Marrucini. But all, whether fighting for or against Rome, had frequently proved themselves formidable warriors. Their country, too, seems almost designed by Nature to make the task of an invader as hard as possible—as the invaders of Italy in the Second World War found to their cost.

It was in this region that the Romans first learned the techniques of mountain warfare, later to prove useful in regions as far apart as Scotland and Turkey. Some of Rome's most important early military towns and roads were built with the object of controlling the mountain tribesmen. Subsequently the resulting network across central Italy proved very useful indeed to Rome, as Pyrrhus of Epirus, and later Hannibal, found to their cost. Both these invaders imagined that if Rome's armies could be defeated in the field, her allies would collapse and make possible a speedy career of conquest. Pyrrhus failed even in the first part of his plan; the Romans fought him to a standstill, and eventually he left Italy in disgust and returned to Greece. Hannibal on the other hand did defeat the Roman armies, most resoundingly, but it did him no good. The Central Italians refused to yield, and Rome was saved. The belief still sometimes heard, that Rome ruled all her territories entirely by force, is simply not true.

About the Fifth and Sixth Regions of Italy little need be said. Each had a name of its own. The Fifth Region, on the east coast of Italy, roughly corresponding to the district now called *Marche* or 'the Marches', was anciently called Picenum. In Latin this means 'Woodpeckerland' and one ancient tradition has it that the Picenes were led down from the highlands of central Italy by a woodpecker. Modern scholars, however, incline to believe that they reached Italy from what is now Yugoslavia, bringing with them a language of their own; what 'Picenum' meant in this language remains a mystery. The Picenes' most considerable town was called Asculum (its modern name, Ascoli Piceno, still preserves its founders' memory) and the chief port of the Fifth Region, then as now, was called Ancona (a Greek word meaning 'elbow'), for here the eastern coast of Italy makes an abrupt change of direction and provides one of the few good harbours all along its length.

The Sixth Region of Italy was called Umbria; part of it, indeed, is still called Umbria. The Umbrians in ancient times claimed to be the most ancient race in Italy: they, they said, had always been there while everyone else—Greeks from Greece, Latins from Troy, Picenes from some-where-or-other, Etruscans, Sicels and the rest from Asia Minor—had arrived in comparatively recent times from foreign parts. Archaeologists today would give at least a kind of basis to this old boast; the Umbrians preserved what is technically called the 'Villanovan culture', a way of life once widespread throughout central Italy, long after it had disappeared in other parts of Italy. Though under Roman rule an important road, the Flaminian Way, Rome's great route to the north, ran right across it, Umbria like Picenum remained something of a backwater.

Above: Street in Herculaneum

Left: Coin of Nero, showing ships at Ostia

Opposite: Pompeii—Via di Stabia. Note the raised pavement and stepping stones

Like the Fifth and Sixth Regions, the Seventh had a special name of its own; it also long possessed a pronounced character of its own. It was the home of the famous Etruscans, whose origin and whose language remain to this day two of the greatest unsolved mysteries of Italian archaeology. The Etruscan cities (twelve of them according to tradition, though in fact there seem to have been thirteen of prime importance) were older than Rome, and the legend has it that when Rome was founded Etruscan priests had to be called in to ensure that the correct religious and magical observations were made. Somewhat later, by which time they had a royal dynasty actually ruling at Rome, the Etruscans made some more tangible contributions to the city. By means of the famous drain called the Cloaca Maxima, they turned a stretch of marshy ground into the Forum, the heart of the city; and close by, on top of the Capitol hill, they set up the great temple of Jupiter, Juno and Minerva, destined to become Rome's holiest shrine. No Roman colony thereafter was complete without its *capitolium*, dedicated to the same three deities and always set on the highest ground available.

But the Etruscans possessed the same lack of unity that was also to bring the Greeks to ruin. The *one* city of Rome broke the *twelve* cities of Etruria, because the 'League' of the twelve never translated itself into practical politics. Thereafter Etruria, like Umbria and Picenum, turned into a quiet provincial backwater. The strange Etruscan language slipped out of use so gently that few noticed its passing.

The Eighth, Ninth, Tenth and Eleventh Regions were comparative newcomers to the Italian scene. In the days of Augustus' great-uncle Julius Caesar they were not recognized as part of Italy at all, but formed an ordinary Roman province, paying tribute and being ruled by a governor. The boundary between Italy proper and this province of 'Cisalpine Gaul' was marked on the west side of the peninsula by a river called the Macra. At its mouth stood the important Roman outpost of Luna, famous under the Empire for its marble—what is now called 'Carrara marble'. On the east side of Italy the boundary was marked by a smaller but better-known watercourse, the famous Rubicon. By crossing it in 49 BC Caesar was leading an army out of his own province and on to the sacred soil of Italy; this amounted to an act of war against the Roman state, which could end only in victory or death for himself—hence the profound social importance of this physically insignificant stream.

Caesar himself gave Roman rights to several communities beyond the Rubicon, and Augustus completed the process by giving the whole region the same rights as those of Italy. It responded by producing some remarkable men. Catullus was a native of Verona, Virgil of Mantua, Livy of Padua, the elder and the younger Pliny both came from Como, and numerous inscriptions survive to inform us that in business and in the Roman army, other less famous northern Italians were achieving successes of their own. In Strabo's description of Italy, the north is the only part treated with any sort of enthusiasm, the only part where the general conditions of life seem to be improving instead of degenerating. Thus Milan is described by Strabo as 'formerly a mere village, but now a considerable city'—though unfortunately he does not say just *how* considerable. At a later period, after the great provincial reforms of the emperor Diocletian, Milan became the capital of a quarter of the Empire, and more important politically than Rome itself. Earlier still it had become the industrial headquarters of Italy, as of course it still is to this day. Verona, too, is called 'a large city' in Strabo's account. Padua seems to have been larger and richer still, for it contained more members of the equestrian order (more 'super-tax payers' would be roughly the modern equivalent) than any other city of the Empire except Rome and Cadiz.

Further east lay the region's chief port, Aquileia, which for a time had had the honour of being the most remote outpost of Roman power in Italy. Unlike almost all its neighbours, Aquileia has failed to maintain its importance into modern times; it was destroyed by the Huns in AD 452, the few survivors of the massacre taking refuge in the marshes along the coast—where in due course they built the city of Venice.

The countryside of the north enjoyed as much prosperity as the cities. Before the Roman conquest it must have presented a somewhat dismal and forbidding appearance; the Po river and its numerous tributaries caused vast tracts of land to be waterlogged, and other extensive regions were covered with thick forest. But when the Romans, with their genius for practical engineering, had cleared some of this away, the underlying soil proved remarkably fertile—more so, indeed, than that found in much of peninsular Italy, in as much as it had not been exhausted by generations of over-cropping. Corn could be grown on it in great abundance. The uncleared land, too, could be used for the breeding of livestock, particularly pigs and sheep; it was Paduan wool that gave Livy and his fellow citizens much of their outstanding wealth. Northern Italy gained under Roman rule an economic lead over the rest of Italy (Rome itself not excepted) which it has never since lost.

The Lands of the Upper Danube

Taisez-vous, roi de Bavière.

Napoleon

'What do you think the Alps *are*?' asked Hannibal as his army approached them in 218 BC. 'Are they anything worse than high mountains? Say, if you will, that they are higher than the Pyrenees, but what of it? No part of earth reaches the sky; no height is insuperable to men.' Thus inspired, the army pressed on over the mountains into Italy, to bring upon Rome her greatest crisis since the invasion of the Celts (also from beyond the Alps) nearly two centuries before.

So the mountains, though a formidable barrier, have never been an insuperable one. They failed to hold back the Celtic-speaking peoples, or Hannibal, or his brother Hasdrubal (though the latter's expedition against Rome soon afterwards came to a sticky end). And though the Romans themselves, moving in the opposite direction, accepted the Alps as the limit of their influence for nearly two centuries (from about 200 down to 15 BC) the time came at length when they broke through this barrier and extended their power right up to the Danube many miles further north.

In describing these newly-conquered lands, one meets a problem that has hitherto not arisen. Ancient Italia is still called Italy; Britannia is still Britain; Hispania is Spain (except of course the part which is now Portugal); and Gallia corresponds at least roughly to modern France. Along the Danube, however, ancient and modern boundaries have nothing in common. The 'upper-most' of Rome's Danubian provinces (the one nearest to the source of the river) was called the province of Raetia: its territory is shared today by Switzerland, Germany and Austria. Next to Raetia, further downstream, lay Noricum—a province corresponding roughly to what is now central Austria, though one of its principal towns (anciently called Celeia, now Celje) today belongs to Yugoslavia. Further downstream still the Danube makes a sudden right-angled bend, ceasing to flow eastward and instead flowing southward. Tucked into this angle was the

Above: Roman bridge over the Adige at Verona

Opposite above: Ostia

Opposite below: Diocletian's Palace at Split

land known as Pannonia. This region took in a small part of modern Austria (including its present-day capital, Vienna), about half of Hungary, and the piece of Yugoslavia called Slovenia. Most of the rest of Yugoslavia belonged to yet another Roman province, Dalmatia. This is counted with the 'Danube lands' here for convenience, but was not really a Danubian province at all. Its most important part, containing the vast majority of its population and nearly all its cities, was the Adriatic seaboard. Between this and the Danube stretched a horrible wilderness of mountain and forest, visited on occasion by Roman armies but hardly at all by Roman civilization.

It was this Dalmatian coast which of all these territories first attracted the attention of Rome. Whereas the Italian side of the Adriatic Sea is almost dead straight, without a single satisfactory harbour between Brindisi and Ancona, the Dalmatian side is full of bays, capes, fiords and islands. It seems to be designed by nature, indeed, as a lair for pirates—and for prolonged periods it was the most formidable nest of pirates in the Mediterranean. There had been a tradition, amounting almost to an unwritten rule, that any strong sea-power—Athens, Rhodes, Carthage, Rome or whatever—should take on the job of suppressing piracy and keeping the seas safe for international trade as a whole. The Romans, however, were most reluctant to undertake the task which tradition imposed upon them. Nevertheless, the piracy along this 'Illyrian' coast grew every now and then more than Rome could ignore: there was an 'Illyrian War' in 229 BC, another in 219 and a third in 168, in which the chief trouble-maker of this coast, one Gentius, was deposed and his kingdom came 'under the jurisdiction of the Roman People' (in Latin, *sub dicione populi Romani*), an odd sort of limbo-land, not exactly a Roman province but not quite not-a-province either.

In subsequent years the Romans scrabbled round a little more at the edges of this vast territory; but the steps that brought it under permanent Roman rule were all taken by one man, the emperor Augustus. He began his attack on the Danubian world in 35 BC, when he was not Augustus but still merely Octavian. In the course of this campaign he defeated one of the most powerful of the tribes on this Dalmatian coast, the Iapodes, and went on to take an important stronghold, sometimes called Segestica and sometimes Siscia.

Put like that, the achievement all sounds very far away and long ago. Where, you may well ask, is Siscia? and does it matter? In fact, it does matter. In the course of Rome's northward expansion, there had often been *one* town that was the key-point in the next phase of operations, one position, as it were, that on a military map would be eroded by the constant tapping of pointers and pinning-in of little flags. In one of the earlier stages of the Roman Republic, this key-point was the city of Veii, little more than ten miles from Rome itself; somewhat later Roman power advanced to Rimini, last outpost of Italy proper on the frontier of the Celtic-speaking world; later again a new outpost was established at Piacenza, on the very bank of the great river Po itself; and later still the port of Aquileia marked the terminus of a new departure, again starting from Rimini but turning eastward instead of west. Julius Caesar had based two legions for a time at Aquileia, probably intending to use them for an attack on the lands of the middle Danube. Only a last-minute accident (the sudden death of its governor) added the province of Transalpine Gaul to his territory and diverted his attention from the north-eastern frontier of Italy to the north-western. It was left to Augustus to make Caesar's plan an actuality.

The Roman capture of Siscia in 35 BC was highly important. The town (today called Sisak) was not only a place of great natural strength, protected by a maze of water-channels at the confluence of the river Kulp with the river Save, but also had great strategic significance; the

Save flows into the Danube, and provides one of the best lines of communication across Pannonia.

In 15 BC the Roman army began the gigantic task of extending Rome's frontier from the Alps to the Danube. This time Augustus did not take the field in person, but gave the command to his two stepsons Tiberius (the future emperor) and Drusus. The operations of these two were brilliantly successful; but the details of what they did are largely unknown. Of the numerous tribal groups between Alps and Danube, one (the Norici, holding a large part of what is now central Austria) seems to have surrendered without a fight. The Norici had long had fairly friendly relations with Rome. Businessmen often used to come up from Aquileia to their capital to buy the fine iron that was found in the surrounding mountains. After the conquest the tribe may have been allowed to keep its own rulers and enjoy a certain independence; not till the reign of Claudius, over fifty years later, do we hear of Noricum as a fully-organized Roman province.

Most of the Alpine tribes, however, were bitterly hostile to Rome; but, being neither numerous nor closely united, they could not put up any prolonged resistance. Once again we know little of the details of the fighting save that it involved, among other things, a Roman naval victory on Lake Constance. A great monument was set up, at a place called La Turbie near Nice, in honour of the final conquest, recording for us the names of the numerous Alpine tribes who had submitted.

Pannonia and Dalmatia proved the hardest task of all. Their inhabitants were divided into fairly large tribes, nearly all of them strongly anti-Roman. The Pannonian campaign continued until AD 9, and on one occasion the Roman forces were nearly thrown out of the country altogether. In the campaign three strongholds played a vital part: all in due course developed from military bases into large cities of the Empire, but unfortunately none of the three has maintained its importance down to our own day, and their names are known only to the specialist. One of these has just been mentioned, Rome's first foothold in the region, the town of Siscia, now called Sisak. The second stood on the same river as Siscia (the river Save), but further downstream, not far from the junction of this river with the Danube at the better-known city of Belgrade. The Romans called it Sirmium: its modern name is Sremska-Mitrovica. Under the later Empire Sirmium was to become an even greater town than Siscia; it was the capital of the Praefecture of Illyricum, the official residence of an Emperor, and the centre of administration for nearly all the Danube lands. The third corner of this Roman 'triangle of force' did not make its appearance till some years later. It stood many miles north of Siscia and Sirmium, on the bank of the great river Danube itself.

The name of this new Roman outpost (it was, as things turned out, the farthest north that Rome was ever to reach in this particular direction) was Carnuntum; the nearest modern site to it is the village of Petronell, some thirty miles down the Danube from Vienna and not far from the Iron Curtain where Austria meets Hungary. The Romans liked to set their frontier on the largest river they could find; they also liked to put the chief strongholds of that frontier at points where a lesser river comes out of hostile territory to join the main river. We have already noticed this along the Rhine frontier. Mainz, the military headquarters of the Roman province of Upper Germany, stands at the confluence of the Rhine with the Main; Vetera, which served the same purpose in Lower Germany, guarded the confluence of the Rhine with the Lippe. Close to Carnuntum the Danube is joined by a considerable river. The Germans call it the March; the Slavs call it the Morava. Like the Main and the Lippe, it flowed down to the Roman frontier from German territory; and the inhabitants of its valley (the land now called Moravia) were the

ITALIA

DACIA

Danuvius
Sirmium
Singidunum

Savus
Drinus
Margus
Angrus

MOESIA

Strymon

Doclea

Scodra

Ulcinium
Lissus
Axius

Dyrrhachium
MACEDONIA
Thessalonica

Apollonia
Haliacmon
Byllis
Olympus Mons
Aulon
EPIRUS

Larisa

Corcyra

Nicopolis
Acheloüs

Athenae

MARE
IONIUM
Patrae
Corinthus

ACHAEA
Sparta

Methone

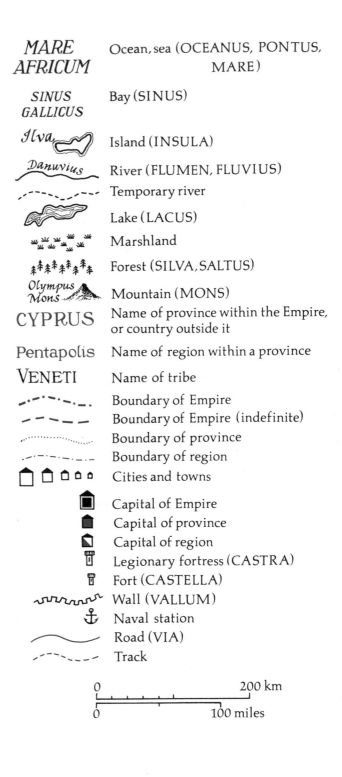

MARE AFRICUM	Ocean, sea (OCEANUS, PONTUS, MARE)
SINUS GALLICUS	Bay (SINUS)
Ilva	Island (INSULA)
Danuvius	River (FLUMEN, FLUVIUS)
	Temporary river
	Lake (LACUS)
	Marshland
	Forest (SILVA, SALTUS)
Olympus Mons	Mountain (MONS)
CYPRUS	Name of province within the Empire, or country outside it
Pentapolis	Name of region within a province
VENETI	Name of tribe
	Boundary of Empire
	Boundary of Empire (indefinite)
	Boundary of province
	Boundary of region
	Cities and towns
	Capital of Empire
	Capital of province
	Capital of region
	Legionary fortress (CASTRA)
	Fort (CASTELLA)
	Wall (VALLUM)
	Naval station
	Road (VIA)
	Track

0   200 km
0   100 miles

German tribe called the Quadi, one of the most numerous, fierce and anti-Roman in all that turbulent land.

Augustus realized at once the importance of Pannonia. There was no question here of leaving it in a kind of limbo, as may have happened with Raetia and Noricum; no sooner was it conquered than it became an official Roman province. Originally the land seems to have made up one single vast block, reaching from the Great Bend of the Danube down to the frontiers of Macedonia, called simply Illyricum; soon after, however, a distinction was made between the southern half (called Dalmatia, and recognized as at least *potentially* peaceful) and the northern half (Pannonia, which from its very nature could never be anything but military). The emperor Trajan subsequently split the Pannonian province into an 'Upper' and a 'Lower' part; the emperor Caracalla made a further readjustment. But these were administrative details, with the object of preventing any one governor from seizing too much power for himself.

For Pannonia was the Roman Empire's supreme military territory. Winston Churchill once called Italy 'the soft under-belly of the Axis', but subsequent events proved his analogy not altogether apt; he may have been right politically and economically, but physically Italy is far too mountainous to be the 'soft under-belly' of anything. But, taking another analogy from anatomy, one might say that the Roman Empire was an organism, the Danube and the road along it its spinal cord, and Pannonia its lumbar region—the weakest spot along the whole column, unsupported by either ribs or pelvis, where a single sharp blow might have the most crippling results. A hostile force over the Danube and into Pannonia would not only be excellently placed for an attack on Italy, but by its mere presence would cut off all land communication between the western and eastern halves of the Empire. To prevent this, the province throughout its history had to have an unusually strong military garrison. In the second century, the comparatively short stretch of river between Vienna and Budapest, about 150 miles long, required no less than four legions to guard it—X Gemina at Vienna itself, XIV Gemina Martia Victrix (the same that had won distinction against Boudica in Britain) at Carnuntum, I Adiutrix at a place called Brigetio, the modern town of Szöny, and II Adiutrix at Aquincum (modern Budapest). By contrast, all Roman Britain in the second century required only three legions; Roman North Africa managed with a single one.

So much for the military importance of the Danube. What, then, about civil life along it? What about the communications that knitted the system together?

Raetia, the uppermost of the Danubian provinces, had little of either. Its capital, and its only city of any great importance, was Augsburg, part of whose ancient name—Augusta Vindelicum —is preserved in the first syllable of its modern one. (Munich, the present-day capital of these regions, did not make its appearance till the Middle Ages.) The emperor Claudius, who seems to have been the first to set Raetia up as a province, also improved its communications with Italy by building a new road, named the Via Claudia Augusta after himself. Starting from Verona, it crossed the Alps by the Resia (Reschen Scheideck) Pass, and an alternative route was also available using the Brenner. But despite this improved line of communication civil life in Raetia developed very little. As the province also lacked military importance (although on the frontier, it managed without a legionary garrison until the late second century) it remained a backwater, thinly-populated and largely cut off from the activity of the rest of the Roman world.

The next province, Noricum, had a slightly more lively existence. Like Raetia, it was officially established by the emperor Claudius, and several of its cities owed their existence to him. The provincial capital was a place called Virunum (modern Zollfeld, not far from Klagenfurt). It had replaced an older settlement nearby on the hill of the Magdalensberg, the former chief place of the Norican tribe, which like many other hill-top settlements (Maiden Castle in Britain, Mont-Beuvray in France, Manching in Germany) went out of use when the *pax Romana* made fortified sites unnecessary.

Virunum, and most of the other towns of Roman Noricum, lay in the southern half of the province, where the Alps are pierced by the two large rivers Drave and Save and their numerous tributaries. The northern part—Noricum Ripense or 'Noricum along the Banks' as it was later called—was more sparsely inhabited, possessing only two cities of any substance, Salzburg and Wels. Like Raetia, Noricum was on the whole a peaceful province, and was long able to manage without a legionary garrison. Only near the end of the second century, during the great Marcomannic War which raged all along the upper course of the river, did the emperor Marcus Aurelius find it necessary to strengthen the garrison of the two upper provinces. Raetia received the new Legio III Italica based at Regensburg; the Legio II Italica was sent to Noricum, and after some moving about established itself at Lauriacum (modern Lorch) where the Danube is joined by a river called the Enns. Each province thus acquired an extra city, for both Regensburg and Lorch, like many legionary bases throughout the Empire, attracted civil settlement and eventually received the official status of cities. They were, moreover, the first Roman cities in either province to be established actually *on* the Danube; hitherto there had been no town of any size on the river further upstream than Vienna, and one cannot but feel that much of the potential of this great river as a highway was being wasted. Even with the addition of Regensburg and Lorch, however, cities on the upper Danube were still few and far between. The land was caught, so to speak, in a kind of communication squeeze, hemmed in between the mountains and the Imperial frontier. Only long after the fall of Rome, with the opening-up of Germany so that the Danube ceased to be a boundary, could it realize its full potential.

In these two upper provinces of the Danube civilization was allowed to develop at its own pace—on the whole, a slow pace. In Pannonia the situation was different. Here, as in Britain and along the Rhine, and in Rome's other military provinces, the Roman Army had a forcing effect upon the growth of towns, causing them to develop at a speed which no wholly peaceful province could have contrived. Almost every town in the two provinces of Upper and Lower Pannonia had military connections, some growing on the sites of abandoned military bases, others alongside fortresses still in use, others again first appearing as settlements officially founded for ex-soldiers. Remember, after all, that four Roman legions amounted to some 20,000 fighting men, add some more for the auxiliary troops who supported the legions along this critical bend of the Danube, then double your answer to take into account all these soldiers' wives, mistresses, children and slaves. Then add another large figure for all the people whom British India called 'box-wallahs'—the tradesmen who followed the Army into new lands hoping for useful contacts with the soldiers and the 'barbarians'. The final total begins to approach 100,000 people, enough for one fairly substantial town even by the standards of our own world. In the Roman world, here was material for at least half-a-dozen towns developed in the highest Roman style.

Yet several centuries of Roman military influence were not sufficient to cover Pannonia *uniformly* with towns. The Roman cities in the land formed a square pattern, bounded on the north and east by the Danube, on the south by the Save river, and on the west by the foothills of the Alps. The centre of the square, round Lake Balaton, possessed no towns of any consequence, much of it being still covered by the primaeval forest and swamp. The third-century emperor Probus set his troops to clearing some of this country—whereupon they promptly murdered him. By this time, Roman soldiers had developed a strong sense of their own importance; already the seeds had been sown of the mediaeval idea that fighting was for gentlemen, while raising walls, digging ditches and improving the landscape were the duty of a very much lower class.

The last of these provinces, Dalmatia, had yet another pattern of settlement. It is a universal rule that the lands of the Roman Empire that border the Mediterranean have many more officially-recognized cities than those far removed from it. They are not necessarily *larger* communities, but they are invariably more *numerous*. So it was with the provinces that border Italy. Raetia possessed four or five official cities, Noricum nine, the two Pannonias had about twenty between them. Dalmatia had at least fifty, and there may well be more that have not yet been discovered. Nearly all of them lay on or very near the sea. The largest of them, in area though perhaps not in population, was the town which present-day Yugoslavs call Zadar, and Italians Zara; the Roman name for it was Iader. The district in which it stands, anciently called Liburnia, was one of the most fertile and prosperous parts of the Adriatic coast. It was particularly famous for shipbuilding; Liburnian light galleys helped Octavian to win the battle of Actium in 31 BC, and later on the word 'liburna' came to mean simply 'ship'—just as in our time all fine porcelain is called 'china', after the country where it was originally made.

The administrative centre of the province was further south, at a place called Salona, which the Romans had seized in about 75 BC as one of their first footholds on this coast. The site, now called Solin, is today virtually a suburb of the city of Split. The ancient situation, however, was just the other way about; Salona was a considerable town (it is thought to have had between 40,000 and 60,000 inhabitants, the latter figure being just twice the estimated population of Roman London) while Split was a mere village dependent on it. Only when the emperor Diocletian retired to Split in AD 305 and built himself a large palace there (still very well preserved) did the village begin to acquire an importance of its own.

Though we cannot be certain, it is probable that Diocletian was born in Salona, and retired to live near his own home town. He was almost certainly a native of *some* place in what I have called the 'Danube provinces', as were most of his predecessors in the third century and successors in the fourth. For by this time the influence of these provinces on the Army, and hence on the governance of the Empire, had become overwhelming. The tail, so to speak, had begun to wag the dog; instead of Rome controlling the Danube frontier, it would be nearer the truth to say that men from that frontier controlled Rome. Diocletian's own great provincial reforms made this state of affairs official. Trier, Milan and Sirmium became the official capitals of Europe. Rome, too far removed from the theatres of military operation, sank to the level of a provincial city seldom visited by the emperors if they could possibly avoid it. Lovers of paradox have sometimes claimed that Christ was not a Christian, or that Freud was not a Freudian: similarly, one could say that after about AD 300 the city of Rome was no longer a part of the Roman Empire.

VII

MACEDONIA

ONE GLANCE AT THE MAP of Greece is enough to show its most outstanding physical feature—the extraordinary way in which it is disjointed, fragmented and altogether broken in pieces. It is a land of innumerable capes and bays and islands and straits and isthmuses, of little pockets of ground cut off from their neighbours by the sea or towering mountains.

In such a country, it is not surprising that communications by land have always been difficult at best, and at worst appalling. The Greek myths are full of horrible incidents encountered by the roadside. One of the hero Theseus' first heroic deeds was to rid the world of a bandit named Sciron, who used to terrorize the road from Corinth to Athens. He later disposed of a better-known character with the same habits, named Procrustes:

> Procrustes was a man to dread;
> He strapped his victims to a bed,
> And those who were too short, 'tis said,
>
> He stretched until they fitted it;
> Nor did he fail to chop a bit
> Off those who were the opposite.
>
> He never wore a bowler hat,
> Or used a ballpoint pen. In that
> He differed from a bureaucrat.

Oedipus similarly won glory (and the right, as prophesied, to marry his own mother) through his conquest of the Sphinx, who dwelt by a road near Thebes and, more subtle than Sciron or Procrustes, terrorized travellers thereon with mental as well as physical torment. Somewhat earlier Oedipus had already fulfilled another part of the prophecy by killing his own father in a quarrel about who should have right-of-way at a crossroads on the road from Delphi to Daulis. There was evidently no need, in those heroic days, to rush up mountains or into forests or marshes or deserts in search of adventure: it could descend on the traveller along some of the best-known of early routes.

Even after these mythical times had given place to an age of sober and well-recorded history, we still find the roads of Greece to be the scenes of repeated and violent conflict. One of the most famous battles in Greek history, Thermopylae, in 480 BC, deals with the attempt by three hundred Spartans to hold back an entire Persian army at a narrow place between the mountains and the sea. (Visitors to the site today, however, find it much altered: so many trees have been cut down in Greece, and so much earth loosened thereby and washed down the rivers, that in many places the coastline has profoundly changed. The pass of Thermopylae is now several miles wide.) Further south, but still on the same road which forms the principal north-south axis of Greece, the ancient traveller found himself in another confined space, with mountains on one side of him and a large lake called Copaïs (now drained) on the other. The small town of Chaeronea in this area was famous as the scene of *two* important battles: one in 338 BC, when Philip of Macedon beat the combined forces of Thebes and Athens and made himself overlord of all Greece; and another in 86 BC, when the Romans under Sulla defeated the forces of king Mithradates of Pontus, with the Greeks on this occasion standing by as helpless spectators. Not for nothing was the whole region of Boeotia, in which Chaeronea stood, grimly nicknamed 'Mars's Ballroom'. Further south still, the roads of the Peloponnese were marked by a string of battlefields, where at various times the Spartans had attempted to expand their gaoler-like influence and their neighbours had desperately sought to thrust them back again.

Though land travel in Greece was always difficult and sometimes horrible, sea travel could be more pleasant. The Mediterranean can be squally and choppy at times, particularly in winter, but it lacks the prolonged gales and towering waves that can make the 'Outer Ocean' so intimidating, and the Aegean Sea enjoys the same clear sparkling light that shines on the Greek mainland. So, whereas the mariner of the north often found himself blundering about in visibility almost nil, his greatest fear that of discovering land by collision, the Greek mariner saw the land as his friend and was at first very unwilling to lose sight of it. Fortunately, Greece is so made that one can travel a long way while sticking to this rule. By 1000 BC or even earlier Greeks had spread across the Aegean to its eastern side and planted settlements there; cities like Smyrna and Ephesus, Miletus and Halicarnassus, which now stand on Turkish soil, were originally Greek. Somewhat later this colonizing spread further afield, all round the inland seas. Marseille in France and Syracuse in Sicily, Cyrene in Libya and Naucratis in Egypt, Trebizond in what is now eastern Turkey and Kertch in what is now Russia, were all part of the Greek-speaking world just as much as Athens or Sparta or Thebes. Many such overseas cities grew larger and more important than the towns which had originally founded them.

In defiance of the conventional histories, I propose to skip any account of Classical Greece and take up its story at the point where many writers end it—with the Macedonian conquest and the end of Greek independence.

Macedonia lies on the northern fringe of the Greek world. Whether it should be called a part of Greece is to some extent a matter of opinion; most scholars, however, seem to think not. (While collecting material for this chapter I found several books supposedly describing 'Northern Greece' which nevertheless deal mostly with what I should have called 'Central Greece', with Macedonia hardly receiving a mention at all.) The Macedonians certainly *spoke* Greek, but they did not share in many of the customs that made the Hellenic world what it was: their southern neighbours regarded them as a set of hicks and hillbillies, the type who, in modern terms, would eat peas with a knife and pass the port the wrong way.

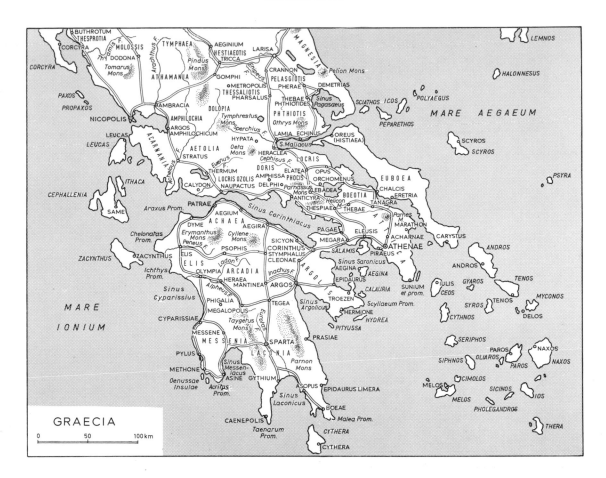

But Macedonia was too powerful to be altogether a joke, By the standards of the time it was an extremely large country, almost as big as all the Greek mainland states put together. Its boundaries were never precisely defined, but took in all kinds of wild tribesmen—Illyrians, Thracians and the like—who could not be called Greek even by courtesy. And it possessed enormous natural resources of timber, livestock, minerals and fighting men. To the Greek states it appeared somewhat as Czarist Russia (or, for that matter, Soviet Russia) appears to the nations of western Europe. Czarist Russia provides the closer analogy, for Macedon had a hereditary monarchy, another custom which her southern neighbours thought very old-fashioned and quite out of keeping with the spirit of modern Hellenism. Unfortunately for them, the Macedonian royal dynasty threw up in the fourth century BC two men of outstanding military genius—Philip II and his son Alexander the Great.

Philip ascended the throne of Macedon in 359 BC, and at once set about aggressive expansion of his kingdom. Northward, he conquered numerous Illyrian tribes, north-eastward many tribes of the country now called Bulgaria, but in those days Thrace. (Thereby he came to resemble even more closely a Russian Czar of the old school: this newly-acquired territory, even larger, colder and more barbarous than Macedonia itself, he used mainly as a deporting-ground for criminals.) Southward, he pressed steadily deeper into the territory of Greece proper. Finally, at Chaeronea in 338 BC, he broke the last Greek army capable of opposing him (the decisive blow in the battle being struck by the cavalry under Alexander, a field-marshal at the age of eighteen). After a century of confused indecision, the Greeks at last had their minds made up for them by an outsider.

Philip's last and most ambitious plan, for an invasion of the Persian Empire, was held up by

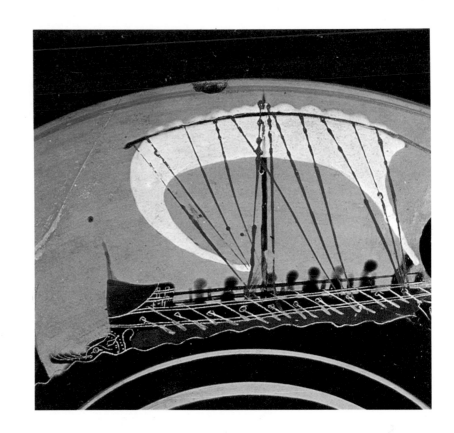

Opposite : Temple of Apollo at Delphi

Right : Greek warship, sixth century BC

Below : Ruins of Corinth with Acro-Corinth in the background

his assassination in 336 BC, but Alexander the Great carried his father's project forward to an extent beyond all that could have been imagined. His Empire, at its height, was the largest that the world had ever known, reaching from the Danube to the Indus, from the Nile (and the city called 'Alexandria-in-Egypt') to the Jaxartes (and the city called 'Alexandria-the-Last', now called Leninabad, in one of the remotest parts of the USSR). Its existence as a united empire, however, was brief. When Alexander died in 323 BC it passed, *officially*, to the joint rule of his son, Alexander IV, and his half-brother Philip III, but the former was a new-born babe and the latter an imbecile. *Real* power rested with the Macedonian generals, who at once began to fight among themselves.

In the ensuing power-game Macedonia itself was an important part of the board, valued as a source of excellent fighting men. It changed hands several times. One of its rulers, named Cassander, made an important contribution to its geography by founding a large new city, named after his wife—Thessalonica. It prospered, and under Roman rule became a provincial capital, as it still is today.

Cassander's chief rivals were a family called the Antigonids, who had unusually chequered careers even by the standards of the time. Antigonus I (nicknamed Monophthalmios or 'The One-Eyed') had built up power in Asia Minor and for a while looked as if he might reunite the greater part of Alexander's empire, but in 301 BC he met defeat and death at the battle of Ipsus. His son, Demetrius called Poliorcetes or 'The Besieger', managed to take over Macedonia and a large part of Greece, but was at length deposed and died in captivity. Only with the third generation, represented by Antigonus II called Gonatas, did the family succeed in firmly establishing itself.

It was Philip V, grandson of the second Antigonus, who sowed the seeds of his country's destruction by making an alliance with Hannibal against Rome. The resulting 'Macedonian Wars' outlasted his reign and went on to involve his son Perseus. Most of the campaigning was done among the Pindus Mountains in central Greece—a region where communications were exceptionally poor even by Greek standards, and the 'fog of war' correspondingly thick. The two critical battles, Cynoscephalae or 'Mount Doghead' in 197 BC and Pydna in 168 BC, both began almost by accident, with neither side well aware of the other's position. On both occasions the Romans won crushing victories, largely because the Macedonian *phalanx* (a close-packed, porcupine-like body of pikemen) failed to keep its formation on rough ground and was destroyed piecemeal by the quicker-moving Roman legionaries. Roman flexibility, in fact, beat Greek rigidity—just the opposite of the state of affairs one usually imagines.

The fourth, last, shortest and most one-sided of the Macedonian Wars ended in 147 BC, when Rome finally annexed the territory and made it into a province—her first foothold in the eastern half of the Mediterranean world. In the following year (the same that saw the fall of Carthage) Greece proper was overrun. A Roman army under Mummius sacked Corinth, and vast amounts of loot were sent off to raise the social and aesthetic taste of the Roman upper class. (Tradition has it that Mummius, a simple soul, arranged a contract by which any priceless masterpiece of art lost on the voyage to Rome should be replaced.)

One of the Romans' first acts in their new province—begun, perhaps, even before it officially became a province—was to build a military road across it, the famous Egnatian Way, linking the Adriatic Sea with the Aegean. Its western termini, both of Greek origin, were the two Adriatic ports called Epidamnus and Apollonia, both in the country now called Albania, and thus more than a little inaccessible to the modern traveller. Apollonia is no longer a port, or indeed an inhabited place at all; like many ports of the ancient Mediterranean world, it was killed by the silting-up of the river on which it stood. Epidamnus, however, still survives, though not under its original name. The Romans considered this, with its suggestion of damnation, to be unlucky, and changed the name of the town to Dyrrhachium, the name of the headland on which it stood. Now called Durrës, it is still the principal port of Albania.

The two roads from these ports met on the banks of the Genusus river (now called the Shkumbin) and then ascended it into the high mountains which the ancients called Candavia, and which today form the frontier between Albania and Yugoslavia. Then it worked its way across central Macedonia—an awkward piece of land where high mountains alternate with deep valleys, often containing lakes of great size and often presenting the ancient engineers with problems of poor drainage and road-subsidence.

At Edessa (a very old town, perhaps going back to pre-Greek times, which preserves its ancient name and importance to this day) the road descends from the highlands into the plain which the ancients called Emathia or 'Sandiland'. Like most Greek plains it is larger now than it used to be, through the continued silting of the rivers which cross it. Here was the heartland of the Macedonian kingdom, containing all its largest cities. Aegae, the oldest capital and burial-ground of the royal family, was long thought to be the same place as Edessa; this was a misunderstanding, however, and its actual remains (including, it is thought, the tomb of the great Philip himself) have recently been found near Vergina, some way further south. Pella, Alexander the Great's capital, stood on a mound almost entirely surrounded by the waters of Lake Ludias, another Greek lake which no longer exists. The Egnatian Way was built to pass through the town, crossing some very treacherous ground. Thessalonica, the region's principal city in Roman, mediaeval and modern times, lies at the eastern end of the Emathian plain, where it joins the rocky peninsula known as Chalcidice. This position, though making the city subject to earthquakes (as has recently been disastrously shown) has at least saved it from the fate that has overtaken Aegae and Pella—abandonment through the blockage of its water-borne lines of communication. Thessalonica was the original terminus of the Egnatian Way; it was later extended, however, past the gold-mining town of Philippi (though when the Romans appeared on the scene the mines were almost exhausted) and so along the north Aegean coast to Byzantium.

Like nearly all Roman roads the Via Egnatia was originally built for military reasons. From the earliest times the Macedonian kingdom had had to beat off attacks from the wild tribes to the north of it; and the hostility of these tribes was in no way lessened when the kingdom came under new management. There was hardly a single Republican governor of Macedonia, so Cicero tells us, who returned from his term of office without celebrating a triumph for some campaign or other, and in all such campaigns the Egnatian Way would have formed his principal line of communication. When Rome acquired territory in Asia the road became even more important. One of the favourite routes to the east, for soldier and civilian alike, was from Rome down the Appian Way to Brindisi, then by ship across the neck of the Adriatic to Durrës, then across Macedonia via the Egnatian Way. From Thessalonica or one of the other north Aegean ports one could then take ship to Ephesus, the capital of Roman Asia and the usual starting-point for journeys to the interior. Under the Emperors, however, the pattern began to change. Augustus' conquest of the Danube lands meant that troops could be withdrawn from Macedonia and stationed much further north; the Via Egnatia became a purely civilian, no longer a military, highway.

Left: The Via Egnatia near Philippi

Opposite: The Corinth Canal, proposed but never built by several rulers of the Ancient World

Below: Roman aqueduct at Kavala, the port of Philippi

The history of Roman rule in Greece proper—the lands south of Macedonia and the Egnatian Way—makes melancholy reading. In the first century BC the country had the misfortune to be closely involved in Rome's terrible Civil Wars. Three decisive battles, Pharsalus, Philippi and Actium, were all fought on Greek territory, each preceded by the inevitable marching and counter-marching, requisitions of animals, food and money, and that habit that makes civil war so particularly unpleasant—that each commander regards anyone who helps the other side, however unwillingly, as a traitor. Much of Greece was reduced almost to a desert. A partial recovery took place under the Emperors, but it was slow. Nero's scheme, by which Greece became 'free' and immune from Roman taxes, does not seem to have greatly helped; Vespasian subsequently cancelled the scheme, but instead of keeping Greece (or the province of Achaea, as it was officially called) for himself, he handed it over to the Senate, taking the province of Sardinia-with-Corsica instead. And Vespasian was a man who seldom made a bad bargain.

A few cities, with support from Rome, prospered despite the general depression. One of these was Corinth which from very early times had been the leading commercial and industrial city of Greece. Sacked by the Romans in 146 BC, the city was restored by Julius Caesar. Under Augustus it became the capital of the newly-created province of Achaea, and once more a great centre of commerce and industry, for which its natural position admirably suited it. The only thing lacking was a canal across the isthmus, but though Caesar, Caligula and Nero all at various times tried to construct one (as several Greek rulers had done earlier) their attempts all failed. (The present Corinth Canal dates only from 1893.) As a kind of substitute, however, there was a slipway across the isthmus in ancient times, linking the harbours of Lechaeum and Cenchreae, and boats of moderate size could be hauled across on that.

A second prosperous city of Roman Greece was Patrae, some seventy miles west of Corinth. In classical Greek times this city had been of no special importance; the Emperor Augustus raised it to a place of substance (as it still is today) by making it a Roman colony and putting several smaller nearby communities under its control, a process technically known as synoecism. Whereas in the outer parts of their Empire the Romans were concerned to create cities, in regions like Greece they sometimes found more cities already existing than they thought desirable, and tried to cut down the number by amalgamating small communities to form larger ones.

Further up the west coast of Greece was another city that had been enlarged by the same method. This too was a foundation by Augustus, built to celebrate his naval triumph off nearby Cape Actium, and named Nicopolis, 'City of Victory'. To swell its population, several settlements in the neighbourhood—including the old and important town of Ambracia, now called Arta—were deprived of their official status and reduced to the rank of villages. The part of Greece in which the city stood, known as Epirus, 'The Mainland', was suffering at the time from an unusually intense poverty and depression, for which the Romans themselves must take most of the blame. In 167 BC, after the Third Macedonian War, the land had been systematically plundered—150,000 Epirotes were sold into slavery—and from this blow it never fully recovered. In the second century AD Epirus was made a province in its own right, but it must have been one of the poorest and most sparsely-inhabited provinces in the Empire; Nicopolis, the capital, was almost its only city of any consequence.

Other parts of Greece besides Epirus suffered from a general feeling of gloom and depression under Roman rule. Sparta, deprived of the military power that had been her chief claim to fame, emerged as merely a nondescript provincial town. Thebes, once even more powerful than Sparta, was a still worse case, only the acropolis of the city being inhabited at all—though here it was not the Romans who were to blame, but Alexander the Great, who had systematically razed the place in 335 BC. Athens enjoyed a kind of prosperity as a famous university town and tourist attraction, but she was feeding on the glories of the past rather than building up anything new for the present. Her harbour of Piraeus, once among the busiest ports in Europe, had become a backwater. Some time in the middle of the second century AD one of the huge Egyptian grain-ships was blown off course and fetched up at Piraeus, whereupon nearly everyone in Athens, including the writer Lucian who tells us about it, came down to stare at the wonder. This single ship, it was said, held enough grain to feed all Athens for a year. Imperial Rome needed a whole fleet of them.

Before one concludes, however, that Rome's annexation of Greece brought nothing but poverty and stagnation, it must be noted that the land had not been especially rich at any time. Its 'Golden Age' was famous for quality of civilization, not quantity of material possessions: it was common knowledge even then that the Greek cities overseas (in Italy, in Russia, in Asia and in Africa) had far greater potential and actual resources than those of the Greek homeland. The operations of Alexander and his successors opened up still further opportunities abroad, and by Roman times all the most enterprising Greeks had long since left their homeland and were earning a brisk living either in the Near East or, much to the disgust of many native Romans, at Rome itself.

The Provinces of the Lower Danube

An Austrian army awfully array'd,
Boldly by battery besieged Belgrade.
Cossack commanders cannonading come
Dealing destruction's devastating doom:
Every endeavour engineers essay,
For fame, for fortune fighting—furious fray!...

Alaric A. Watts

Even in heroic times, well before the beginning of reliable history, the Greeks took an interest in the Black Sea. The famous tale of Jason and the Argonauts describes a voyage from Iolcos (modern Volo, in Thessaly) to Colchis at the extreme eastern end of the Black Sea, in quest of gold (the 'Golden Fleece'). The sea can be stormy, and early voyagers called it the Pontus Axeinos or 'Inhospitable Sea': the name was later changed to Euxeinos ('Hospitable') as being politer to whatever deity was responsible for the bad weather.

In the seventh century BC exploration began to be followed by permanent settlement. Byzantium, at the gateway to the Euxine, is supposed to have been founded in 660 BC. It was followed, about a century later, by other towns further north—among them Odessus (modern Varna, the chief port of Bulgaria), Tomis (modern Constanza, the chief port of Romania) and Istros or Istria (now uninhabited, though its ruins are well preserved). Istros stood near the mouth of the Danube, and from it trading expeditions went a considerable distance up the river. Herodotus, writing in the fifth century BC, describes it very clearly, with its tributaries, up as far as the place now called the 'Iron Gate'. Here the Danube forces its way through a narrow gorge between the Balkan Mountains and the Transylvanian Alps, with a powerful current and many whirlpools. Beyond this obstacle to navigation Greek knowledge was very sketchy. Herodotus himself put the source of the river in 'the fountain of Pyrene, in the country of the

Left: Nicopolis, the capital of Epirus

Opposite: Temple of Zeus at Athens completed by the emperor Hadrian

Below: The Acropolis of Athens viewed from the air

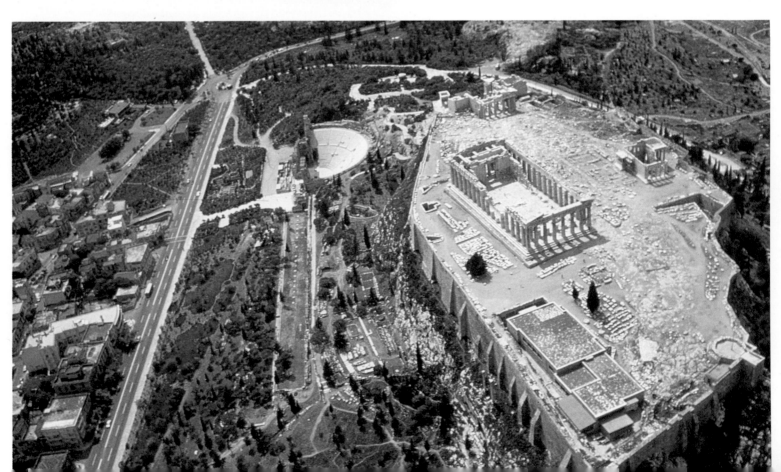

Celts'; he may have had the Pyrenees in mind. Other Greeks supposed that a branch of the Danube entered the Adriatic Sea (there was indeed an important early trade route from the middle Danube to the Adriatic, but it did not, of course, follow the same river all the way). Yet another geographical red herring of the Greeks was the belief that from some high mountain in the interior one could see both the Black Sea and the Adriatic. (Such a peak, according to my calculations, would have to be at least two or three thousand feet higher than Mount Everest.) The geography of the upper Danube lands was never fully understood until the Romans conquered them.

The people who lived between the lower Danube and the Aegean Sea, who were collectively known as Thracians, were also observed with attention by their Greek neighbours. Rugged and mountainous though their land might be, they existed in fair numbers. Herodotus, indeed, calls them the most numerous of the nations of the earth save only for the Indians. They were also remarkably backward. They played the same part in Greek popular talk as the 'Kings of the Cannibal Isles' did among the Victorians. They were the fiercest, most savage, most primitive, most 'barbarous' in every sense of the word, of all known peoples under the sun. Even the Aethiopians of the far south and the Celts of the far west seemed to have more inklings of civilization.

Philip II of Macedon conquered most of Thrace in the 340s BC, and founded several new towns there, peopleing them largely with condemned criminals—the largest, officially called Philippopolis, was commonly nicknamed Poneropolis, meaning 'City of Baddies' or 'Crooksville'. But his successors as kings of Thrace, Alexander the Great and then a general named Lysimachus, had other and richer fish to fry in the continent of Asia; they left the inner part of Thrace very much to its own devices. The death of Lysimachus (in 281 BC) was soon followed by an invasion of Celts from further up the Danube, which flung the whole region into disorder. By the time the Romans appeared on the scene, most Thracians were leading much the same sort of life that they had before the Macedonians came.

As was mentioned in the previous chapter, the Roman conquest of the Danube under Augustus is ill-documented, and operations on the lower river are outstandingly so. Hostilities began in 29 BC when Licinius Crassus (grandson of the famous millionaire who had shared power with Caesar and Pompey) defeated a tribe called the Moesi and captured the town of Serdica (modern Sofia). Later, we do not know exactly when, came further campaigns under a general named Lentulus. By about AD 6 Rome had officially established what was called the province of Moesia—a huge block of land, reaching from Constanza on the Black Sea some 400 miles west up the Danube to where it joins the Save river at Belgrade, and then from Belgrade some 200 miles south to Skopje and the border with Macedonia.

A large piece of Thrace, though now surrounded on the north and the east and the west and the south by land under direct Roman rule, preserved a precarious kind of existence under its own kings for forty years more. The Romans themselves called it a 'client kingdom'; the Middle Ages would have called it a 'vassal kingdom'; its equivalent in modern times is usually known as a 'satellite state'. In AD 46 the emperor Claudius finally suppressed it and turned it into the Roman province of Thrace. The old Greek city of Perinthus, on the Sea of Marmara some fifty miles west of Byzantium, became the new provincial capital. (Byzantium itself, which was larger than Perinthus and at first sight might have seemed a better choice for the capital, did not belong to Thrace at all; by an odd administrative quirk, it remained attached, throughout the early Empire, to the province of Bithynia, the rest of which lay on the Asian side of the Straits.) A fair number of Thracians were sufficiently enamoured of Roman rule to join the Roman army, mostly as cavalry troopers; some work was immediately found for them at the other end of Europe in Claudius' earlier acquisition, the Roman province of Britain.

Beyond the Thracians, on the northern side of the Danube, lived another large body of people closely akin to them, collectively called sometimes Getae and sometimes Dacians. Their heartland was the mountainous triangle of country which today belongs to Romania and is called Transylvania—best known today as the backdrop for innumerable films about vampires and werewolves. To the Romans, however, it often presented a more tangible, if less mysterious, peril.

Under their king Burebista, a contemporary of Julius Caesar, the Dacians achieved a remarkable degree of political unity, more than that of their Thracian kinsmen to the south of the Danube. Caesar himself twice made plans to wage war upon Burebista, first in 59 BC when he received his first important military command, and again in 45 when he had become supreme ruler of Rome, but his plans were upset the first time by events in Gaul (page 116) and the second time by his death.

On Burebista's own death, soon afterwards, the Dacian kingdom broke up, and for about a century ceased to be a danger to Rome. In the eighties AD, however, when Domitian was emperor, it was reunited under a ruler named Decebalus, even more formidable and aggressive than Burebista. A Dacian army invaded Roman Moesia, killed its governor and wiped out a legion (number V on the lists, known by the odd name of Alaudae, 'The Lark'). Reinforcements had to be brought into the lower Danube zone from Dalmatia, from the Rhine and even from as far afield as Britain. (One result was that as described on page 40 the conquest of that last province, despite a recent crushing victory for Rome, was never completed.)

Domitian was succeeded as emperor by Nerva, who began to reign at the age of sixty. He was in poor health, and survived less than two years; no one expected him to embark upon a major war. But *his* successor, the emperor Trajan, was positively bursting with military urge, and the first target for it was the kingdom of Dacia. In AD 101 the Roman invasion began. It is marked by one unusual fact: the chief document describing it consists not of writings on paper, but of carvings on stone. This is none other than Trajan's Column at Rome, set up by the Emperor himself in honour of his victories and surviving almost intact to this day.

The Romans' principal base for the campaign was a fortress called Viminacium; its modern name is Kostolac (pronounced Kostolatz). It was the capital of the province of Upper Moesia (for Domitian had subdivided the earlier single province of Moesia into two parts). Here a bridge of boats was built across the river; one of the best-known carvings on Trajan's Column depicts a force of Roman legionaries crossing it. A second bridge was thrown across the Danube some seventy miles further east: this one was originally also a bridge of boats, but was later rebuilt in permanent form by the famous engineer-architect who designed the Column—Apollodorus of Damascus, one of the few members of that happy band of brothers described at the end of Chapter I whose name we actually do know. (Thus a Greek born in Syria, acting on orders from a Roman born in Spain, improved communications between Yugoslavia and Romania.) The bridge, nearly three-quarters of a mile long, was the longest to be found in the Empire—probably anywhere in the Ancient World. Though its wooden superstructure was destroyed by Trajan's successor Hadrian, the stone piers in the river survived and were visible until fairly recent times. At each end of it were Roman fortified strongholds, that on the south being called simply

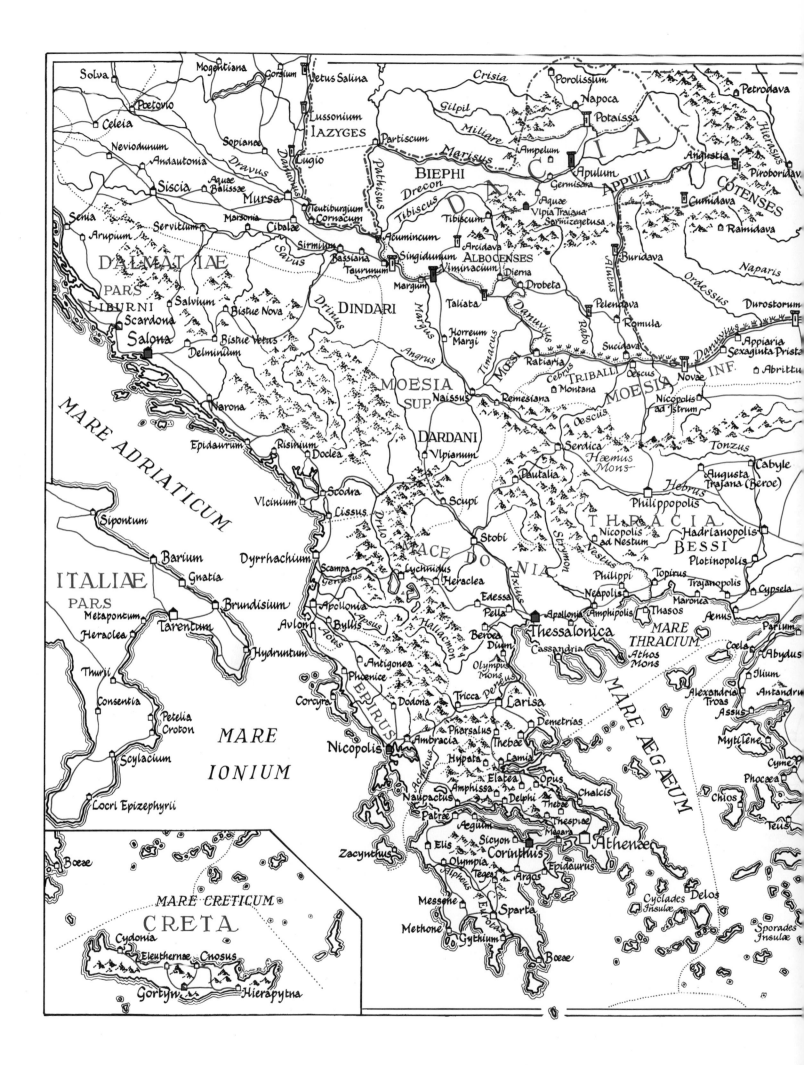

Solva · Mogentiana · Gorsium · Vetus Salina · Crisia · Porolissum · Petrodava

Poetovio · Napoca

Celeia · Sopianae · Gilpil · Miliare · Potaissa

Neviodunum · Angustia · Piroboridava

Andautonia · Dravus · Lugio · IAZYGES · Partiscum · Marisus · i Ampelum · DACIA · Apulum · APPULI · COTENSES

Siscia · Aquae · Balissae · Mursa · BIEPHI · Drecon · Germisara · Aquae · Vlpia Traiana · Sarmizegetusa · Cumidava

Senia · Marsonia · Teutiburgium · Cibalae · Tibiscus · Tibiscum · Ramidava

Arupium · Servitium · Cornacum · Acumincum · Arcidava

Sirmium · Singidunum · ALBOCENSES · Buridava

DALMATIAE · Savus · Bassiana · Taurunum · Viminacium · Diema · Naparis

PARS · Salvium · Bistue Nova · Margum · Drobeta

LIBURNI · DINDARI · Margus · Taliata · Danuvius · Pelendava · Durostorum

Scardona · Bistue Vetus · Horreum · Margi · Romula · Danuvius

Salona · Delminium · Angrus · Moesi · Ratiaria · Sucidava · Appiaria · Sexaginta Prista

Cebrus · TRIBALLI · Oescus · Novae INF. · Abrittum

MARE ADRIATICUM · Narona · MOESIA · Naissus · Remesiana · Montana · MOESIA · Nicopolis ad Istrum

SUP. · Oescus · Serdica · Tonzus

Epidaurum · Risinium · Doclea · DARDANI · Vlpianum · Haemus · Mons · Augusta

Vlcinium · Scodra · Scupi · Pautalia · Hebrus · Cabyle · Trajana (Beroe)

Sipontum · Lissus · Philippopolis · THRACIA

Drilo · Stobi · Nicopolis · Hadrianopolis

Barium · Dyrrhachium · MACEDONIA · ad Nestum · BESSI

ITALIAE · Gnatia · Scampa · Lychnidus · Strymon · Nestus · Philippi · Topirus · Plotinopolis

PARS · Genusus · Heraclea · Neapolis · Trajanopolis · Cypsela

Metapontum · Brundisium · Apollonia · Edessa · Apollonia · Amphipolis · Maronea · Aenus · Parium

Heraclea · Tarentum · Avlon · Byllis · Aous · Pella · Beroea · Thessalonica · Thasos · Coela · Abydus

Thurii · Hydruntum · Antigonea · Hallacmon · Dium · Cassandria · MARE · Ilium · Antandrus

Consentia · Phoenice · Olympus · THRACIUM · Athos · Alexandria · Troas

Petelia · Corcyra · Dodona · Mons · Peneus · Mons · Assus · Mytilene

Croton · EPIRUS · Tricca · Larisa · Cyme

Scylacium · MARE · Ambracia · Pharsalus · Demetrias · MARE AEGAEUM · Phocaea

IONIUM · Nicopolis · Hypata · Thebae · Chios

Locri Epizephyrii · Achelous · Lamia · Teus

Amphissa · Elatea · Opus · Chalcis

Naupactus · Delphi · Thebae · Thespiae

Patrae · Aegium · Megara · Athenae

Zacynthus · Elis · Sicyon · Corinthus · Epidaurus · Cyclades · Delos

MARE CRETICUM · Olympia · Tegea · Argos · Insulae

CRETA · Messene · Alpheus · Eurotas · Sporades

Boeae · Cydonia · Methone · Sparta · Insulae

Eleuthernae · Cnosus · Gythium

Gortyn · Hierapytna · Boeae

CARPI

Tyras

Tyras

Pyretus

Noviodunum

Troesmis

Carsium

Histria

Axiopolis

Tomis

Tropaeum Traiani

Callatis

Dionysopolis
(Cruni)

Odessus

Marcianopolis

PONTUS

EUXINUS

Mesembria

Anchialus

Apollonia

Deultum

Salmydessus

Bizye

Selymbria Byzantium
Rhaedestus Calchedon

Apri

Perinthus

PROPONTIS Cius

Cyzicus

Apamea Myrlea

Apollonia Prusa

A S I AE

PARS

Pergamum

Thyatira

Elaea

Magnesia Sardes

Smyrna Hypaepa

Ephesus

Tralles

Magnesia

Priene Alabanda

Miletus

Stratonicea

Halicarnassus

Rhodus

Amastris

Tieum

Heraclea

Nicomedia

BITHYNIAE

PARS

MACEDONIA

A drawing of a scene from Trajan's Column

Pontes, 'The bridges', while the northern one was called Drobeta. This latter developed into a substantial Roman town, and still survives under the name Turnu-Severin or 'Tower of Severus': the Romanians correctly ascribe it to a Roman Emperor, but incorrectly to one who ruled nearly a century after the real originator of the place.

Even more impressive were the transverse works linking the lower bridge with the upper, for these had to pass the formidable Danube gorge of the Iron Gates. For water-borne traffic Trajan built a canal that by-passed the worst of the rapids, so that the two great Roman Danube fleets—the *Classis Pannonica* based near Belgrade, and the *Classis Moesica* near the river's mouth— could now for the first time make easy contact with each other. A new road was also built, through the gorge itself. As there was not one inch of level ground between the waters and the cliff-face, part of this had to run through a gallery cut into the solid rock (entirely by hand, of course; blasting powder and dynamite lay many centuries in the future). The other part of the road rested on a wooden platform, projecting over the whirlpools of the gorge. Unfortunately the remains of this work, even more remarkable than Hadrian's Wall as a piece of Roman military engineering, are no longer visible, being submerged beneath the waters of a hydro-electric scheme.

After these tremendous preparations, the details of the campaign itself seem a little tame. The First Dacian War (AD 101–2) involved two Roman armies converging on the Dacian capital, Sarmizegetusa, and ended with the surrender of Decebalus himself. Failing to profit from this warning, however, the Dacians yet again began to raid Roman territory; the resulting Second Dacian War (AD 105–6) culminated in the storming of Sarmizegetusa, the death of Decebalus and total Roman victory.

Rome thereby gained control of an enormous piece of territory, six hundred miles long from Budapest at the great bend of the Danube to Odessa on the Black Sea, and four hundred miles wide from the Lower Danube frontier to the crests of the Carpathian Mountains. The question was: how much of this should be permanently retained?

Trajan himself had no doubts on the subject. He was one of the last Roman emperors to hold the old-fashioned view that unlimited Roman expansion was both possible and desirable, or, in the words of the anthem,

Wider still and wider,
Shall thy bounds be set;
God who made thee mighty,
Make thee mightier yet!

Hadrian, the next emperor, held different views. One of his first acts on coming to power was to abandon all the conquests made by Trajan in the last years of his life, east of the Euphrates; and he also proposed likewise to abandon all Trajan's conquests north of the Danube. He changed his mind, however, about Dacia proper—the mountainous land now known as Transylvania. This formed a kind of natural bastion beyond the Danube which was the Empire's moat; if Rome did not hold it, some other power would—and the events of the past fifty years had amply shown what kind of a threat *that* could be. Also, the mountains contained valuable minerals, including gold. So Transylvania was allowed to continue as the Roman province of Dacia, and perhaps (unlike most provinces along Rome's northern frontier) even paid the expenses of its own military garrison—Legio XIII Gemina at Apulum (Alba-Iulia).

The lands to the west and south and east of Transylvania were another matter. Though some geographers included them all together in a sort of 'Greater Dacia', they differed very obviously from Dacia proper. They are not mountainous lands, but almost dead flat; not forest country, but grassland; and all through ancient and much of mediaeval history they have been occupied by tribes of nomadic horsemen. The particular group of these that held power during the days of the Roman Empire were collectively known as Sarmatians, and their grazing-grounds reached from the Great Plain of Hungary in the west to the banks of the river Volga in the east. To put such people under regular provincial government would be like trying to carry water in a sieve, and they were left independent. Hence the odd shape of the Roman frontier line in their area.

More lasting in effect, though less spectacular, than Trajan's conquests on the lower Danube was his contribution to civil life in the region. The new province of Dacia was repopulated by transferring settlers from other parts of the Empire, and as a result became a bastion of Roman civilization as well as of Roman military power. To replace its old capital of Sarmizegetusa (the hill-fort now called Grădiştea Muncelului) Trajan built a new one, some miles further west on more accessible ground. The new capital was also called Sarmizegetusa, but with the honorary prefix Ulpia Traiana (Ulpius was Trajan's family name). Other towns grew and flourished, to receive official recognition from later emperors. Though one of the last Roman territories to be occupied and one of the first to be given up (Aurelian abandoned it to the Visigoths in AD 271), Dacia acquired a remarkably strong Roman character in a comparatively short time. To this day its inhabitants speak a language derived from Latin, and are proud to call their country *Rom*-ania.

One by-product of the Dacian conquest was that part of the lower Danube frontier was a frontier no longer. Two military bases on it, Ratiaria and Oescus, accordingly had their garrisons removed and developed into purely civil settlements. Ratiaria, like the Dacian capital, received the honorary title of Colonia Ulpia Traiana. Upstream from it, in Upper Moesia, lay legions IV Flavia at Belgrade and VII Claudia at Kostolac. Down the river, in Lower Moesia, were I Italica at Novae (Steklen), XI Claudia at Durostorum (Silistra) and V Macedonia at Troesmis (Iglitza).

Further south, in the province of Thrace, Trajan was also active. Cities in these parts had been developing only very slowly. Claudius, on annexing the province, had founded a colony at

Above: Battle between Roman auxiliaries and Dacians seen on Trajan's Column

Opposite: Graeco-Roman ruins at Eforie, Romania (on the coast south of Constanza)

Apri (modern Inecik, in European Turkey); Vespasian had founded another at Deultum (modern Debelt, near Burgas); and Domitian yet another at Scupi (Skopje) in the neighbouring province of Upper Moesia. But the first two of these stood very near the sea, the third at no great distance from the Macedonian frontier. The interior of Thrace had only one city—Philippopolis—worthy of the name.

Trajan founded ten new cities in the region. Trajanopolis and Augusta Trajana he named after himself, Plotinopolis after his wife, Marcianopolis after his sister, two cities called Nicopolis after his victories; four other towns (the most important being Serdica, the modern Sofia) received official city-status and the title Ulpia. With the founding of Hadrianopolis in the next reign, the opening-up of Thrace was virtually complete. The province, previously somewhat off the beaten track, could become an important link in the Empire's system of communications.

Under the Republic and early Empire, the chief link between East and West had been the Egnatian Way across Macedonia, already described. But as more and more troops came to be established on the Danube, this road was to some extent superseded by a more northerly one, approximately following the line taken in more recent times by the Orient Express. From Belgrade, on the frontier between Lower Pannonia and Upper Moesia, the road followed the Danube downstream as far as Kostolac, the provincial capital. Here, while one route continued to follow the Danube, another ascended a tributary of it called the Morava to reach the town of Nish, an important crossroads. From here a road led down to the Dalmatian coast, and another back to the Danube; the main road, however, continued straight on into the Balkan Mountains, across the frontier between Latin-speaking Moesia and Greek-speaking Thrace, to Sofia. Descending again, it followed the river which the Greeks now call Hebrus and the Bulgarians Maritsa, past Philippopolis (or Plovdiv, as it is called now) to Hadrianopolis (Edirne, a town about which little is known, because it stands near the place where Turkey, Greece and Bulgaria meet each other, and politics makes archaeological study almost impossible). At Perinthus, the capital of Thrace, the road reached the sea, which it followed for the last stretch to Byzantium and the crossing into Asia.

All the cities along the road flourished. Philippopolis in the third century is said to have had at least a hundred thousand inhabitants—that at all events is the figure given for those killed or enslaved when the Goths sacked it in AD 250, though very probably exaggerated. In the great administrative reforms of Diocletian at the end of the third century, the city became a provincial capital, as did its neighbours up and down the road, Serdica (Sofia) and Hadrianopolis. The former is a national capital today.

It was the city at the end of the road, however, that ultimately received the greatest benefit from it. Looking at a modern map, with knowledge of its recent history, one thinks of Byzantium (or Constantinople, or Istanbul, call it what you will) as almost designed by Nature to be a great city, and, standing as it does at the junction of two seas and two continents, a great centre of communications as well. Its founders, however, did not see it that way at all. The city's most obvious natural advantage was its splendid harbour, the Golden Horn; its chief sources of wealth, originally, were agriculture and fishing (for, through some oddity in the pattern of currents in the Bosphorus, many more fish were found on the European side than on the Asian). A little later, when Greek colonies developed on the Black Sea and began to export goods to the Greek homeland, the sea route via Byzantium did become important; as a centre of communication by land, however, the city was a non-starter. The Thracians on one side of the straits were among the most savage and backward peoples in Europe; their kinsmen on the other side, the

Mysians and Bithynians, very little better. The road out of Classical Greek Byzantium led nowhere.

Roman Byzantium was a modest provincial town, fairly large but by no means outstandingly so. The opening up of Thrace by Trajan and the new roads that this entailed slowly caused it to grow, now that at last it had a hinterland; but then at the end of the second century it took the wrong side in one of Rome's numerous civil wars, and was razed by the armies of Septimius Severus. It recovered, but a century later was still only a modest provincial town. When Diocletian wanted a capital from which to rule all Rome's eastern territories, he chose not Byzantium but Nicomedia (modern Izmit) some fifty miles further east, in Asia.

So perhaps the traditional view, that it was Constantine who made Byzantium great by an act of Imperial will, has something to recommend it. Doubtless he had an eye for its natural advantages, nor would he consider its moderate size a drawback; he aimed to found a *Christian* city, and larger communities were very often important centres of the old—and from his viewpoint the wrong—religion. Afterwards, of course, the advantages of the site made it seem more and more the obvious choice. But observe what a complex series of events—exploration of the Danube, military ambition in Romania, road-building in Bulgaria, even the appearance of a new religion—had to happen before something so 'geographically obvious' could come about.

Mosaic from Piazza Armerina, Sicily. Probably commissioned by a professional catcher and trainer of wild animals

VIII

AFRICA

The whole desert he described as being like a gravelled drive carelessly weeded, of infinite breadth and leading to nowhere.

Lord Dunsany, *Travel Tales of Mr. Joseph Jorkens*

THE GEOGRAPHER STRABO noted the contrast between the two sides of the Mediterranean—the European coast angular, with many changes of direction, the African coast forming a smooth curve with hardly any breaks in it at all, and as a result hardly any satisfactory harbours. Later explorers found that Africa's other coasts were just the same, often being even harder to approach than the Mediterranean coast. More recently still the underlying cause of this has been found: whereas Europe is, geologically speaking, an assemblage of odds and ends with very diverse histories, Africa is a single continental block that has preserved the same basic shape for many millions of years. All its rough edges, so to speak, were long ago smoothed off.

In North Africa the difficulties of communication are increased still further by the great Sahara desert. In many places this reaches right down to the sea, leaving no room for any settlement of consequence; here and there, however, are regions where water makes human habitation possible. Towards the east side of the desert the river Nile creates the land of Egypt, which requires a map and a chapter all to itself. Somewhat further west, a range of hills called the Jebel Akhdar or 'Green Mountains' attracts to itself a certain amount of rainfall and makes habitable the land of Cyrenaica. Further west still, the Jebel Nefusah performs the same service for the land of Tripolitania. The westernmost of all these 'islands' in the desert is the largest. It is formed by two parallel mountain ranges, known as the Maritime and the Saharan Atlas, which start in Tunisia and run away to the west, steadily gaining height, to reach the Atlantic coast in Morocco. The block of land enclosed and watered by these mountains is known to geographers today as the Maghrib, from the Arabic *Jezirat al-Maghrib* meaning 'Island of the West'. Even the Arabs, more accustomed to it than most peoples, saw the desert as a barrier at least equal to that of the sea.

The history of North Africa west of Egypt, like that of several other parts of the Mediterranean world, begins with the exploration of the Phoenicians and Greeks, and the conflict that developed between them. The first Phoenician settlement in Africa, at a place called Utica (modern Bou Chateur, about ten miles north of Tunis) is supposed to have been founded as early as 1101 BC, while the more famous city of Carthage, now virtually a suburb of Tunis, dated its foundation to 814 BC. (Archaeological study, however, suggests that these traditional dates are much too early.) In the course of time Carthage gained a predominancy over the other Phoenician settlements; her ships monopolized trade in the western Mediterranean, and some even passed the 'Pillars of Hercules' to enter the Atlantic. One of her explorers named Himilco sailed at least as far as Brittany and may have reached the British Isles; another, named Hanno, is supposed to have voyaged a considerable distance down Africa's Atlantic coast, though just how far is disputed. (All this region was long the abode of myth and magic—the island of the Gorgons, the Gardens of the Hesperides with their golden apples, and the giant Atlas who held up the sky were all located somewhere hereabouts—and it is very hard to disentangle real from fictitious exploration.)

Greek settlement in Africa began later than Phoenician, and was never anything like so widespread. Tradition has it that the first Greek colonist in the continent was a man named Battus, from the island of Thera in the Aegean Sea, and that (after two unsuccessful attempts) he established a permanent colony at Cyrene in about 630 BC. Other cities were later founded a little further to the west—first Barca, then Tauchira (the modern town of Tokra) and finally Euesperides (the modern town of Benghazi). What is now eastern Libya (or Cyrenaica) thus became a Greek preserve, while western Libya (or Tripolitania) was controlled by Carthage. The boundary between the two spheres of influence was set at a place called Arae Philaenorum, better known to many Englishmen today as 'Marble Arch', after the great monument set up there by Mussolini.

The great conflict between Carthage and Rome has already been described from several points of view; it remains now to consider its African aspect. In the First Punic War (264–241 BC) the chief theatre of operations was Sicily. A Roman attempt to shorten the war by direct invasion of Africa ended in miserable failure.

The Second Punic War (218–201 BC) was more wide-ranging. Its principal battles were fought in Italy and Spain; Africa did not come into the action until almost the very end of the war, when the great Roman general Scipio invaded the continent and the still more famous Punic leader Hannibal was recalled from Italy to confront him. The last battle of the war was fought near a small town called Zama (its modern name is Jama). It had something of the decisiveness and excitement of Waterloo in more recent times, being the first (and, as things turned out, the last) clash between two commanders, each of whom had shown himself virtually invincible against opponents of lesser ability. In the battle itself the Romans (rather unusually) had more cavalry than their opponents; these mounted men so conducted themselves as to win the battle, and with it the war.

One side-effect of this great conflict was to bring on to the stage of history some of Carthage's immediate neighbours, the tribes collectively known as Numidians. They formed two main tribal groups, the Masaesyli in the west and the Massylii in the east, who despite their similar-sounding names were bitterly hostile to each other and invariably took opposite sides in the larger clash between Rome and Carthage. The final victory of Rome was also a victory for the Massylii and their king Masinissa: it was he, indeed, who had supplied the horsemen who saved the day for Rome at the crucial battle of Zama. He was rewarded with an enlarged kingdom and the valuable official title of 'Friend of the Roman People'. Thus armed, he set to work converting Numidia from a collection of disorganized nomads into a powerful and modern nation. His capital was Cirta (the town now called Constantine), a place well suited to be a centre of communication, yet at the same time extremely defensible; it was surrounded on three sides by the precipitous gorge of a watercourse now called the Wadi Rummel. The town became an important centre of Roman business even while still independent; under direct Roman rule its importance increased still further, and to this day it is still one of the largest cities in Algeria.

Masinissa was able to enlarge his kingdom still further by gradually nibbling at territories that still ostensibly belonged to Carthage, well aware that Rome would almost certainly support her former ally against her former enemy. This is precisely what happened: the anti-Carthage party at Rome, led by the famous Cato with his constantly-repeated slogan of *Delenda est Carthago* or 'Carthage must be destroyed', gave the unfortunate city notice to quit. Its inhabitants were to scrap it and move to a new site—anywhere they liked, but not less than ten miles from the sea. The 'Third Punic War' that this harsh decree provoked merely prolonged the agony. In 146 BC Carthage was sacked, the ruins ploughed into furrows and these sown with salt, as a sign that even the site of the place was accursed.

Thus came into existence the Roman province of Africa. Utica, Carthage's old rival, was its first capital.

Despite its grandiose name, Roman Africa was not a large province. Compared with the continent as a whole (or even with the part of the continent known to the Ancient World) its size was diminutive. It corresponded roughly to the northern half of what is now Tunisia. On the north and east it was bounded by the sea; westward it reached as far as the town of Thabraca (now called Tabarka, close to the frontier between Tunisia and Algeria); southward it reached the town of Thenae (now called Thyna, not far from Sfax). The frontier between Roman Africa and independent Numidia was marked by a construction called the *fossa Scipionis*, 'Scipio's Ditch'—the oldest example of a permanent Roman frontier-work, and for several centuries the only work of its kind.

The expansion of Roman power in Africa was remarkably slow. The Roman conquest of Britain took forty years; of Gaul, seventy; Spain required just under two centuries. But though the province of Africa was founded in 146 BC, the last additions to its territory were made no less than three and a half centuries later, by the emperor Septimius Severus.

Even after their victory over Jugurtha of Numidia in the late second century BC, the Romans (unusually) took no new land for themselves. The next annexation in Africa was not to be made until 46 BC, when Julius Caesar defeated the supporters of Pompey at the battle of Thapsus. Among these was king Juba I of Numidia, who committed suicide; his kingdom was promptly annexed to form the province of Africa Nova. Caesar's other great contribution to African history was his order to restore the city of Carthage—just a century after it had been destroyed and solemnly cursed. Though he himself did not live to see much work done on it, the new foundation was a tremendous success; it soon replaced Utica as the provincial capital, and for the second time became one of the largest cities in the western Mediterranean.

Among his many provincial reforms, the emperor Augustus amalgamated Africa Vetus (the original Roman province) with Africa Nova (Caesar's addition) to form a single province, still of no great size, which reverted to the older and simpler name of Africa. He handed it over to the control of the Senate, thereby creating something of an anomaly. Most other 'Senatorial' provinces—southern Spain, southern France, Sicily, Greece—were completely pacified and required no armed forces; provinces with large numbers of troops in them were normally 'Imperial'—strictly under the Emperor's own control. But Africa, though Senatorial, was far

Opposite: The Cherchell Museum

Left: Detail of picture below: Carthage—guardian lion at entrance to Roman road

Below: Carthage—Roman road

from being wholly peaceful: throughout its history it required a garrison of one legion (Legio III Augusta) plus a large number of auxiliary troops. The provincial governor in Augustus' time thus had the unusual distinction of commanding an army, albeit a small one, in his own right and not as a deputy of the Emperor. This made him eligible for a triumph—for the rules about granting this high military honour insisted that only the supreme commander could receive one, never a subordinate officer, however worthy. In 19 BC the governor of Africa, Cornelius Balbus, was indeed awarded a triumph, being both the first non-Italian (he came from Cadiz) and the last private citizen, unconnected with the Imperial family, to be so honoured. (The loophole in the system which made his triumph possible was eventually blocked by the emperor Caligula, who decreed that in future the armed forces in Africa should be directly responsible to himself as emperor, not to the provincial governor.)

Balbus' triumph is described for us by the elder Pliny, who unfortunately omits, however, to give us any details of the campaigns that earned it. All we have is a list of the places which, in his triumphal procession, Balbus claimed to have captured; they are in no obvious order, and a fair number of them cannot be identified. The campaigns, however, do seem to have covered a lot of ground. In one direction, Balbus was active in the district of southern Libya now called the Fezzan, where he defeated a powerful tribe called the Garamantes; further west, he took the oasis of Ghadames and may have penetrated as far as the settlement of Ghat, over 500 miles from the sea. Further west still, he seems to have been active also round Biskra, in Algeria. We may picture a series of raiding patrols, moving out through the desert in various directions from the as yet ill-defined southern frontier of the Roman province.

But the consolidation of new territory, the conversion of mountain and forest, steppe and semi-desert into respectable parts of a Roman province, lagged far behind the long-distance raids of Balbus. We have already seen in this book various relationships between *tribe* and *town* in different parts of the Empire: Gaul, for instance, where tribe and town were closely linked, and Spain, where each tribe had numerous tiny settlements which the Romans hoped to amalgamate into larger ones. North Africa, however, saw a third and sadder pattern of habitation, repeated more recently in several parts of the world: when the townsman moves *in*, the tribesman is compelled to move *out*. He then retaliates by raiding, and a prolonged guerrilla war is the result. In the reign of Augustus' successor Tiberius, Roman Africa was plagued by a particularly active *guerrillero* named Tacfarinas, whose operations extended all over the southern part of the Maghrib where the mountains of the Saharan Atlas come down to the desert. Three successive governors of the Roman province received what are called 'triumphal ornaments' (the next highest honour after a full-scale triumph) for defeating him, but each time he re-emerged to continue his raids. Only after seven years of this did a fourth general, Cornelius Dolabella, end the situation by actually killing Tacfarinas himself.

In AD 42 (the year before the conquest of Britain) Rome's territory in Africa was made much longer, though not very much larger, through the annexation of Mauretania. This country, the land of the Mauri or Moors, reached from the Atlantic to the frontiers of Roman Numidia. In the reign of Augustus it had been under a king named Juba—the son of the Juba whom Julius Caesar defeated at Thapsus. The younger Juba spent much of his early life at Rome, where he became an enthusiastic (but not, so far as we can tell, a very accurate) scholar and developed a great interest in Greek art and the Greek way of life. He married another royal refugee, Cleopatra Selene the daughter of Mark Antony and Cleopatra. On receiving their new kingdom among the Moors, these two set up a capital at an old Phoenician settlement called Iol, which they enlarged, renamed Caesarea after their patron (Caesar Augustus) and turned into a little outpost of the Greek world many hundreds of miles from any true member of the Greek-speaking community. The site of Caesarea-Iol (now called Cherchell) has yielded some of the finest artistic works in all Roman Africa.

Juba was succeeded by his son Ptolemy, who fell foul of the emperor Caligula and was put to death. The ensuing rebellion in Mauretania, however, outlasted the emperor, and it was left to his successor, Claudius, to restore order. A Roman army scored a notable 'first' in the history of ancient exploration by crossing the High Atlas Mountains of Morocco, emerging into the desert on the far side and penetrating as far as a watercourse called the Gir—nowadays spelt Guir. (The army's commander, Suetonius Paullinus, subsequently became governor of Britain: perhaps his experiences in the mountains of Morocco helped him deal with those of Wales.) But this expedition, like that of Balbus sixty years earlier, was in the nature of a punitive raid, not a permanent annexation of territory. The part of Mauretania brought under direct Roman control was of more limited extent. The province of Mauretania Caesariensis, named after its capital Caesarea-Iol, was a ribbon of land following the Algerian coast, some 500 miles long but nowhere more than 50 miles wide (its southern boundary at first was ill-defined). Mauretania Tingitana, further west, took its name from its capital Tingis (Tangier): it consisted, in effect, of a stretch of Atlantic seaboard, about 150 miles long, from Tingis down to Sala (now a suburb of Rabat, the present-day Moroccan capital). Between the two provinces lay the mountain massif of the Rif, which even in our own times has shown its admirable suitability for guerrilla warfare: no Roman remains have been found in this area, and Roman control over it can have been little more than nominal. The usual way of reaching one Mauretanian province from the other was by sea. Under the later Empire, indeed, Tingitana was reckoned for administrative purposes as a part of Spain, with which it had closer links than with the rest of Roman Africa.

Meanwhile back in Africa proper (always more important than Mauretania, from a military, social or economic point of view) Roman power was still slowly extending itself. In Tiberius' time the headquarters of the Third Legion was at a place called Ammaedara (modern Haïdra) linked by a military road to the port of Tacape (Gabès) on the shores of the Lesser Syrtis. (It was the building of this road, right across their traditional grazing grounds, that led the tribesmen under Tacfarinas to revolt). Vespasian's reign, in the seventies AD, saw the legionary headquarters shifted further to the south-west, to Theveste (modern Tébessa). A road linked the new base with the coast via the oasis-town of Capsa (Gafsa): Roman occupation was now leaving behind the zone of steppe and semi-desert and approaching the desert proper. The abandoned fortress of Ammaedara took on (like Lincoln and Gloucester a generation later) a new existence as a colony for retired soldiers.

One reason why the Romans moved so slowly in their take-over of Africa may have been the difficulty of finding a suitable halting-place. Anxious not to bite off more than they could chew, they took only a little nibble at a time. The Maghrib appeared as a complex and very awkward tangle of mountains, with nothing in it comparable with the Rhine, the Danube or even the Forth-Clyde line in Britain, at which one could say 'Thus far, and no further'. But in Vespasian's time a makeshift solution was found, for the elder Pliny, writing in that reign, can say that 'Roman Africa includes . . . the whole of Gaetulia, as far as the river Nigris which separates Africa proper from Aethiopia'. This river is *not* the one we know today as the Niger; that flows on the far side of the Sahara, many hundreds of miles from the Roman frontier, and few if

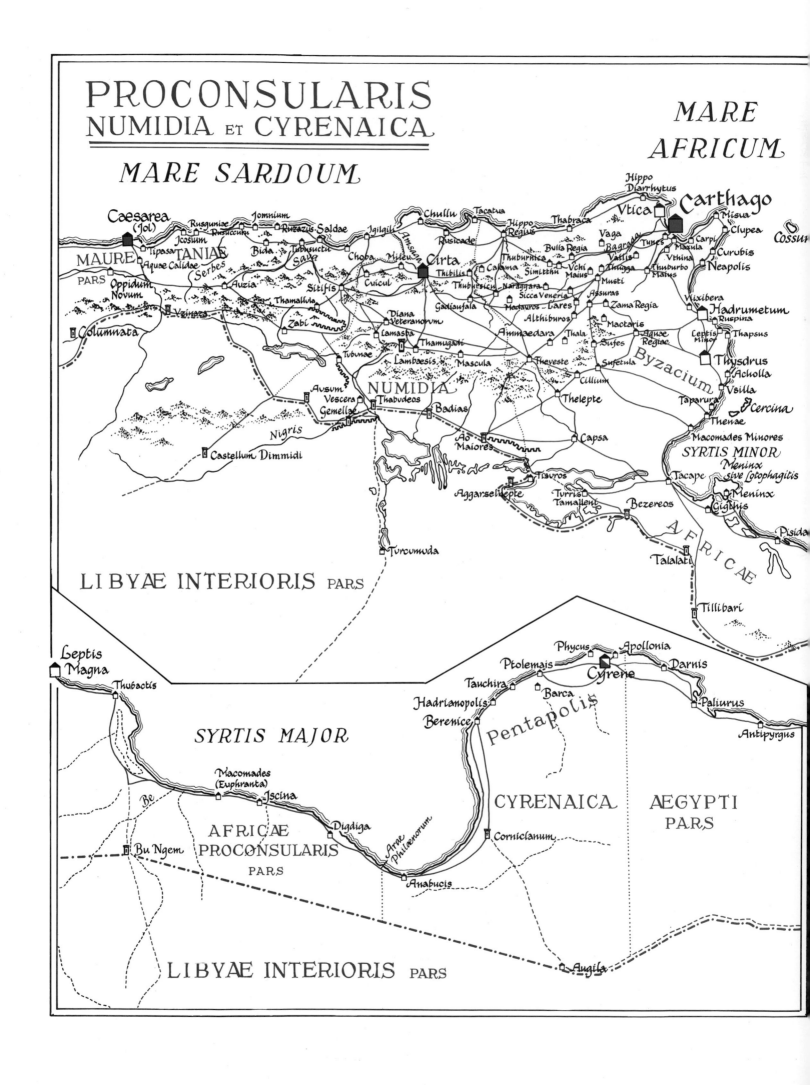

ITALIAE PARS

Messana
Panormus
Tyndaris
Drepanum
Cephaloedium
Halaesa
Segesta
Agyrium
Centuripae
Lilybaeum
Henna
Catana
Thermae
Leontini
Selinuntiae
Agrigentum
Syracusae
Neetum

Locri
Epizephyrii
Regium
Julium
Tauromenium

SICILIA

Gaulus
Melita

Lopadusa

MARE
LIBYCUM

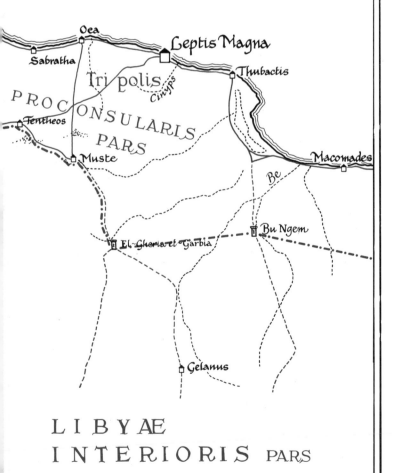

Oea
Leptis Magna
Sabratha
Thubactis
Tripolis
Cinyps
PROCONSULARIS
Tentheos
PARS
Macomades
Muste
Be
Bu Ngem
El Gheria-el-Garbia
Gelanus

LIBYAE
INTERIORIS PARS

MARE AFRICUM	Ocean, sea (OCEANUS, PONTUS, MARE)
SINUS GALLICUS	Bay (SINUS)
Ilva	Island (INSULA)
Danuvius	River (FLUMEN, FLUVIUS)
	Temporary river
	Lake (LACUS)
	Marshland
	Forest (SILVA, SALTUS)
Olympus Mons	Mountain (MONS)
CYPRUS	Name of province within the Empire, or country outside it
Pentapolis	Name of region within a province
VENETI	Name of tribe
	Boundary of Empire
	Boundary of Empire (indefinite)
	Boundary of province
	Boundary of region
	Cities and towns
	Capital of Empire
	Capital of province
	Capital of region
	Legionary fortress (CASTRA)
	Fort (CASTELLA)
	Wall (VALLUM)
	Naval station
	Road (VIA)
	Track

0   200 km
0   100 miles

any Romans can ever have heard of it. The ancient Nigris was a much more insignificant water-course, now called the Djedi, which rises in the Saharan Atlas and flows across the desert to fall into a salt lake called the Chott Melrhir. Compared with the great permanent rivers of northern Europe, the Djedi was a very feeble apology for a frontier-line; still, it was the best available, and the Romans gradually moved up to it.

The advance, as usual, was slow, and it is not until about AD 100, in Trajan's reign, that we see substantial changes. The Third Legion abandoned its base at Theveste (which, like Ammaedara before it, became a colony for military veterans) and moved west, along the flank of the mountain massif called the Aurès, to find its third and last home at Lambaesis (now called Lambèse). Here it was well placed not only to guard the Aurès itself (an ill-explored region, many of whose inhabitants were strongly anti-Roman) but also to work round one side of the massif, through the pass of Biskra, and thus reach the desert and the banks of the river Nigris. At the same time an advance was made along the opposite side of the mountains, the key point here being a fort with the odd name of Ad Maiores, 'To the Ancestors'. This and other forts were linked together by a road, destined to become the final frontier of Roman Africa. The land of the salt lakes, further south still, was not considered worth annexing.

Hadrian, taking the same policy with Africa as with Britain, further strengthened this southern frontier by means of walls. It was neither necessary nor practicable to fortify the whole system in this way (it would have needed something like fifteen Hadrian's Walls placed end to end) but we do know of several stretches of walling, similar in style to the British wall but less massive, placed presumably where tribes happened to be unusually numerous or hostile. Africa, even more than Britain, suffered from the drawback that some tribes *within* the province were quite as dangerous as those *outside* it: there could be no question of a single linear frontier, however strongly fortified, with 'Us' on one side of it and 'Them' on the other. The African frontier system had rather to take the form of an elaborate network of roads, forts, semi-military towns, block-houses, watch-towers and signal stations. The system steadily developed into this form throughout the second century.

The last emperor to make significant additions to Roman territory in Africa—or, indeed, in any part of the Empire—was Septimius Severus, who reigned at the beginning of the third century AD. He was himself an African, born at Leptis Magna in the Tripolis, and as emperor paid particular attention to his native land. The city of Leptis was enlarged, adorned with an improved harbour and many impressive new buildings, and, along with its neighbours Oea and Sabratha, protected against attack from the desert by means of a new military road, the *limes Tripolitanus*, sweeping round the arc of hills called the Jebel Nefusah. Further south still, at places now called Ghadames, El Gheria el-Garbia and Bu Ngem, were three forts in the desert itself—eyes on stalks, so to speak, projecting forward from the network of forts and roads that formed Roman Africa's nervous system.

Further to the west Severus was also active. The long ribbon-like province of Mauretania Caesariensis was almost doubled in width by means of a new road with forts, the *limes Mauretaniae*, running some way to the south of the old frontier. Numidia (now a province in its own right, independent of the governor of Africa proper) also acquired new military works—these being a little out of the ordinary. Instead of running north-west to make a direct junction with the Mauretanian frontier, the new works in Numidia tended to the south-west, thrusting deep into enemy territory. We have here, in fact, a 'ladder-pattern' of advance similar to that used in the Roman conquest of northern Britain (page 39); the two overlapping *limites*, of Numidia and of Mauretania, forming the sides of the ladder, with numerous cross-connecting roads forming the rungs. Thus the Gaetuli, Bavares and other tribes of what is now central Algeria were caught and held in a network of Roman roads, just as the Brigantes had been in what is now northern England.

As a result of all these works, the map of Africa differs slightly from the others in this book. The rest of them try to show the situation as it was round about the middle of the second century AD—a convenient period, when nearly all the major towns and forts that were *going* to be founded by Rome *had* been founded, and peace and stability reigned not only in the Roman Empire but also among most of its neighbours. Septimius Severus' works in Africa, however, are so interesting that it seemed a pity to omit them: accordingly, the Africa map shows the situation early in the third century AD, some fifty or sixty years later than its companions in the book. The situation shown was not a long-lived one: by AD 235, when the last member of the Severan dynasty perished, most of Septimius' new conquests in Africa had been abandoned again.

Behind the Roman military road-network lay the civilian network. To a large extent the one had grown out of the other: roads built originally to link forts later proved equally convenient to link the towns that replaced those forts.

Africa possessed a remarkable number of such towns. An official list quoted by Pliny states that the province contained 516 officially recognized communities. (All Spain, a much larger area, had 513; the three northern provinces of Gaul, sixty between them; Britain, twenty or twenty-five at the very most.) The communities in question were far from being evenly distributed over the province, and had very diverse sizes and origins. Some were of Phoenician origin, older than Rome herself; some were founded by native rulers of Africa, considerably younger than the Phoenician cities but still dating from well before the Roman conquest; others (a particularly large group) were developed by the natives under the umbrella of the Pax Romana; others again were built *by* Romans *for* Romans; and others yet again were purely tribal units without any kind of central built-up area—though many of these subsequently developed capital cities of their own, either willingly—as native settlements, or unwillingly—as new semi-military colonies planted on their land by order of the central Roman government.

The largest towns were also the oldest, those of Phoenician origin. Without exception they were on the coast: most of them, indeed, were so sited as to make access from the sea as easy, from the land as difficult as possible. Some, like Utica and Leptis Magna, were built at river-mouths, using the sea and the river to form two sides of a defensive triangle; others, like Iol, stood on islands; others again, like Carthage, Rusicade, Rusazus, Rusuccuru and all the other towns with this characteristic prefix (which, like *Ras* in modern Arabic, means 'cape') stood on peninsulas. (The Phoenician mother-cities, Tyre and Sidon, occupied sites of exactly the same sort.) In some parts of the Empire the coming of Rome, essentially a land-based power, saw a growth of inland cities at the expense of the older maritime ones; but in Roman Africa, though numerous inland towns did develop, the older ones on the coast never lost their primacy. Carthage, as already mentioned, was among the largest cities to be found in any part of the Empire, with something like a quarter of a million inhabitants. Leptis Magna may have had 80,000 or so, Utica and Hadrumetum (modern Sousse) almost as many—nothing very much by modern standards, but in the ancient world very considerable indeed.

Starting from these great maritime cities, Roman civilization had gradually percolated inland, like ink across blotting-paper—or more precisely like water through the veins of a leaf, following

Above: Dougga—the main road leading to Carthage
Opposite above: Volubilis, in Morocco
Opposite below: Amphitheatre at Thysdrus (El Djem)

certain preferred lines of communication. (As a result, Africa even at the height of Roman power was a land of contrasts: not many miles from a highly civilized and sophisticated Roman city one might find oneself among tribesmen who had learned nothing from Rome save a feeling of thinly-veiled hostility.) One road of the highest importance led from Carthage up the valley of a river called the Bagrada, eventually reaching the important city of Cirta (Constantine), capital of Numidia, and thence pressing on into Mauretania. Towns were strung out all along this road; but on its northern side it was bordered by a mountainous region with hardly any Roman settlements at all.

An even more important road left Carthage in a south-westerly direction, passing through the three successive encampments of the Third Legion: first Ammaedara, then Theveste, and finally Lambaesis far away in southern Numidia. This was perhaps the most important line of communication of Roman Africa; all along its course, and all over the country on both sides of it, towns grew up at such a rate as to produce almost an ancient equivalent of 'ribbon-development'. This was the heart of the corn-growing belt of Africa, the 'granary of Rome', whence innumerable ox-carts carried the grain down the once-military road to Carthage for shipment to the Imperial capital. Some Roman writers, indeed, maintained that Africa was naturally designed, as it were, to produce corn and corn only; but fortunately for themselves the Africans never took this theory seriously. Corn was the staple crop, at least in the north of the province, but cornfields always had to share the land with vineyards and orchards, the latter producing such exotic fruit as dates, figs, almonds and pomegranates, which also found a ready market at Rome.

One town, just a few miles off the 'Great South-West Road', may be taken as typical of the whole region: it is unusually well preserved, but not so far as we know unusual in any other way. Its name today is Dougga; the Romans called it Thugga. So many inscriptions have survived from the site that we can actually trace its progress up the Roman municipal hierarchy. It already existed when the Romans arrived, but was known at first merely as the 'village of Thugga'—in Latin, *pagus Thuggensis*. Later it became *Civitas Thugga*, the 'City of Thugga'; in the early third century it received the title of *municipium*, and in AD 261 the still higher title of *colonia* (this at a time, be it noted, when most cities in other provinces of the Empire were stationary or declining). Its physical appearance grew to match its political status: all through the second and third centuries it was being adorned with public buildings (a theatre, a circus, a bath-house and no less than ten temples) by its rich and public-spirited citizens. For though Thugga was a small town (having something like five thousand inhabitants) we can see from its houses that it was a rich one. Under the later Roman Empire, and in the Middle Ages, and in some countries (such as Great Britain) down to recent times, the Lord of the Manor has preferred to live in his manor, well away from everybody else. Under the earlier Roman Empire, however, African lords preferred to live with their fellow lords in cities, enjoying the advantages of urban life. Peasants remained on the estates outside the city, coming in only on market-days and holidays (to watch entertainments for which their landlords, as town councillors, had paid).

South of the region of intensive corn-growing and concentrated settlement, the land grows drier and the towns more widely spaced. The region called Byzacium, where the Tunisian coast bellies out to form the northern shore of the Lesser Syrtis, was suited to a more mixed kind of cultivation than the lands further north. It grew corn well (according to the elder Pliny, outstandingly well) but it was also good for growing olives in large quantities. And instead of possessing a multitude of small communities, inland Byzacium was dominated by a single large one, the city of Thysdrus, now called El Djem. This town has one of the largest and best-preserved amphitheatres known in the Roman world, with seating for sixty thousand people—only half, it is thought, living in the town itself, the actual built-up area; the rest lived outside, coming in on market-days to watch the games after selling their farm produce at the market. Still, even a resident population of thirty thousand made Roman Thysdrus about the same size as Roman London—and probably much more impressive to look at.

Further south still, in Tripolis and along the Numidian frontier, the olive was the staple crop, and a very lucrative one. The oil sheikhs of Leptis Magna became quite as rich as the oil barons of Cordoba and Cadiz, though their product never reached such a high standard. Spanish oil was considered the finest in the world: African oil was regarded by upper-class Romans of the first century as disgusting (though later its quality seems to have improved). Still, it was cheap, and it succeeded in capturing what advertising men now call the 'down-market' levels of Roman society, while leaving the Spanish product in control of the 'up-market' sales.

Ground too dry or too rough even for olives could provide useful grazing land. Keeping flocks and herds, after all, had been the principal business of most Numidians until the Roman conquest. Cattle and sheep (of rather indifferent quality) were bred and also horses of excellent quality: the African light horse, with his rider, supplied a valuable ingredient in many Roman armies, and with three similar horses and a chariot, made a brave show at the games all round the western half of the Empire.

As one went southward and westward in Roman Africa, away from Carthage and the great cities of the coast, the 'wild country' gradually began to make its appearance. Among the cattle-ranches, the olive-groves, the orchards and the cornfields—sometimes, even, within easy walking distance of a highly civilized town—were tracts of high ground, keeping much of their primaeval forest and its inhabitants. Many types of animal—lions, leopards, ostriches, antelopes, gazelles, even elephants—that we now associate particularly with eastern Africa, were in those days found also north of the Sahara. The Romans hunted them with vigour, and made much money from it. There were unusual types of plant, too: one tree became highly valued at Rome for making tables, the top formed by a single slice through the tree-trunk. It grew among the mountains of Mauretania. At Mogador, on the Atlantic coast of Morocco some way beyond the official Roman frontier, shellfish were found whose bodies, suitably treated, yielded the highly prized dye called Imperial Purple, used on the clothes of emperors and other great men.

And all these exotica formed part of Africa's exports. Besides the everyday cargoes of corn, oil and dried fruit, on an African road, one might meet a wagon groaning under the weight of high-quality Moorish logs; or a caged lion, off to kill and be killed for the delight of spectators at the Colosseum; or a load of ivory, carefully wrapped for concealment from the eyes of sneak-thieves and bandits. Or, at sea, a sudden horrible smell might announce the presence of a ship with a cargo of Gaetulian purple shellfish.

Africa, in parts, could be among the most conventional of Roman provinces. In other parts, however, it could be one of the most exciting.

Compared with the history of Roman Africa, that of Roman Cyrenaica to the east is simple, not particularly interesting and at times a little depressing. The country was taken over by Rome, quietly and without any fuss, in 96 BC, by bequest of its king Ptolemy Apion. In due course it became a province, or rather a demi-province, since for administrative purposes it was included in a single unit with the island of Crete. Like its western neighbour Africa proper, Cyrenaica was always under senatorial control.

Above: Leptis Magna—Roman ruins

Left: Timgad—theatre and part of the town

Opposite: Arches at Leptis Magna

The pattern of settlement in the region was a simple one. The most important part of Cyrenaica, the narrow tract of fertile land between the Green Mountains and the sea, was known to the Greeks as the Pentapolis or 'Five Cities' (a counterpoise, so to speak, to the Phoenician Tripolis or 'Three Cities' further to the west) and it continued to be a Pentapolis for the first two centuries of Roman rule. There was never a great expansion of new towns in Cyrenaica as there was in Africa; the number of sites suitable for town-building was strictly limited by nature. The 'Five Cities', in order from east to west, were Apollonia, the port of Cyrene; Cyrene itself, the capital and only inland town of importance; Ptolemais (originally the port for the older city of Barca, which had declined to the level of a second-class community); Tauchira, sometimes also called Arsinoe; and Berenice, the modern Benghazi, immediately next to the older Greek settlement of Euesperides. (The names Ptolemais, Arsinoe and Berenice all came from members of the Ptolemy family, Greek-speaking Macedonian rulers of Egypt: we shall meet them again in Egypt itself.) The emperor Hadrian founded a sixth city, Hadrianopolis, but it seems never to have achieved any great success.

The road system was correspondingly straightforward. From Leptis Magna a route followed the coast to the frontier at Arae Philaenorum, then ran through all the cities of the Pentapolis, then through the desert once more in the direction of Alexandria and the Nile delta.

The economic basis of life in Cyrenaica was the same as that of Africa and most other Mediterranean lands. Corn, wine and olive oil were the three staples, the olive (as in Tripolis) being of especial importance. Until about the time of Christ, there was also something much more unusual, indeed unique, to export—the herb sometimes called lasarpicium and sometimes silphium. It grew on the dry southern slopes of the Green Mountains, where little else would grow, and was valued as a cattle-fodder, a medicine and above all as a flavour in cooking, particularly of fish dishes. It was still abundant in Caesar's time, but soon afterwards died out through overcropping: a single stalk was brought to the emperor Nero as a great curiosity. The plant is now totally extinct, and botanists have been unable to say precisely what it was. With its disappearance, Cyrenaica lost a major source of revenue; under the Roman Empire it always gives the impression of being something of an economic backwater.

IX

AEGYPTUS

This was the way the world walked in the beginnings of recorded time, Roman, Arab, Assyrian, Greek; if you could talk to everyone who used this road you could write the history of the human race. Everyone was here, except the Children of Israel who made it the hard way, farther south. And now they were trying to make it again, from a different direction, over the sea from Europe and elsewhere—still the hard way, they being Jews.

George MacDonald Fraser, *Night Run to Palestine*

EGYPT, SAID HERODOTUS, is the gift of the Nile. The phrase has been repeated so often that it has become almost a cliché, but is worth saying again because it is so profoundly true.

It is true not only in the obvious sense—that without the river the whole land would be a desert—but in a more subtle one. The Blue Nile, a faster and more powerful stream than the White Nile although not so long, causes (or to be precise, *did* cause) the whole valley of Egypt to be flooded every summer (a phenomenon that constantly baffled ancient geographers); in addition, it brings down from the highlands of Abyssinia a vast quantity of silt, much of which was left lying on the Egyptian fields after the floodwaters had receded. There was thus no need for manuring, crop rotation or any of the other devices normally used to prevent soil exhaustion. Hence Egypt's vast agricultural potential, and her tremendous economic importance to the Ancient World. This state of affairs, however, no longer exists; it was stopped by the building of the famous High Dam at Aswan. The lower Nile no longer floods, and the silt no longer reaches Egypt at all, piling up instead in the large lake behind the Dam. What the consequences will be for the land's ecology and economy is uncertain.

Like most of the Near East, Egypt came for a time under the rule of Alexander the Great. He entered it in 332 BC without the slightest opposition, and remained there for about a year—during which time his greatest achievement was the founding of a large city named after himself, destined to become the capital and chief port of all Egypt.

On Alexander's death (at Babylon, in 323 BC) civil war among his generals broke out almost immediately. In the resulting power-struggle some, so to speak, were aiming for the jackpot—complete suppression of all rivals, and reunion of Alexander's empire in its entirety under their own governance. Others, more cautious, were prepared to content themselves with a firm grip on *part* of the empire. Among these last was a general named Ptolemy, who also knew exactly which part he wanted—it was Egypt, one of the most naturally defensible countries in the world. To the east and west it is shut off by desert; in the south the Sudanese were too few to be a serious danger; a direct seaborne attack on the north would find itself floundering among the lakes and marshes of the Delta. Only in the north-east was Egypt exposed, where the great coast road runs up to Palestine and Syria, and in an age without tanks or aircraft this possible

Above: The Nile Delta photographed from space. Behind it can be seen the Gulf of Suez and Mount Sinai

Opposite below: Coins of Antony and Cleopatra

Opposite above: Bust of Cleopatra given to her son-in-law Juba the Second, now in the Cherchell Museum

line of invasion was easier to defend than it is now. And within these natural barriers the Nile provided a storehouse of vast agricultural wealth and industrial potential.

So the Ptolemy family became Pharaohs of Egypt. Their reign lasted for just three centuries less a quarter—from 305 BC when the first Ptolemy had himself officially proclaimed king, to 30 BC when the last of the family, Cleopatra, commited suicide. The earlier members of the family ruled with great vigour, making the 'Egyptian Empire' almost as large as it had ever been; the later members, however, fell into slackness and decadence. Meanwhile the power of Rome in the eastern Mediterranean was steadily increasing. Greece was annexed in 146 BC, western Asia Minor in 133, Cyrenaica in 96, Crete in 67; Pompey the Great's victories brought Roman armies all over Asia Minor, Syria and Palestine, and down to the very gates of Egypt herself. Only the Sudanese in the south, who were insignificant, and the Parthians to the east, who were a long way off, remained outside the Roman net. Cleopatra's father, Ptolemy XI nicknamed the 'Piper', was virtually a puppet of the Roman Republic: when *they* piped, *he* danced.

It was therefore only natural that Cleopatra herself, a woman of remarkable intelligence and character (and by no means the straightforward sex-goddess of popular plays and films today) should try to influence Rome by influencing the great men of the Roman Republic. With Julius Caesar she was wholly successful; with Mark Antony she backed the wrong horse, or at any rate the losing horse.

So the family of Ptolemy ceased to rule Egypt, and their place as heir to all the Pharaohs was taken by the family of Caesar. To put it another way, Egypt became a province of the Roman Empire. From the very beginning it had a special status: whereas some provinces were 'senatorial', administered by action of the Roman Senate, and others 'imperial', run by deputies directly responsible to the emperor himself, Egypt was what one might call 'ultra-imperial'. Caesar Augustus, like Ptolemy I before him, was well aware of the province's vast natural wealth and defensibility; and he had no wish to see it made the rallying-ground for his political opponents. He accordingly decreed that no senator was even to set foot in Egypt without special permission. Even the governor, who normally in a province of such size would without doubt have been a senator, belonged instead to the lower order of Roman society called the equestrians (sometimes translated as 'the Knights' though this can be misleading: most equestrians were rich businessmen, the ancient equivalent of 'upper-middle classes', certainly not heroes in shining armour). The post of governor of Egypt (*Praefectus* of Egypt, as it was technically called) was one of the highest to which a Roman equestrian could aspire.

Egypt was a remarkably conservative country—in agriculture, in art and in obeisance to its supreme Pharaoh—and it was equally conservative in the pattern of its principal towns. From time immemorial the country had been divided into forty-two administrative districts, known to the Greeks and to modern scholars as 'nomes'—twenty in the Nile delta and twenty-two upstream in the valley. The system probably goes back earlier than 3000 BC, to a time before Egypt was unified; for each nome had its own special patron deity, and often too its own special sacred animal. Hence arose the odd-sounding names given by the Greeks to some nome-capitals —'City of Zeus', 'City of Apollo', 'City of the Sun', 'City of Dogs', 'City of Crocodiles'. An animal regarded as sacred in one nome might be wholly secular and even edible in another. Nevertheless the Ptolemies found the nome-system useful for administration, as did the Romans after them. Despite some subdivisions and amalgamations, many of the original forty-two were still on the official lists at the time of the Arab conquest, after a run of almost four thousand years.

A few cities lay outside the regular pattern of nomes and their capitals. One such was Naucratis, near the north-western corner of the Delta, founded in about 610 BC by Greeks with the permission of a then independent Egypt. It was designed as a treaty-port to be the centre of Graeco-Egyptian trade (somewhat analogous to Hong Kong or Shanghai in more recent times), and was always Greek, not Egyptian, in its appearance and general way of life.

The Macedonian take-over of Egypt deprived Naucratis of its chief raison d'être; the city was superseded by a new port, also of Greek design but enormously larger—Alexandria. This city was planned from the very first to be the capital and chief port of a country, which function it fulfilled admirably. The island of Pharos (with its famous lighthouse, the seventh wonder of the world) gave shelter from the prevailing northerly wind, and an artificial causeway linked it with the mainland, separating the Great Harbour from the Harbour of Eunostos or 'Safe Return'. From the latter a canal ran to the Canopic river, westernmost of the seven branches which the Nile delta possessed in ancient times (it now has only two of importance). So Alexandria had the benefit of connexion with this great watercourse without the drawback of its constant silting.

Bills of lading and statistics of gross annual output are among the many types of ancient document that we have to do without, but it seems likely that, in terms of gross tonnage of shipping handled, Alexandria was either the largest or the second largest port in the Mediterranean (its only possible rival being Ostia, the port of Rome). The geographer Strabo noticed in addition that ships leaving the port were noticeably lower in the water than ships coming in, and this is not to be wondered at. Egypt imported very little except timber, tourists and (under Roman rule) Government officials; her exports were enormous and varied. There was the Roman corn-levy, for a start, about ten per cent of every corn-crop grown in the land; in earlier times it had been stored in vast granaries (as recommended by Joseph in the Bible, in case seven fat years should be followed by seven lean ones); now it was sent away in enormous ships (the supertankers of the Ancient World) to feed the people of Rome. Other goods exported included salt, soda, paper, scent, glass and fine silverware—for the city of Alexandria was as great in industry as in straightforward commerce. Then there were the goods that passed through Egypt on their way from remoter lands: ivory from East Africa, incense from Arabia, pepper and spices from India and the islands of the furthest East, even sometimes silk from China (though this could also travel overland and reach the Mediterranean by a more northerly route). The Chinese themselves were long under the impression that Alexandria was the capital of the Roman Empire—unfortunately, because whereas 'Lo-ma' might have slipped quite easily over their tongues, 'A-li-xan-tu-li-a' proved unpronounceable and had to be shortened to 'Li-jien'.

The city was as famous for its intellectual as for its commercial life; its university, after that of Athens, was the most renowned in the Greek world. The two differed somewhat as Oxford and Cambridge have traditionally done; Athens had the higher prestige because it dealt with higher-sounding subjects—the nature of the Real and the Ideal, the principles that distinguish Existence from Non-Existence, the nature of the gods, and the best way to lead a Good Life (with a capital G and a capital L). In the Mouseion at Alexandria (whence comes our word 'museum') the inmates were more concerned with the material than the immaterial world. Euclid developed systematic geometry; Aristarchus proved that the sun was larger than the earth, and upset conservative opinion by suggesting that the earth revolved round it; Herophilus was the first to propose that the brain, not the heart or the liver, was the seat of intelligence; Eratosthenes

AEGYPTUS PALAESTINA ET ARABIA

MARE LIBYCUM

MARE AEGYPTIUM

Phycus Apollonia
Cyrene Darnis

CYRENAICAE PARS

Paliurus

LIBYARCHAE Antipyrgus

ANIRITAE

Marmarica Catabathmus Zagilis
MARMARIDAE ZYGRITAE

Parætonium Alexandria Nicopolis Pachnamunis
CHATTANI Canopus Buto
Pedonia Xois
Antiphrae Marea Naucratis Sais

Libya Andropolis Tava Thmu
ADYRMACHIDAE Nitriotis Bubastis Delta
Niciu Athrib

Letopolis Heliopolis
Babylon

Ammoniace Memphis

Moeris Aphroditopolis
Lacus
Arsinoe Nilopolis
Ammonium (Crocodilopolis)

Heracleopolis Magna

Hepta nomia

Psobthis Oxyrynchus

LIBYA Cynopolis

Oasis
DESERTA Minor Antinoopolis

Hermopolis
Magna

Lycopolis

LIBYAEGYPTII Hypselis
Antæopolis

LIBYA Aphroditopolis

INTERIORIS

PARS Mothis Hibis

Oasis
Major

Cysis

LIBYA DESERTA

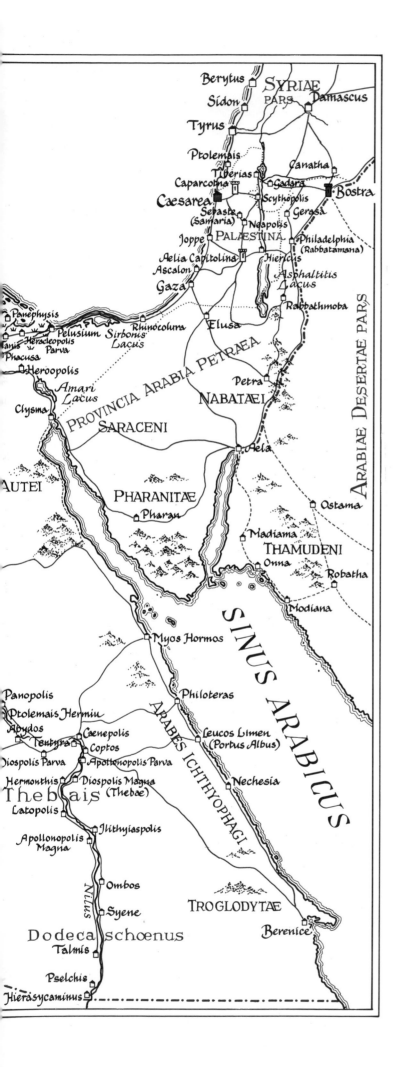

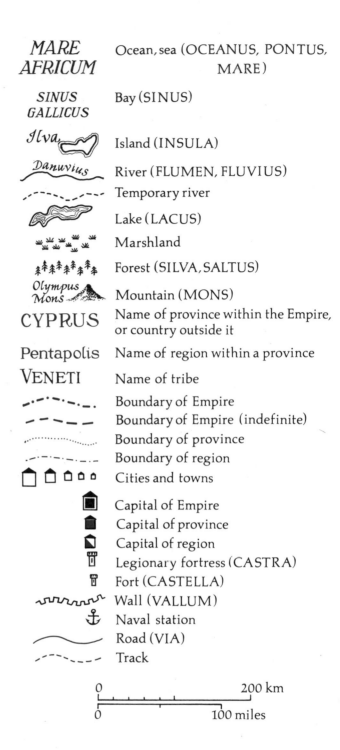

MARE AFRICUM	Ocean, sea (OCEANUS, PONTUS, MARE)
SINUS GALLICUS	Bay (SINUS)
Ilva	Island (INSULA)
Danuvius	River (FLUMEN, FLUVIUS)
	Temporary river
	Lake (LACUS)
	Marshland
	Forest (SILVA, SALTUS)
Olympus Mons	Mountain (MONS)
CYPRUS	Name of province within the Empire, or country outside it
Pentapolis	Name of region within a province
VENETI	Name of tribe
	Boundary of Empire
	Boundary of Empire (indefinite)
	Boundary of province
	Boundary of region
	Cities and towns
	Capital of Empire
	Capital of province
	Capital of region
	Legionary fortress (CASTRA)
	Fort (CASTELLA)
	Wall (VALLUM)
	Naval station
	Road (VIA)
	Track

0				200 km
0		100 miles		

The Pharos (Lighthouse) of Alexandria

measured the circumference of the earth, coming within fifty miles of its true value; Hero built numerous mechanical devices, including forerunners of the theodolite and the steam-engine; and Claudius Ptolemy, whose geographical work we have already mentioned several times, was even more distinguished as a mathematician and astronomer than as a geographer. His system of the universe won world-wide acceptance until finally challenged by Copernicus in the sixteenth century.

National capital, provincial capital, harbour city, industrial city, university city—Alexandria was always on the boil, always coming up with something new, often with something new and violent. Of the city's half-a-million or so inhabitants, about 300,000 were Greek, the rest mostly Jews, and this alone made a perfect recipe for riots and civil strife. The principal garrison of Roman Egypt, Legio II Traiana was stationed not on the frontiers, but only a few miles from the capital itself. Here, evidently, was the place of greatest danger.

Most of the rulers who shared among themselves what had been Alexander's empire were great enthusiasts for building new towns (or, at the very least, enlarging old ones) and renaming them after themselves and their relations. The Ptolemies, however, were not, at any rate not in Egypt proper. In Cyrenaica to the west, in Sinai and Palestine to the north-east, and all along the Red Sea coast we *do* find towns with the typical dynastic names of Ptolemais, Berenice and Arsinoe: but in the Nile region itself (apart from Alexandria and Naucratis, which existed before the first Ptolemy arrived) we find only one Greek foundation, Ptolemais Hermiu, occupying the site of an old nome-capital called This. The reason for such restraint was a simple financial one. A Greek city had to have a Greek constitution; it had to have territory to support it; and it had to have at least some political autonomy and freedom from taxation. All this meant money out of the pockets of the central government. Far better, surely, to stick to the old-fashioned nome, paying regular tribute to the Pharaoh in the time-honoured way.

No more cities of the Greek type were founded, therefore, either by Ptolemies or by Romans, until the second century AD when the emperor Hadrian founded Antinoöpolis. This took its name from his paramour Antinoüs, who was drowned in the Nile: Hadrian laid it out generously, and in due course it became possibly the largest city in the Nile valley. Its remains were still impressive at the end of the eighteenth century, when Napoleon's army passed them, but by now have almost completely disappeared.

The pattern of roads linking these various towns was, and still is, a straightforward one. Nature has set the scene in Egypt with little scope for variation. From Alexandria, the capital, one Roman road ran south-east, following the Canopic branch of the Nile up to Memphis at the head of the Delta (an important natural junction of routes, often the capital of Pharaonic Egypt, and still a large and important town under Roman rule.) Thence the road continued to follow the left bank of the Nile, throwing off only one important branch to serve the region known today as the Fayyum, and in ancient times as Crocodilopolitis after its principal city. Here an offshoot of the Nile dropped into a lake called Lake Moeris (larger in those days than it is now) whose shores were able to grow corn in even greater abundance than the rest of Egypt. The main road carried on, past Oxyrhynchus (the 'City of Sharp-nosed Fish', where many interesting papyri have been found), past Hermopolis the Great, to Lycopolis ('City of Wolves', modern Asyut) where the valley begins to narrow. Further upstream still we find Ptolemais Hermiu, that solitary Greek city in an Egyptian surrounding, Diospolis the Lesser and Apollonopolis the Greater, then nothing in particular until the Roman frontier is reached at Hierasycaminos (El-Maharraqa, whose original site was submerged by the building of the Aswan High Dam).

An exactly corresponding road followed the opposite bank of the river. From its terminus at Pelusium, the port at the north-east corner of the Delta, it followed the eastern, or Pelusiac, branch of the Nile to Babylon (Old Cairo, not to be confused with the much larger Babylon in what is now Iraq). Thence it carried on past Antinoöpolis (Hadrian's new foundation), Coptos (an important road junction, as we shall presently see), Diospolis the Greater, better known as Thebes and on several past occasions the capital of all Egypt, though now sadly fallen from its former glory; Ombos (now called Kom Ombo); and Syene (now called Aswan) before, like its opposite number, reaching the Roman frontier. Neither this road nor the one on the opposite side of the Nile, however, can ever have been particularly popular; for ordinary travel the Nile itself provided a far smoother and more comfortable highway. The great boats used on it may not have been strong enough to face the open sea, but in their own element they were unrivalled. They had been used, after all, to carry statues, obelisks and blocks for building pyramids long before Greece, much less Rome, was in existence. The Nile, too, so beneficent to humanity in other ways, seemed to have a kindly approach to that ever-tedious problem of managing a sailing boat. The prevailing wind in Egypt is 'light airs from the North'; to go upstream the Nile boatman simply hoisted a single large, heavy square sail. To come downstream again he furled the sail and let the current do the work.

Besides these longitudinal roads parallel with the Nile, there were also some at right angles to it. It was possible to make one's way from Alexandria to Pelusium directly across the Delta, though this road can hardly have been popular either. It had to cross six major branches of the river, plus several minor ones, almost all too deep to ford and too wide to bridge, and the Delta was

Above: Bust of Antinoüs, the emperor Hadrian's paramour who was drowned in the Nile and had a large Egyptian city built and named after him

Right: Figure of Anubis in Roman military dress from Kom el Shugafa

Opposite: Pompey's Pillar—Alexandria

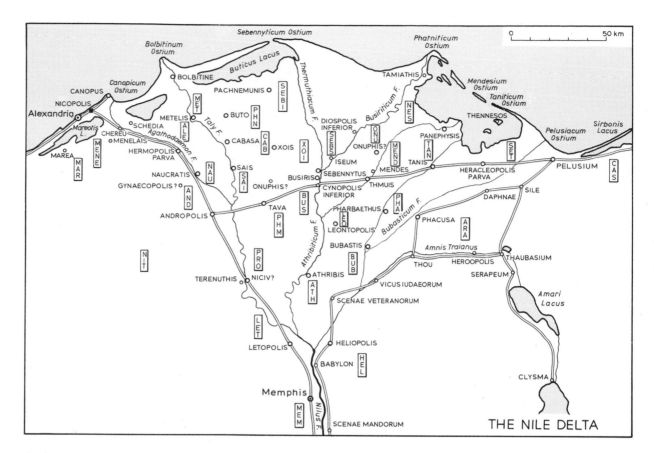

THE NILE DELTA

Regions of
Lower Egypt

ALE	Alexandriae Regio	LET	Letopolites	PHA	Pharbaethites
AND	Andropolites	MAR	Mareotis	PHM	Phthemphuthi
ARA	Arabia	MEM	Memphites	PHN	Phthenetu
ATH	Athribites	MEND	Mendesius	PRO	Prosopites
BUB	Bubastites	MENE	Menelaites	SAI	Saites
BUS	Busirites	MET	Metelites	SEBI	Sebennytes Inferior
CAB	Cabasites	NAU	Naucratites	SEBS	Sebennytes Superior
CAS	Casiotis	NES	Nesyt	SET	Sethroites
HEL	Heliopolites	NIT	Nitriotis	TAN	Tanites
LEO	Leontopolites	ONU	Onuphites	XOI	Xoites

remarkably short of suitable bridging material. For most purposes it was quicker to move from place to place in the Delta by sailing up one river-branch or canal and down another.

A few roads avoided the Nile region altogether and plunged into the desert itself. West of the river, there was the important route leading from Alexandria along the coast through the desolate regions of Libya and Marmarica, eventually to reach comparatively fertile ground in the neighbouring province of Cyrenaica. Other routes, ill-defined tracks rather than true Roman roads, cross-linked the various oases of the Western Desert. Originally the word 'Oasis', like 'Archipelago' and 'Volcano' was not general but specific. The early Egyptians referred to *the* two Oases: the Greater, now called El-Kharga, and the Lesser, now called El-Bahariya. Only later did the term become generalised to apply to other similar formations— the Dakhla Oasis, the Farafra Oasis and the Oasis of Siwa or Ammonium. This last was the remotest from Egypt proper, and also the most romantic. Cambyses of Persia, the conqueror of Egypt for the Persian Empire, is reported to have sent an expedition there, which never arrived; somewhere between Bahariya and Siwa all the men were overwhelmed in a tremendous sand-storm. Alexander the Great went to Siwa too, by a different route and with better success: he arrived without mishap, consulted the famous oracle of Zeus-Ammon, and *may* (this is disputed) have acquired from the oracle the belief that he himself was some form of god.

The roads of Egypt's Eastern Desert were more substantial, and in more general use, than those of the Western. In the first place, whereas most of the Western Desert conforms to the popular idea of what a desert should be—sandy—the Eastern Desert is on the whole not sandy but rocky, and across it runs a range of mountains containing some valuable natural products. And secondly, the Eastern Desert lies on the way to the Red Sea, up which came so many cargoes of fascinating foreign goods.

The most obvious way of dealing with such cargoes would seem to be to unship them at Suez (a port already in existence, under the name of Clysma) and then carry them by land either due north, following the line of the present Suez Canal, to the great port of Pelusium on the Mediterranean, or else due west, to the Nile itself, and so down the river to Alexandria. This latter route was followed by an artificial canal—a sort of precursor of the Suez canal—but this does not seem to have been as much help as it might have been. First, receiving as it did the silt of the Nile, it repeatedly became blocked and had to be cleared: the emperor Trajan was one of several potentates who had this job done, and for a time the canal came to be called after him, the *amnis Traianus*.

But the real trouble with Trajan's Canal, or Ptolemy's Canal, or Darius' Canal, or whatever you call it, lay in conditions on the Red Sea itself. The same persistent northerly winds that make the Nile so easy to navigate make the Red Sea remarkably troublesome, for ancient ships were not good at sailing against the wind. There was also the danger from reefs, shoals, sharks and pirates to be considered. Normally, therefore, ships in the Red Sea did not go all the way up to Suez, but instead unloaded their cargo at some port on Egypt's east coast, whence it could be carried across the desert to the Nile and so down to Alexandria. There were several suitable ports, different ones being popular at different times. Myos Hormos ('Mussel Harbour') was the most northerly and for a long time the most popular; then came Philoteras; then Leucos Limen ('the White Harbour'); and finally, very near the southern frontier of Egypt, Berenice. Roads from these ports converged on the cities of Coptos and Caenepolis, where the Nile makes a great bend and has its closest approach to the sea. Hadrian built a new road, named the Via Hadriana after himself, which ran from Berenice northward along the Red Sea coast, then swung inland to reach his new foundation of Antinoöpolis. This road does not seem to have been much used, however, and a glance at the map will suggest why. Compared with the old and reasonably straight road from Berenice to Coptos, the Via Hadriana was horribly long and roundabout. Antinoöpolis was simply not in the right place to be a shipment point.

The Eastern Desert also contained some valuable mineral wealth. The Mons Porphyrites, near the road to Myos Hormos, yielded porphyry, particularly valued by the emperors because its dark-red colour approximated to that of Imperial purple. Mons Claudianus, somewhat further south, yielded a kind of grey granite. Further south still were mines of gold, amethyst, and a substance called *smaragdus* (sometimes translated 'emerald', but here probably meaning the less precious green stone called amazonite; true emeralds were found only in Asia.) All these, like other minerals throughout the Empire, were the personal property of the Emperor.

Examination of Egypt's economic history sometimes gives the impression of a vast, beautifully made, smooth-running machine, whose sole object is to produce wealth for the Pharaoh. Whether the said Pharaoh's name be Rameses, or Ptolemy, or Tiberius Claudius Drusus Nero

Above: Shrine at El Kab

Opposite: Boats on the Nile using a technique that has changed little for centuries

Germanicus—or, for that matter, Khedive Ismail or Prince Farouk—is immaterial. The machine runs on regardless, even supplying its own fuel; all it needs is a small amount of repair and maintenance.

This certainly is how the Romans saw Egypt. Other provinces were allowed, even encouraged, to develop on their own with a modest amount of freedom under Roman law; in Egypt this was discouraged as leading to loss of revenue. Everything was centralized, and everything was taxable. The poor paid the taxes; the rich had the thankless task of collecting them (unpaid) and making up any deficiency out of their own pockets. They also had to devote time and money to maintaining and improving the towns: this was standard practice throughout the Empire, but in most other provinces (Roman Africa, for instance, with its five hundred ever-growing cities) was regarded as a privilege. In Roman Egypt it was a burden. Numerous papyri tell us of the horror with which an eminent man faced the possibility of being made a local councillor; at times he would willingly surrender two-thirds of all his property to someone else who would do the job instead. Even then he might find no takers.

The alternative, for rich and poor alike, was flight. Egypt grew fuller and fuller of roving *lazzaroni* displaced from their homes by the burden of central government. We have an edict of AD 154 (the very middle of what Gibbon called the Golden Age of Roman prosperity) issued by a man with the ironic name of Liberalis: it offers a three-month amnesty to such wandering peasants, then ends, 'If anyone is found roaming away from his home, after this great manifestation of my clemency, he shall be arrested as an acknowledged, no longer as a suspected, criminal . . .' But the flights continued. Another papyrus of about AD 170 records that the population of one village near Mendes, in the north-eastern Delta, had fallen from fifty-four to four; that of another from twenty-seven to three. In Ptolemaic times the town of Theadelphia, in the Fayyum, had been a considerable settlement; by the fourth century AD it had only twenty-five inhabitants on the assessment-lists, and all but three of those had fled. Roman emperors, in other words, were simply failing to supply the small amount of repair and maintenance that Egypt required; the machine was gradually running down.

Alexandria alone retained its prosperity and its liveliness, to a large extent living on the rest of the province. Roman Egypt, in fact, must have been a little like one of the poorer countries of Africa or Latin America today—all the wealth and sophistication and flourishment concentrated in the capital, while out in the 'back country' the peasants carry on their immemorial lives but one step removed from slavery.

X

ASIA

The man who makes his entry by leaning against an infirm door gets an unjustified reputation for violence. Something is to be attributed to the poor state of the door.

J. K. Galbraith, *The Affluent Society*

I N ELEMENTARY GEOGRAPHY, Turkey is one of the easier countries to understand. It has a neat shape on the map—roughly rectangular; its inhabitants are all Turks; the language they speak is Turkish. It possesses two memorable cities: Ankara, the present capital, which is plumb in the middle, and Istanbul (or to old-fashioned persons, Constantinople), the previous capital, which is tucked away in one corner.

When the Romans first came to Turkey (or Asia, as they themselves rather vaguely called it) the physical background was very much the same, but the political pattern was vastly more complicated. The Turks themselves were not on the scene at all, nor would be for another thousand years; their ancestors at the time were living far to the east, somewhere in the neighbourhood of the Great Wall of China. Instead we find a remarkable medley of peoples of at least a dozen different races and as many languages. Ancient Turkey was rather like a rocky beach: every now and then a vast wave swept over it from one direction or another, seemingly carrying all before it, only to subside again—but leave behind, caught in odd pools and crevices, specimens of the flora and fauna it had carried.

The most widespread of these 'fauna' were the Greeks. They had established themselves on the west coast of Turkey (which in physical form and in climate is similar to the Greek coast on the opposite side of the Aegean Sea) very early indeed, perhaps as early as 1500 BC. Somewhat later they spread along the south coast of the peninsula, reaching as far as Cyprus; later still they built settlements along its north coast.

The Greeks, however, were a maritime folk, and all their new foundations lay on or near the sea. The inner part of the country, from the Pontic mountains in the north to the Taurus range in the south, was fought over by other peoples, some highly civilized with abundant historical records, others not civilized at all. Lycians and Hittites entered the peninsula from the east; Phrygians, Mysians and Bithynians from the north-west; Cimmerians from the north, crossing the Black Sea from the land that still bears their name, the Crimea. Though on occasions a single unitary government—Persian, Greek or Roman—lay like a blanket over the land, beneath the blanket all kinds of vigorous, though invisible, activity persisted.

The other piece of country to be described in this chapter I propose to call the Levant—the region shared today, with no good grace, by Syria, Lebanon, Israel and Jordan.

In contrast with the remarkable ethnic and linguistic melée in ancient Turkey, the people of the ancient Levant had closely similar origins and at times even spoke a common language—not that this made them any better-disposed toward each other than they are today. All, or nearly all, had at one time or another in the past emerged from the great Arabian desert, thereupon gradually giving up their nomadic habits and taking to settled life. The books of Joshua and Judges in the Bible show how this happened to one particular group of these Semitic peoples, the Hebrews; other groups (Amorites, Canaanites, Aramaeans and later Nabataeans) at various times changed their pattern of living in exactly the same way.

The Levant forms a bridge, the only convenient land-bridge with the sea on one side of it and the desert on the other, between three regions—Egypt, eastern Turkey and Mesopotamia—all with greater potential wealth, power and military strength than itself. As a result it has frequently been subjected to rule from outside. The reign of Solomon round about 950 BC occupies a special place in Biblical history not only for its intrinsic glories but also for the rarity of the situation: for once there was no power, either to north or to south, strong enough to threaten the new-formed Kingdom of Israel. Subsequent years saw the danger of foreign invasion increase once more. Palestine, and indeed all the Levant, became subject in turn to Assyrians, Babylonians, Persians, Greeks, Romans, Byzantines, Persians again, and finally Arabs. Only with the establishment of the Ommayyad caliphs at Damascus in the eighth century AD could it again be said that the Levant contained a state both powerful and autonomous.

The whole of this region was unified from the mid-sixth century BC (when Cyrus the Great incorporated it into his Persian Empire) down to 323 BC (when Alexander, also called Great, died). Thereupon almost all the various generals who had set themselves up as Alexander's 'successors' became involved in it. Lysimachus, king of Thrace, was interested in the north-western regions; Seleucus, king of Iran and all the former eastern Persian provinces, had designs on eastern Turkey; Antigonus called 'the One-Eyed', who can best be described as king of everything he could lay hands on, had hopes of seizing the whole peninsula. Even Ptolemy, king of Egypt, was involved, for one of the few things lacking in that almost wholly self-sufficient land is timber, and some of the best timber could be found in Cilicia and Cyprus. Hence arose much warfare both by land and by sea.

By the 270s BC the situation had become comparatively stable. The Antigonid family, descendants of Antigonus the One-Eyed, ruled Macedonia and much of Greece, but had been forced out of Asia. The Ptolemies ruled Egypt, Palestine and Cyprus. The third of the great successor-dynasties, the Seleucids, controlled (at least in theory) most of the rest of what had been Alexander's empire—a huge block of territory, reaching from the Aegean Sea to the Khyber Pass. Formidable on paper, the Seleucid kingdom was in fact beset by terrible internal weaknesses; like an old elm-tree it was constantly shedding parts of itself. Alexander's conquests in India were given up by Seleucus I as early as 304 BC (in exchange for which the latter ruler received a strong force of Indian elephants, which proved useful to confuse his enemies at the other end of his kingdom). Bactria, the next province to the north of India, broke away under a Greek ruler of its own in about 248 BC, forming a strange enclave, deep in the heart of Asia, in which Greek, Persian, Indian and Chinese ideas on life and art met and mingled with remarkable effects. A few years later Parthia, the land to the south-east of the Caspian Sea, also broke away, this time not under Greek but Iranian leaders. The kingdom of Parthia was destined eventually to replace that of the Seleucids altogether and become the greatest

Detail of mosaic at Pompeii showing Alexander the Great at the battle of Issus

enemy of the Roman Empire.

At the opposite end of the Seleucid kingdom the situation was also shaky. In the northern parts of Turkey, where Alexander had had little influence, small non-Greek kingdoms began to appear soon after his death—Bithynia in the north-west, Pontus next to it along the Black Sea coast, and Cappadocia inland, on the central plateau. Then, in 278 BC, the already well-mixed ethnic stew that made up ancient Turkey received yet another new ingredient—a body of Celts from the Danube region, who settled themselves round Ankara in the centre of the Anatolian plateau and made a living largely by plundering their richer and more peaceful neighbours.

But the kingdom that was eventually to make the greatest contribution to destroying Seleucid power was none of these. The important city of Pergamum (now called Bergama) broke away from Seleucid rule in 262 BC and gradually gathered round itself a small but rich territory. So began yet another 'successor-dynasty' to Alexander, this one being known as the dynasty of the Attalids. Despite several attempts the Seleucids never succeeded in suppressing the Attalids; at length, indeed, these attempts led to their own destruction, by bringing in the all-consuming power of Rome.

How and why the Romans became involved in Asian affairs is by no means easy to explain in simple terms. It came about through a complex network of interlocking alliances (of the sort that did so much to start the First World War). Rome hated Carthage, and particularly hated Hannibal, who had brought her to the verge of total destruction. Philip V, king of Macedon, had made an alliance with Hannibal; so Rome hated him too, and was to launch a series of wars ending with the permanent annexation of his kingdom. And Antiochus III, king of the Seleucid territories, had made an alliance with Philip, whereby Roman hostility, now at two removes, extended to him also. Worse still, the dreaded Hannibal, expelled from his native city of Carthage, was now residing at the court of Antiochus: dark stories went round at Rome that he might reappear in Italy, with a new army and all the wealth of the East behind him—like the second attack of a fever that proved almost fatal the first time.

Antiochus III, sometimes called *Megas* or 'the Great' was certainly great in ambition and in ability, but not, unfortunately, in achievement: he lacked one quality vital to a really great world conqueror—luck. His master-plan was to restore the Seleucid kingdom to the size and glory it had had under his great-great-grandfather, Seleucus I; and in the east this plan was largely successful. He utterly defeated the Parthians, and advanced right up to the frontiers of Bactria and India. But his campaign in the west entailed the taking (or as he said, the re-taking) of certain cities on the European, as well as some on the Asian, side of the Straits: and the Romans, having just defeated Philip of Macedon, regarded all Greece in Europe as being under their control. This apparently trivial dispute developed into open war, culminating late in 190 or early in 189 BC with a battle near the town of Magnesia-by-Sipylus (modern Manisa) on the Hermus river about twenty miles from Smyrna. Thanks largely to the cavalry of their ally, the king of Pergamum, the Romans won a crushing victory—and afterwards imposed a crushing peace. Antiochus was deprived of all the territory he had controlled north of the Taurus Mountains: nothing was left to him in Turkey except Cilicia and Pamphylia, confined spaces between the said mountains and the sea.

The kingdom of Pergamum took advantage of the sudden power-vacuum to expand and occupy most of western Turkey; its only rival here was the great maritime republic of Rhodes, which suffered from the disadvantage of unpopularity at Rome. At its height it controlled almost half the Turkish peninsula, but in 133 BC a curious fate befell it—Attalus III, its last king, died and left his possessions to Rome.

Just as thirteen years earlier the Roman province acquired from Carthage had become simply Africa, so this new foothold in yet another continent was called simply Asia. Its relations with its neighbours were soon to produce highly elaborate and dangerous problems for its Roman governors. Immediately to the east of the new province, three Celtic tribes still occupied the region round Ankara. They were less of a nuisance than they had been, for shortly after the battle of Magnesia a Roman army had soundly thrashed them—to the great relief and thanksgiving of all their neighbours. To the north-east of Roman territory, separated from it by the towering mountain of Mysian Olympus, lay the kingdom of Bithynia, which was usually friendly to Rome; beyond it lay the kingdom of Pontus, which was not. The eastern part of the peninsula, beyond the Gauls, formed the kingdom of Cappadocia. The south coast, save for some small pieces that still belonged to the Seleucids, was an array of little communities almost independent, with a distressing habit of supplementing their livings by piracy. (This was largely Rome's own fault: she had squashed the republic of Rhodes, which had previously acted as *guarda-costa* in these waters, and then refused to take on herself the job that the Rhodians now could not do.)

The real nigger in the Asian woodpile, however, was king Mithradates of Pontus. This remarkable monarch had gained control of the Greek cities on the north side of the Black Sea, in what is now the Crimea; also of the land of Colchis at the eastern end of the sea, where the Golden Fleece was once sought. Thus armed, he began to press upon his two weaker neighbours in Asia, Bithynia on the west side of his kingdom and Cappadocia on the east. This was in 90 BC, a convenient time since Rome was preoccupied with the violent conflict in Italy that is generally called the 'Social War'. The Romans unwisely attacked in Asia with insufficient forces, and were catastrophically defeated. Mithradates overran Roman Asia, most of which hailed him as a liberator from Roman usurers and tax-collectors. Eighty thousand Italians were massacred. Mithradates' forces pressed on into the Roman province of Macedonia, hoping to repeat the same exercise there.

The situation was saved by the great Roman general Sulla. Landing in Epirus with a smallish force, he seized Athens, then made his way to the plain of Boeotia—already the scene of many famous battles. Two further ones were now fought, at Chaeronea and Orchomenus, both of which Sulla won. The Pontic armies were expelled from Greece. After some further confused fighting in Asia, Mithradates at length decided that the game was up; he agreed to pay an indemnity, give up his conquests and retire to his own kingdom of Pontus. Only gathering threats of civil war at Rome itself (in which Sulla was determined to play—and did play—an important part) saved him from a much harsher fate. As it was, cities in Roman Asia that had hailed him as liberator were soon made to wish they hadn't.

Meanwhile the problem of piracy in the eastern Mediterranean was growing steadily more acute. Of the three great national fleets that had previously, by unwritten agreement, maintained the 'Freedom of the Seas' in these parts, the Rhodian fleet had been suppressed by Rome soon after the forming of Roman Asia. The Egyptian fleet, once powerful, had steadily declined as Egypt became more and more a puppet of Rome. The Seleucid fleet, drawn from Syria and Phoenicia, was in even more of a decline: the Seleucid kingdom by this time resembled Poland in one of the darker phases of its history—cut by a partition here and a partition there, menaced on all sides by stronger neighbours (Romans to the west, Armenians to the north, Parthians to

Above: Road through the Syrian mountains between Alexandretta and Antioch

Opposite: Ephesus—entry to street

the east, even Jews to the south, who under the famous Judas Maccabaeus had made themselves into an independent nation). It was destined very soon to go where a candle-flame goes when the wax runs out.

Rome alone could suppress the pirates; but for a long time she did nothing. In the seventies and early sixties BC, however, some campaigns were launched which achieved at least a partial success, the most important coup being the Roman capture of Crete, one of the pirates' principal strongholds, in 67 BC. Much remained to be done, however; and in that same year Pompey the Great was given a special *provincia*—a word usually translated as 'province', but which originally simply meant 'job'. After serving in high office at Rome, such as the consulship, an eminent Roman was thought eligible for a *job* outside Italy—usually, but not always, entailing the control of some specific piece of territory. Julius Caesar, who was unpopular with the Senate, was at one stage in his career offered the *provincia* of 'Minister of Italian Forestry'—the most insignificant job that the Senate could drag up for him. Only the influence of powerful friends, Pompey among them, gained him a more impressive and encouraging position as governor of Gaul.

Pompey's 'province' of 67 BC was an unusually interesting and challenging one. It was a kind of roving commission, effective throughout the Mediterranean, with the sole object of suppressing piracy. To help him do this, Pompey was granted five hundred ships, a hundred and twenty thousand soldiers and six thousand talents (something of the order of two million pounds today). With such ample resources, his operation was a complete success; in less than a year the pirate danger was over and communications made safe.

Hardly was this job finished when Pompey received another one, this time on the opposite side of the Turkish peninsula. Back in 74 BC the king of Bithynia, Nicomedes, had died, and like Attalus III in the previous century had bequeathed his kingdom to Rome. Mithradates, who had for some time planned to bring Bithynia under his own control, promptly invaded the new province. There followed a prolonged war between him and the Roman commander Lucullus, who slowly but inexorably gained the upper hand. Mithradates was forced out of Bithynia into his own kingdom of Pontus, then out of that into the neighbouring (and still more mountainous) kingdom of Armenia, ruled by his ally and son-in-law Tigranes. Lucullus pursued as far as Artaxata, the old capital of Armenia, but then his troops refused to follow him any further. Soon afterwards orders came from Rome that he should hand over his command to Pompey. He returned home in disgust, and spent the rest of his life giving incredibly lavish parties (so that the adjective 'lucullan' has entered the English language).

Pompey, with a much larger force than Lucullus had had, soon finished what his predecessor had begun. He utterly defeated Mithradates (near the place later named Nicopolis, 'City of Victory') and forced him to flee to Russia: he received the surrender of Tigranes and took from him all his conquests: he campaigned in the Caucasus area, reaching almost as far as the Caspian Sea: he made Syria into a Roman province: and he put an end to an unpleasant civil war that had been raging in Palestine. Rome was now the undisputed ruler—in fact, if not everywhere in theory—of all Asia up to the river Euphrates.

Under the late Republic and early Empire, the political geography of Asia was incredibly complicated. It has been likened to the geography of Germany before Bismarck—a patchwork quilt of tiny states; but a closer analogy is British India: parts of the land being under the direct rule of the overall controlling power, other parts being (ostensibly, at least) independent under their own rulers. Some of these 'rajahs' in turn were controllers of large and powerful states, some small and insignificant; some enjoyed the fullest confidence of the ruling government, some were regarded with considerable suspicion and kept under close watch. Nor was the pattern a static one. Kings, Queens and Viceroys of British India cannot, on the whole, be called whimsical; some Roman emperors were. Herod Antipas, for example, (the ruler mentioned frequently in the Gospels, who ordered John the Baptist's execution and did much to bring about the crucifixion of Christ) was finally deposed and exiled to France through lack of influence with the emperor Caligula; his nephew Herod Agrippa (mentioned in the Acts of the Apostles) *did* have influence with Caligula and later with Claudius, and as a result saw his kingdom steadily magnified.

For despite their violent attacks on those (such as Mithradates) who seemed a danger to them, the Romans regarded Asia with almost as much suspicion as Africa. The reason, though, was different. Africa was a *physically* alarming land, full of myth and mystery; the problem was to deal with wild tribes, some of whom might have odd feet, or talk in the language of bats, or have faces in their chests instead of in their heads. Asia was different: all Asians were well known to have their heads in the usual place, but what went on inside those heads was frequently a mystery to the simple-minded Roman. Not physically, but *mentally*, was Asia alarming.

So, in the early days of the Roman Empire under Augustus, we find Roman *influence* still reaching up to the Euphrates, but Roman *direct rule* covering only a much smaller area. The great Civil Wars had had a strong element of 'East-against-West' about them. In the first round Caesar, conqueror of Gaul, beat Pompey, conqueror of Asia. In the final round, Antony and Cleopatra are supposed to have dreamed afresh the dream of Alexander, seeing a new Empire that once more reached as far as India, with Alexandria as its capital and Rome as a mere provincial city. True or false, this gave their rival Octavian a valuable piece of propaganda: 'Rome for the Romans', he could claim, 'and no damned Asiatics in *my* Empire!'

So when Octavian became Augustus, only a small part of Roman Asia was under direct Roman rule. The whole area contained only three strictly Roman provinces: Asia proper, Bithynia and Syria. The first two were under senatorial control; Syria, through its advanced position confronting the great Kingdom of Parthia, Rome's largest enemy, remained invariably under the direct control of the emperor.

All the rest of 'Roman' Asia was ruled by client kings set up, or confirmed in their power, by Augustus himself. They were very numerous. Those who like to hear the strange resonance of ancient names, of foreign kings and battles long ago, might try reading aloud the list of those vassal-kings in the East who acknowledged the rule of the only, the almighty, the maker of kings, Emperor Caesar Augustus.

Amyntas, king of Galatia
Polemo, king of Pontus
Archelaus, king of Cappadocia
Artavasdes, king of Armenia the Lesser
Artaces, king of Armenia the Greater
Antiochus, king of Commagene
Abgar, king of Osroene
Obodas, king of the Nabataeans [his capital was the famous city of Petra]
and, most famous of them all,
Herod the Great, king of Palestine.

Above: Roman gateway at Hierapolis

Opposite: Ephesus—principal street

By the second century AD (to which these maps refer) all these kingdoms had gone save Greater Armenia, which preserved a delicately-balanced independence, in as much as both Romans and Parthians would have liked to have it, but neither would tolerate for a moment the other's possession of it. Roman Turkey now consisted of six provinces, the Roman Levant of three. As in other parts of the Empire, the slack in the rope had been taken up, and Rome was in face-to-face confrontation with one of her most formidable enemies.

In what is now western Turkey, the Roman province of Asia was still in existence, changed little in size or shape from what it had been under the Roman Republic, still senatorial, still with its capital at Ephesus—and still incredibly rich. To govern Roman Asia or Roman Africa were the two highest pinnacles of administration to which an upper-class Roman could aspire, normally after distinguished military service in one of Rome's more war-like provinces such as Pannonia, Syria or Britain. The contrast between the two sides of the Aegean Sea was astonishing: whereas the Greek side, fundamentally poor economically despite its artistic and intellectual glories, succumbed in the wars before and during the Roman takeover to a state of chronic numb financial misery, the Asian side was able to shake off equal military horrors and emerge each time as rich as before. This comparatively small province had been the seat of three of the Seven Wonders of the World—the Temple of Artemis at Ephesus, the Mausoleum of Halicarnassus and the Colossus of Rhodes: all but the last (knocked down by an earthquake in 225 BC) were still in existence. Ephesus, the provincial capital, had at least a quarter of a million inhabitants, perhaps more, and was the province's chief port: through silting of the river Caÿster, it is now no longer a port at all. Smyrna, which unlike most great ancient cities of western Turkey is still important today, was a close rival of Ephesus in the matter of size; so too was Pergamum, the old capital of the Attalid kingdom that preceded the Roman province. (This was a university town, which for some time had carried on a quiet literary war with the bigger and better-known university town of Alexandria. When the Egyptians, rather meanly, cut off the supply of the ancient world's standard writing material, papyrus, the Pergamenes developed a substitute material, from specially prepared sheepskin. The Romans knew this substance, more expensive than papyrus but much more durable, as *carta Pergamena*; today we call it parchment.)

Some Roman provinces were dominated by their capitals, no other city in the land being anything like so large. Roman Egypt was so dominated by Alexandria; Roman Africa by Carthage; Roman Gaul by Lyons and later by Trier; even Roman Britain to some extent (like modern England) by London. Roman Asia, on the other hand, had no such all-embracing metropolis. Ephesus, Smyrna and Pergamum were merely the three largest cities among a multitude of rivals. Cyzicus, on the southern shore of the Sea of Marmara close to the Bithynian border, was a huge city, and its temple built by Hadrian was reckoned the eighth wonder of the world. Halicarnassus far to the south was an enormous city; so was Rhodes, on its island, which for a time had ruled all the waves of the eastern Mediterranean; so was Miletus, with which the forces of Nature have dealt harshly. Miletus once stood on a peninsula, secure from all land-based attack save on one side; steady silting by the river Maeander (another classical name which has received a general meaning from geographers) has now turned it into a wholly inland site. What was the *Gulf* of Latmus, at whose entrance Miletus stood, has become instead the fresh-water *Lake* of Latmus.

But though Asia was among the richest and most populous of Roman provinces, its wealth and its population were far from being universally distributed. The province's principal roads and principal cities followed the natural lines of communication into the interior—the westward-flowing rivers of Asia, in particular the two longest ones, the Hermus and the Maeander. From Smyrna a road ran up to Sardis, a mighty city dominating, in Roman as in Persian times, the whole of the upper Hermus valley; then, swinging a little to the south it passed Philadelphia (the 'city of brotherly love' founded by the brothers Attalus and Eumenes of the Pergamene dynasty) before climbing up through barren country, past the source of the Hermus and on to the plateau of central Anatolia. The road up the Maeander was still more important, as the main route from the provincial capital, Ephesus, to the interior. Instead of a single giant city like Sardis dominating the valley, we find a string of smaller ones all along the river, and many more on its tributaries: Tralles, Alabanda, Antioch-on-the-Maeander, Laodicea-on-the-Lycus (this town, with its neighbours Hierapolis and Colossae, produced some of the finest wool to be found anywhere in the Empire) and finally, at the head of the river, the great city of Apamea. (Like the other successors of Alexander, the Seleucid kings were fond of founding or refounding cities under their own names: just as cities with names like Ptolemais or Berenice show the influence, further south, of the Ptolemy family, so in Turkey, Mesopotamia and even as far east as Iran a string of Seleucias, Antiochs, Apameas and Laodiceas commemorates various male and female members of the Seleucid family. The Romans, with their Caesareas, Claudiopolises and so forth, were to carry on exactly the same tradition.)

Away from the large west-flowing rivers of Asia, however, settlement, except on the coast, was sparse. In the northern part of the province—Troas, in the extreme north-west, and Mysia next to it—the rivers run not westward to the Aegean but northward to the Sea of Marmara. Behind the great port of Cyzicus lay a tract of land possessing hardly any towns at all, and none of any great size. It was good hunting country—the emperor Hadrian is said to have founded the town of Hadrianutherae ('Hadrian's Hunt') in honour of a particularly good day's sport in the region—but it was too mountainous and forested to be much use for anything else.

Beyond the mountains of Mysia lay Rome's second oldest piece of territory in the peninsula, the province of Bithynia-et-Pontus. On the map it had the shape of a tadpole, Bithynia forming the head and the long, narrow coastal strip of Pontus the tail. Its capital was Nicomedia (modern Izmit)—yet another town with a dynastic name: it was founded by Nicomedes I of Bithynia.

We are unusually well informed about second-century life in this province, since one of its governors was Pliny the Younger (nephew of Pliny the Elder, the encyclopaedist whose geographical remarks have been quoted already several times in this book) and Pliny's letters to the emperor Trajan have been preserved. They give us a somewhat plaintive picture. Looking today at the vast monuments of Roman rule, the Colosseum, the Pont du Gard, the bridge of Alcantara, Hadrian's Wall and all the other ruins that have outlived their builders by so many centuries, one begins to feel that Romans built for all time; the sheer size and weight of their creations overwhelm us. But this was not always the case; Pliny often shows us the opposite—to use a fashionable term, the unacceptable—face of Roman public building. The city of Sinope needed a new water-supply; Prusa needed a new bath-house; down the main street of Amastris flowed a filthy sewer that should have been covered over. Nicomedia, the capital, had spent nearly a million pounds on an aqueduct that had had to be demolished; Nicaea, the second city of the province, had spent even more on a theatre that remained only half built—and the half that was built already showed signs of falling down. Pliny calls repeatedly for engineers and architects, and finally receives a somewhat surprising answer. Trajan's first reply makes the obvious retort:

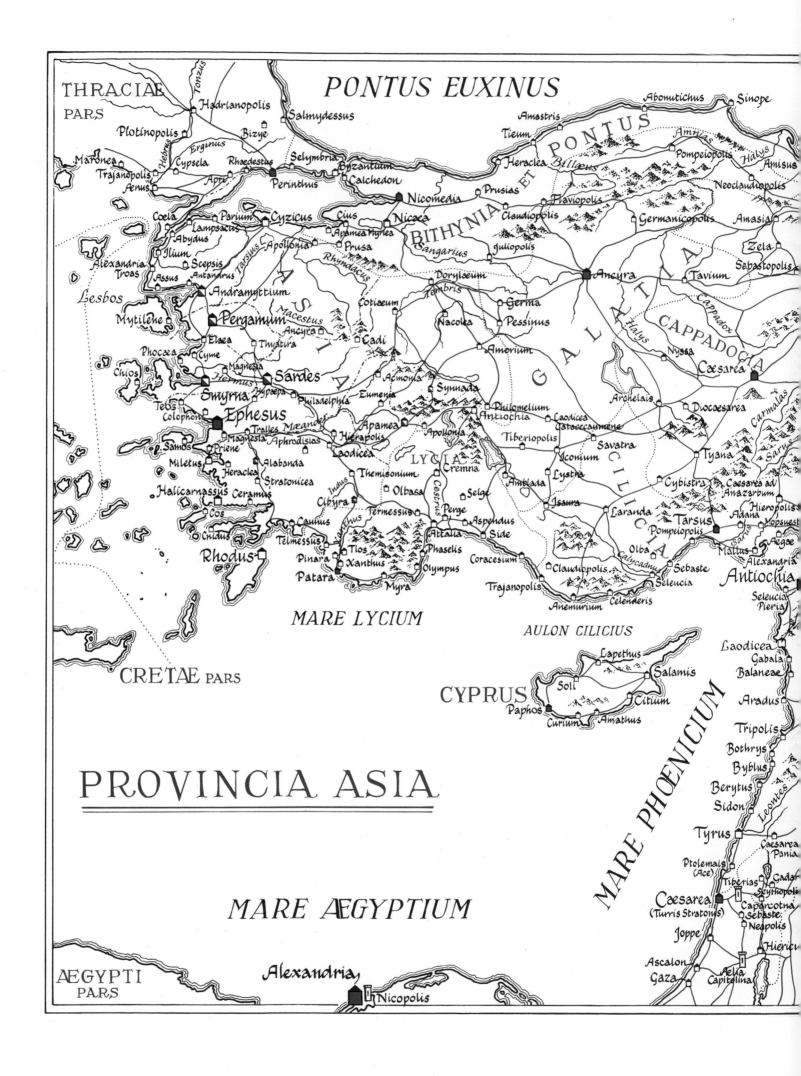

THRACIAE PARS

PONTUS EUXINUS

Hadrianopolis
Plotinopolis
Bizye
Salmydessus
Amastris
Abonutichus
Sinope
Maronea
Cypsela
Rhaedestus
Selymbria
Tieum
Heraclea
Billaeus
PONTUS
Amnias
Pompeiopolis
Hálys
Amisus
Trajanopolis
Aenus
Apri
Perinthus
Byzantium
Calchedon
Nicomedia
Prusias
Flaviopolis
BITHYNIA ET
Claudiopolis
Germanicopolis
Neoclaudiopolis
Amasia
Coela
Parium
Cyzicus
Cius
Nicaea
Apamea Myrlea
Prusa
Apollonia
Sangarius
Juliopolis
Zela
Lampsacus
Abydus
Tarsius
Rhyndacus
Dorylaeum
Ancyra
Tavium
Sebastopolis
Ilium
Alexandria
Troas
Scepsis
Antandrus
Assus
ASIA
Cotiaeum
Sambris
Germa
CAPPADOX
Andramyttium
Lesbos
Macestus
Ancyra
Nacola
Pessinus
GALATIA
Hálys
CAPPADOCIA
Mytilene
Pergamum
Elaea
Thyatira
Cadi
Amorium
Nyssa
Caesarea
Phocaea
Cyme
Magnesia
Hermus
Sardes
Synnada
Acmonia
Archelais
Diocaesarea
Carmalas
Chios
Hypaepa
Philadelphia
Eumenia
Philomelium
Antiochia
Laodicea
Catececaumene
Tiberiopolis
Savatra
Tyana
Sarus
Tebs
Colophon
Smyrna
Ephesus
Tralles
Maeander
Magnesia
Priene
Aphrodisias
Hierapolis
Apamea
Apollonia
LYCIA
Iconium
Lystra
CILICIA
Cybistra
Caesarea ad
Anazarbum
Hieropolis
Samos
Miletus
Alabanda
Laodicea
Themisonium
Cremna
Ambiada
Selge
Isaura
Laranda
Tarsus
Adana
Mopsuest
Heraclea
Stratonicea
Olbasa
Halicarnassus
Ceramus
Cibyra
Termessus
Perge
Aspendus
Pompeiopolis
Olba
Calycadnus
Mattius
Alexandria
Cos
Caunus
Xanthus
Attalia
Side
Sebaste
Aegae
Cnidus
Telmessus
Tlos
Phaselis
Coracesium
Claudiopolis
Seleucia
Antiochia
Rhodus
Pinara
Xanthus
Olympus
Trajanopolis
Seleucia
Pieria
Patara
Myra
Anemurium
Celenderis

MARE LYCIUM

AULON CILICIUS

Laodicea
Gabala
Balaneae

CRETAE PARS

CYPRUS
Lapethus
Soli
Salamis
Citium
Paphos
Curium
Amathus

Aradus
Tripolis
MARE PHOENICIUM
Bothrys
Byblus
Berytus
Sidon

PROVINCIA ASIA

Tyrus
Caesarea
Pania
Ptolemais
(Ace)
Tiberias
Gadar
Scythopolis
Caesarea
(Turris Stratonis)
Capancotha
Sebaste
Neapolis

MARE ÆGYPTIUM

Joppe
Hiericu
Ascalon
Gaza
Aelia
Capitolina

AEGYPTI PARS

Alexandria
Nicopolis

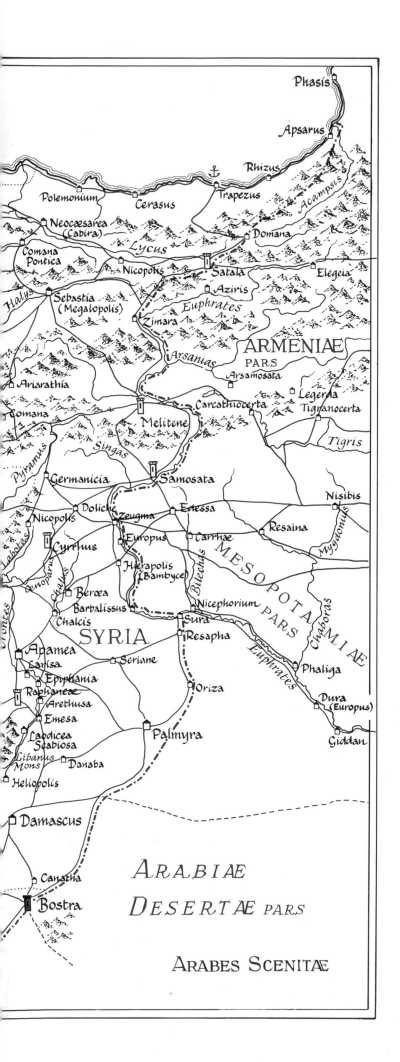

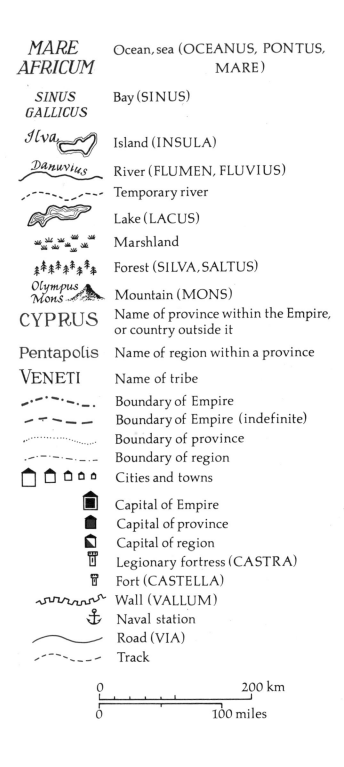

MARE AFRICUM	Ocean, sea (OCEANUS, PONTUS, MARE)
SINUS GALLICUS	Bay (SINUS)
Ilva	Island (INSULA)
Danuvius	River (FLUMEN, FLUVIUS)
- - - - -	Temporary river
	Lake (LACUS)
	Marshland
	Forest (SILVA, SALTUS)
Olympus Mons	Mountain (MONS)
CYPRUS	Name of province within the Empire, or country outside it
Pentapolis	Name of region within a province
VENETI	Name of tribe
—··—··—	Boundary of Empire
— — —	Boundary of Empire (indefinite)
·········	Boundary of province
—·—·—·	Boundary of region
⌂⌂⌂⌂⌂	Cities and towns
⬛	Capital of Empire
◪	Capital of province
◩	Capital of region
⬛	Legionary fortress (CASTRA)
⬛	Fort (CASTELLA)
⌇⌇⌇⌇⌇	Wall (VALLUM)
⚓	Naval station
═══	Road (VIA)
- - -	Track

0	200 km
0	100 miles

'Why ask me, at Rome, for an architect, when most of them come out to Rome from Greece in the first place?' And it does seem odd that, even if Bithynian architects were sub-standard, someone better could not have been found in the much more sophisticated neighbouring province of Asia, from the University of Pergamum, perhaps, or the great metropolis of Ephesus, or the city that had once built itself a Colossus. But we hear nothing of the kind. Instead Pliny writes to the governor of Lower Moesia on the Danube (this being the nearest province with strong Roman armed forces in it) seeking a military engineer. So the Roman Army, we hope, saves the day.

In later years the wealth and importance of this province greatly improved. In Pliny's time it was still somewhat off the beaten track: the main roads across Turkey ran from west to east, starting from Ephesus or one of the other great cities of the Aegean coast. The northern route through Bithynia was comparatively little used; it was longer, and some of it ran through wild and difficult country. It was Pliny's contemporary and overlord, Trajan, who did much to increase the importance of this route, by his opening-up of Thrace (as described on page 144). Byzantium now became a great road-centre, which it had not been before, and the natural way to continue a journey via Byzantium was to cross the Bosphorus to Chalcedon and take the road through Bithynia. The emperor Diocletian made this line of communication still more important by choosing Nicomedia as his capital; the founding of Constantinople made it one of the main approaches to the second largest city in the Empire.

Most of central Turkey, east of Asia and Bithynia, was occupied by the province of Galatia, of a shape so complicated as to defy description. It puts one in mind of the sculptor's maxim 'Take a block of stone, then chip off everything that doesn't look like what you want'. Indeed it had been formed in a somewhat analogous way, as an assemblage of all the pieces of central Turkey that the emperor Augustus did not (for the time being) want: not only Galatia proper (the land of the Celtic tribes who had invaded the country in 278 BC) but also on the north side Paphlagonia, and on the south side part of Phrygia, part of Pisidia and part of Lycaonia. The whole medley was placed by Augustus in charge of a king named Amyntas, who proved something of a disappointment. It was hoped that he would control the fierce and warlike tribes along his southern frontier, but instead (in 25 BC) he was captured and killed by them. Rather than find another candidate, Augustus decided on direct annexation and the whole heterogeneous territory became the province of Galatia.

It was neither a rich nor a populous province. The middle parts of it were too arid for intensive settlement, the fringe regions too mountainous. The Celtic tribes, moreover, had followed the same principle of 'one tribe, one town' (see page 77) as was characteristic of their kinsmen in France and to a lesser extent in Britain and on the Danube. Three Celtic tribes had settled in the peninsula, and each covered a large area with one, and only one, principal headquarters. These were the towns of Pessinus, Tavium and Ancyra (modern Ankara), the last being the largest, not only the provincial capital but also an important staging-point on the great road already mentioned, from Byzantium diagonally across Turkey into Syria.

Paphlagonia, north of the Celtic lands, was even more backward. It possessed only three cities, all with names commemorating Roman rulers—Pompeiopolis, Germanicopolis and Neoclaudiopolis. The second of these was the largest: it had been the capital of Paphlagonia under the name of Gangra, to which name it later reverted (the Turks today call it Çankiri). But none of the three cities was especially large, and the land around them always remained wild and remote from the main currents of civilization.

The mountain lands on the opposite, southern side of the Galatian province were equally wild and possessed even less political unity; they were shared by a number of small and very fierce tribes against whom the Romans themselves had had to wage frequent wars. A multitude of small towns developed. Some were Roman military colonies, similar to those found in many other wild parts of the Empire, founded by Augustus to help pacify the area; others were native settlements that gradually grew and in due course received official recognition. Of the colonies, the largest was a town called Antioch-by-Pisidia, which (as its name implies) was Seleucid before it became Roman, and may in fact date back to an earlier period still. The other Galatian city that gives the impression of having been larger than average is Iconium, the chief place of Lycaonia; under the name of Konya it is still an important city today. Both Antioch and Iconium stood on one of the most important east-west routes across Turkey.

Beyond the province of Galatia lay the province of Cappadocia, more regular in shape than the former, but like it consisting of an assemblage of territories with diverse characters. Cappadocia proper was annexed by Tiberius in AD 17; the land to the north of it, known as Pontus Polemoniacus after its erstwhile ruler Polemo, was taken over by Nero in AD 64; the neighbouring small kingdom of Lesser Armenia kept its independence till Vespasian's reign—AD 72. Thus the *province* of Cappadocia, unlike the earlier *kingdom* of the same name, had a seacoast—quite a long one, stretching from near Amisus (modern Samsun) past the famous city of Trapezus (Trebizond) and so up to a military post called Apsarus, which marked the limit of direct Roman rule on the Black Sea (though many tribes beyond acknowledged Rome's supremacy to a less definite extent).

For Cappadocia, unlike the other provinces of Roman Turkey, lay on a frontier of the Empire. As frontiers go, it was not an especially important or dangerous one, partly because the land on the other side of it, Greater Armenia, was often ruled by a king well-disposed towards Rome and sometimes indeed a virtual puppet of Rome, partly because the lofty mountains on both sides of the frontier make campaigns across it extremely difficult and unpleasant (as the Turks and Russians discovered in the First World War). The Cappadocian frontier was, however, important enough in the second century to have a garrison of two Roman legions. Legio XV Apollinaris occupied the fortress of Satala (now called Sadagh) high up among the Pontic mountains, one of the loneliest military positions in the Empire; Legio XII Fulminata was in a less isolated spot, at Melitene (near the modern town of Malatya). Here several roads converged, and there was an important crossing of the river Euphrates, which formed the frontier-line. This river, like the Rhine and Danube, was paralleled by a military road with forts, about which relatively little is as yet known. Indeed of all Rome's frontier-systems, that of Cappadocia has received the least attention from scholars and archaeologists.

Civilian settlement in the province developed slowly. Cappadocia had the same natural disadvantages as Galatia—parts of it extremely mountainous, other parts excessively arid. Strabo says of the Cappadocian kingdom (before the Roman takeover) that it had only two cities worth the name, Tyana and Mazaca. The former was an extremely ancient town, with a uniquely important geographical position near the approach to the Cilician Gates—the only practicable pass in this region over the Taurus Mountains. A list of eminent persons who passed through Tyana at one time or another, from Hittite kings at one end of the time-scale to Byzantine emperors at the other, would make a very fine 'Who's Who' of the Ancient East.

197

Above: Roman bridge over the Calycadnus at Silifke

Opposite: The Cilician Gates—a difficult stage on the road from North to South Turkey

From the point of view of the early Cappadocian kings, however, Tyana was too much at the centre of things. They were, after all, trying to consolidate a kingdom in the face of powerful enemies, and there was no point in making themselves too conspicuous. They therefore chose a remoter site—Mazaca, later to be renamed Caesarea. The new city flourished, becoming the capital of the Roman province and an important road-centre. Now called Kayseri, it is still important today.

Though other towns existed in Cappadocia (some already under the kingdom, overlooked by Strabo, others appearing later under Roman influence) Caesarea-Mazaca and Tyana always retained their predominance. The new foundations were small, and not numerous: Cappadocia was never, nor could ever be, a highly urbanised region.

North of Cappadocia proper was the land of the Pontic mountains, included by Rome in the same province as Cappadocia, but possessing a very different physical character. In contrast with the arid interior, the northern mountains receive abundant rainfall, in summer as well as in winter, supporting a dense growth of forest and many interesting types of plant not found else-where. (Rhododendrons, azaleas and cherries were all introduced to Europe from this land—the last, reputedly, by the great soldier-turned-gourmet Lucullus. Pontus was also famous for medicinal drugs, and, less innocently, for poisonous ones.) The mountains also possessed great mineral wealth (the first workings of a new metal, destined to end the Bronze Age and replace it with the Iron Age, are thought to have taken place here); the tribes of the Pontic coast were likewise diverse, and sometimes very surprising, in their habits and customs. In fact, ever since Xenophon and his men passed that way (when they cried 'Thalassa! Thalassa!' on first seeing the Black Sea, and became delirious through eating the local poison-honey) or earlier still, when Jason in the Argo sailed along these shores in search of the Golden Fleece, to bring back as his bride the sinister and murderous Medea, this eastern Pontic coast had a special character of its own. Many who have travelled there in modern times maintain that it still has.

Roman administration along the south coast of Turkey had a particularly complex history, not all of which has been adequately worked out. There was an entity called 'Provincia Cilicia' in about 100 BC, but this was a *provincia* of the old-fashioned kind—a job, not attached to any particular piece of territory, and especially not attached to any part of Cilicia. That region did not come under Roman rule until Pompey's victory over the pirates (see page 188). Soon afterwards the administration was reorganized, and Provincia Cilicia vanished from the map: it was not to reappear until Vespasian's reign in the seventies AD, this time in a more appropriate place.

Cilicia proper, as we may now call it, was divided into two parts of very different physical character. The eastern part, called Pedias or 'the plain' was flat and fertile ground, watered by three large rivers and possessing many towns, some of great age and size. Tarsus, the birth-place of St Paul, was the largest and also the Roman provincial capital: Anazarbus, later renamed Caesarea-ad-Anazarbum, was her closest rival. This 'Flat' Cilicia was also a most important land of passage, linked on one side (by the pass of the 'Syrian Gates') to Syria, and on the other side (by the 'Cilician Gates') to the highlands of Cappadocia. To reach Turkey from Syria *without* traversing Cilicia was a very hard slog indeed.

For all these reasons, the Romans had kept a firm grip on Cilicia Pedias ever since Pompey had acquired it for them; it was thought too small, however, to make a province in its own right, and treated instead as an appendage of Roman Syria. Its western neighbour, Cilicia called

Tracheia or 'Rough' was a very different affair. This land is a tangle of mountains, coming down to the sea with many capes and bays forming perfect hide-outs for pirates. Towns were small, Seleucia-on-the-Calycadnus (still in existence under the name of Silifke) being perhaps the largest of an insignificant collection. After suppressing the pirates, the Romans had little wish to control the country themselves, and handed it over to a number of petty dynasts; only with Vespasian (who seems to have disliked governments of this sort—he suppressed them in Syria, Palestine, Greece and northern England as well as in Turkey) were the last of these kinglets removed and Cilicia welded into a single political unit.

Next to Cilicia lay Lycia-et-Pamphylia, the smallest province on the Turkish mainland, but big enough, like Cilicia, to show great diversity of physical and human character. The Pamphylians on the coastal plain spoke Greek, possessed large cities, and were peaceful and prosperous. Their neighbours the Lycians, also a peaceful race, were not originally Greek at all; they probably descended from the people called Luwians, who had invaded Turkey some two and a half thousand years earlier. They kept their own language and customs at least down to the fourth century BC, after which Greek influence gradually filtered in. One custom they kept which the Greeks never knew—the ability to form a league of cities that would not either break up or turn into an empire ruled by one city. Despite numerous attacks from without, some very destructive, the Lycian League carried on for centuries, as best it could, the tradition of 'Independent Jimmy' of Asia: 'You leave me alone, and I'll leave you alone'. When the emperor Claudius finally annexed the League in AD 43 it was already surrounded by Roman territory for at least two hundred miles in every direction.

The last piece of land that had once come within Rome's early, ill-defined 'Province of Cilicia' was the island of Cyprus. It had been annexed (peacefully) in 58 BC, and under the Empire became a province in its own right. Paphos, near the west end of the island, was the capital, but Salamis at the opposite end (near Famagusta) may have been larger: under the late Empire it superseded Paphos as the administrative headquarters, and it has certainly yielded more impressive remains.

Very little is said about Cyprus under Roman rule. Let us hope that, for one span of its existence, it enjoyed the happiness proverbially ascribed to countries with no history.

The Roman Levant, by contrast, has a tremendous amount of history. Political, social, military, urban and even religious reorganization came hard on each others' heels.

The Seleucid kings had begun the process. Syria from the first was one of the most important parts of their empire (at the last, indeed, in the sombre days before the final takeover, it *was* their empire) and they developed it intensively. Seleucus I founded four enormous cities: Antioch (or to give it its full name for once, Antiochia) named after his father; Seleucia, its port, named after himself; Laodicea-on-Sea, the modern Latakia, after his mother; and Apamea, on the river Orontes, after his wife. Great Antioch was one of the twin capitals of the whole Seleucid empire (the other being yet another Seleucia, on the river Tigris in Mesopotamia): after the Roman conquest it became the capital of the province and the third largest city, after Rome and Alexandria, of the whole Roman Empire. It possessed, among other things, a unique public service which even Rome lacked—street lighting. (Critics of the city, who were numerous, claimed that the Antiochenes combined the worst dissipations of the Greek and the Syrian characters, and that the sole purpose of the lighting was to let them indulge in orgies all night as well as all day.)

Besides this group of four extra-large cities (the Syrian Tetrapolis, it was called) numerous

Roman road between Antioch and Aleppo

Baalbek—temple of Bacchus

other cities in the area showed Seleucid influence. Further up the Orontes river from Apamea was a city called Epiphania, after king Antiochus IV Epiphanes ('Antiochus the Illustrious'); further upstream still was another Laodicea. On the Euphrates Seleucus I had founded a town called Seleucia at the Bridge; later, however, the first part of the name was dropped and it became known simply as 'The Bridge' (Zeugma). The bridge in question maintained its importance under Roman rule, being the most usual way of crossing the Euphrates from Roman to Parthian territory or vice versa.

Other towns, instead of bearing royal names, commemorated the Macedonian homeland of their new settlers (in the manner used more recently by colonists in America and Australia). Beroea and Edessa, Dium, Cyrrhus and Europus were all names of places in Macedonia.

Few of these Seleucid foundations were on entirely virgin sites. Often, indeed, the 'foundation' meant in effect no more than giving a new name to a very old city. Beroea, for example, had previously been called Haleb (spelt Chalybon by the Greeks) and today it is called Haleb once more, though for historical reasons Englishmen generally pronounce its name the Italian way— Aleppo. The new name of Epiphania covered the very old city of Hamath or Hama, which similarly has reverted to its original name. The Greek veneer over many such Oriental cities must have been very thin indeed.

Northern Syria had military as well as civil importance, as the principal confrontation point between Rome and Parthia. Three legions guarded it—XVI Flavia at Samosata, IV Scythica probably at Cyrrhus, and III Gallica at Raphaneae. Forts and cities were linked by a complex network of roads running in all directions.

Further south, the presence of the Lebanon and Anti-Lebanon mountain ranges made the pattern of towns and roads a simpler one. A traveller wishing to go south from (say) Antioch while avoiding the mountain heights has three courses open to him. The easiest route is that along the coast itself. This is the land of the famous Phoenician trading-cities: first Aradus, on its island; then Tripoli (so called because three other cities, Aradus, Sidon and Tyre, came together to found it); then Byblos, once a great centre of the papyrus trade (it gave the Greeks their word *biblion* for a book, whence our 'Bible') but now somewhat declined from its old importance. The next city to the south, Berytus (Beirut), had by contrast risen in the world; the emperor Augustus had planted a Roman colony there, and the city became a little outpost of Latinity in a Graeco-Semitic world, famous in the third century for its school of Roman law. Then came the two most famous of them all, Sidon and Tyre: still, under Roman rule, two hives of commerce and industry.

The next city on this coast, Acre, could be regarded either as the last city of Phoenicia or the first of Palestine. Then came the cities of Palestine proper—Caesarea, its new capital; Joppa, the port of Jerusalem; and the old Philistine cities of Ashdod, Ascalon and Gaza. Beyond Gaza came a gap, with no major settlement until the Nile was reached at Pelusium. But this was the only difficult part of the road; all the rest of it was perfectly straightforward to travel.

Another road from Antioch to the south ran further inland, up the Orontes river past Apamea and Hama and other towns already mentioned, to reach the high ground between the two ranges of Lebanon and Anti-Lebanon. Here stood Baalbek, which the Greeks called Heliopolis—a temple city, whose temples have survived remarkably well down to the present day. Then the traveller could descend the Jordan valley and come to the heart of Palestine, the holy but very violent city of Jerusalem.

Even by Eastern standards the history of Palestine is unusually stormy. Since Alexander's death it had belonged first to the Ptolemies of Egypt, then to the Seleucids of Syria, then to the Jews themselves (after the revolt of Judas Maccabaeus), then to the Romans under Pompey. Augustus had given the land to that most famous or infamous of Rome's client princes, Herod the Great, who ruled with a rod of iron till his death in 4 BC. Then Rome tried partition—Herod's kingdom was shared among three of his surviving sons—but this did not work well: in AD 6 the eldest son was deposed and forced to flee. His kingdom thereupon was made a Roman province under procurators (Pontius Pilate being the best known of these). Caesarea-on-Sea was the procurator's capital; Jerusalem his principal headache.

Subsequently yet another member of the Herod family, Herod Agrippa, rose to importance. He was a close friend of the emperor Caligula and of the emperor Claudius, and from them he acquired a territory almost as large as that of his grandfather the original Herod. But on his death Rome repossessed most of it; his son, Agrippa II, was left ruling a very much reduced area.

Then in AD 69 and 70, came the terrible events that the Jews have never since been able to forget: the abortive revolt against Roman rule, the defeats by Vespasian and his son Titus, the sacking of Jerusalem, the devastation of Palestine, and the Diaspora of Jews fleeing from their

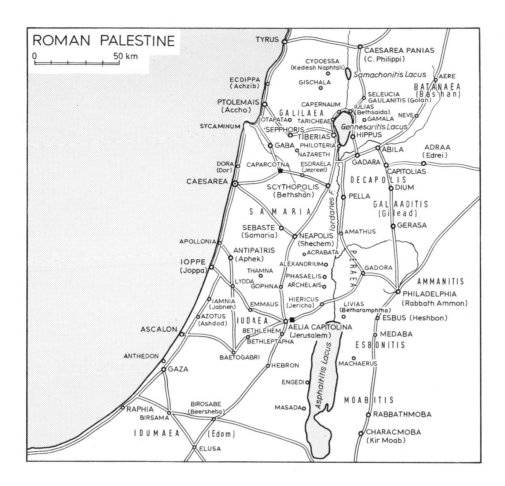

ruined land all over the world. Palestine became an armed camp guarded by legions VI Ferrata and X Fretensis; Jerusalem (rebuilt by Hadrian and renamed Aelia Capitolina) a purely Greek city which Jews were not allowed even to enter. The full power of Rome had been turned on the one small nation that (from Rome's point of view) had persistently refused to fit into the system and behave itself; and the results were devastating.

But to return to our imaginary traveller. If for some reason he does not wish to use the coast road from the north, nor yet the one through Palestine, there is a third possibility. He can take a road further east still, round the far side of the Anti-Lebanon Mountains and through the desert. Here, for obvious reasons, towns are few and far between: but some do exist. There is Palmyra in its oasis, for example, a great entrepot-city for trade between Rome and Parthia. There is Damascus, flourishing in the desert thanks to water brought down from the mountains by the river Abana ('Are not Abana and Pharphar, rivers of Damascus, better than all the waters of Israel?') Further south the road passed a group of cities on the eastern, non-Jewish side of the Jordan, which had escaped the fall of Palestine and become very prosperous.

For this rather ill-defined and unpromising eastern route was in fact an important avenue of trade. The traders in question were a people called the Nabataean Arabs, best known for their rock-cut, rose-red capital city of Petra. From this centre deep in the desert their caravans worked down to the very heel of the Arabian boot, to what is now Yemen, returning with spices and incense valued by the Roman and the Parthian empires alike. Then, by a complex network of tracks in the 'no-man's-land' between the two powers, the goods were distributed. This quiet trade continued till AD 106, when the emperor Trajan annexed the kingdom and called it (with characteristic Roman grandiosity) the province of Arabia. Petra ceased to be the capital;

Above: Rock-cut tombs at Petra
Opposite below: Palmyra—general view
Opposite above: Scene from Arch of Titus: Roman triumphal procession with trophies from Jerusalem

it was replaced by the important Roman military base of Bostra garrisoned by Legio III Cyrenaica, linked by a road (Rome's effective frontier in these parts) to Palmyra and thence to the Euphrates. But the supply of goods was still there, and so was the demand; so the trade continued now through different channels. The Nabataeans' loss was someone else's gain.

Finally, let us try to consider these ten provinces of Roman Asia as a whole; did they have any special character that Roman Europe or Roman Africa lacked?

One very striking impression one receives on reading about the land is that of tremendous industrial activity. Of course there was agriculture too: all parts of the Mediterranean world produced those staples of life, corn, wine and olive oil, and the wine of some Aegean islands—Lesbos, Chios and Cos—had an international reputation. The orchard fruit of Syria and Palestine, too, was as popular in ancient times as it is today. There was stock-rearing: parts of central Turkey and of Syria along the desert fringe were suited to no other form of life. There was mining, though less than there had been; many of the best supplies, such as the gold-works that brought wealth to Midas and Croesus, were exhausted by Roman times. But all these could be matched, and indeed surpassed, by the west: the cornfields of Sicily, the olive estates of Africa, the horse-breeding plains of Gaul and Lusitania, the mineral wealth of Spain and the Danube lands. Where the contrast lies is that western provinces, if they produced anything at all, usually produced raw materials: the Roman East produced manufactured goods.

The cities of the land resounded with industry. The cloth trade alone employed enormous numbers of people. All western Turkey produced woollen cloth; Cilicia concentrated more on linen; Syrians worked both in linen and silk (for Chinese silk as brought from China was too thick and heavy for Roman taste, and was often unravelled and woven anew). Then there were the dyers (particularly numerous at Tyre, where they made the city smell most unpleasant—the most valued type of dye was extracted from rotting shellfish). There were workers in leather, masons and carpenters, potters and glassworkers (the latter concentrated in the city of Sidon), workers in all kinds of metal, and the hundred-and-one other types of odd-job-man that one has to have in an industrial city. *Here*, it would seem, is a distinction between East and West: eastern cities, to a much greater extent than western ones, made their livings not by growing things or breeding things or mining things, but by *making* things. Some scholars have suggested, indeed, that this difference—more cities, more manpower, more industrial urge—helped the Eastern Roman Empire to survive when the Western Empire fell, and to last right through to a time when Asia Minor, by its unaided efforts, carried the vast, complex and expensive superstructure that was the Byzantine Court.

APPENDIX I

Chronology

(Note: most dates in this list before 500 BC are disputable, and should not be taken too literally.)

BC

1184   Greek sack of Troy

(Soon afterwards came a period of much migration and confused fighting throughout the Near East)

1100   Phoenician founding of Cadiz

814   Phoenician founding of Carthage

776   First Olympic Games

(the standard zero-point of Greek dating)

753   Founding of Rome

c.750   First Greek settlements in Italy and on the Black Sea

733   Greek founding of Syracuse and Corcyra (Corfu)

706   Greek founding of Taranto

c.700   Phoenician founding of Sexi (Almuñecar) in Spain

660   Greek founding of Byzantium

654   Phoenician founding of Ibiza

631   Greek founding of Cyrene

627   Greek founding of Epidamnus (Durrës)

612   Fall of Nineveh: Assyrian Empire destroyed by Medes and Babylonians

c.610   Greek treaty-port at Naucratis in Egypt

c.600   Greek founding of Marseille. Phoenicians circumnavigate Africa (?)

574   Phoenicia conquered by Nebuchadnezzar of Babylon. Punic cities in the west become independent. Beginning of Carthage's rise to power

539   Cyrus of Persia captures Babylon. Beginning of the Persian Empire

c.535   Sea-battle off Alalia (Corsica): Carthage defeats the Greeks and becomes the dominant power in the Western Mediterranean

510   Rome becomes a republic

c.500?   Hanno of Carthage explores the west coast of Africa

490   First Persian invasion of Greece defeated at the Battle of Marathon

480–479	Second Persian invasion of Greece: Persians victorious at Thermopylae, defeated at Salamis and Plataea
431–404	Peloponnesian War: Athens against Sparta. Spartan victory
c.400	Celtic tribes invade north Italy
390	Celtic tribes sack Rome
343–290	Periodic wars between Romans and their southern neighbours, the Samnites
338	Battle of Chaeronea: Philip of Macedon conquers all Greece
336	Murder of Philip. His son Alexander the Great succeeds him
335	Alexander destroys Thebes
334–323	Campaigns of Alexander in Asia. Complete conquest of the Persian Empire. Many cities founded, among them Alexandria in Egypt (331) and Alexandria 'the Uttermost' (329)
323	Death of Alexander, the signal for prolonged civil wars
314	Rome founds a colony at Lucera—her first east of the Apennines
312	Building of the first part of the Via Appia—Rome to Capua
304	India lost to Greek rule
300	Founding of Antioch in Syria by Seleucus I
c.300?	Pytheas of Marseille explores the British Isles and perhaps reaches as far as Norway
295	Battle of Sentinum: Rome defeats a confederation of northern and southern Italians
280–275	Pyrrhus of Epirus tries without success to defeat Rome and conquer Italy
279	Celtic tribes invade Greece
268	Rome founds colonies at Benevento and Rimini
264–241	First Punic War (Rome against Carthage) ending in Roman victory and conquest of Sicily
c.248	Independent Greek kingdom established in Bactria
244	Rome founds a colony at Brindisi (to become the terminus of the Via Appia)
241	Building of the Via Aurelia (Rome to Pisa)
c.240	Iranian tribesmen seize Parthia from Greek rule
238	Romans annex Sardinia and Corsica
227	Punic founding of New Carthage (Cartagena) in Spain
220	Building of the Via Flaminia (Rome to Rimini). Victories of Hannibal in Spain
218	Rome founds colonies on the river Po, at Piacenza and Cremona
218–201	Second Punic War (against Hannibal). Romans repeatedly defeated in Italy, but successful in Spain. Hannibal finally defeated by Scipio at Zama (202). Rome acquires control of the southern and eastern coasts of Spain
214–147	Periodic wars between Rome and Macedonia
197	Romans defeat Macedonians at Cynoscephalae
190–189	Romans defeat Antiochus III, Seleucid king of the East, at Magnesia-under-Sipylus
189	Rome founds a colony at Bologna
187	Building of the Via Aemilia (Rimini–Bologna–Piacenza)
181	Rome founds a colony at Aquileia

168	Romans defeat Macedonians at Pydna
160s	Parthian conquest of Iran and much of Iraq. Decline of the Seleucid kingdom
149–146	Third Punic War
148	Building of the Via Postumia (Cremona-Verona-Padua-Aquileia)
147	Final Roman annexation of Macedonia
146	Destruction of Corinth and Carthage by Rome; the latter's territory made into the province of Africa
133	Fall of Numantia: Romans acquire control of central Spain. The province of Asia comes to Rome by bequest of its ruler
121	Roman conquest of southern France
118	Rome founds a colony at Narbonne (the first outside Italy). Building of the Via Domitia to link it with the Rhône
112–105	Jugurthine War in Africa
109	Building of the Via Aemilia Scauri (Pisa to Genoa)
105–101	German invasion of France and Italy, finally defeated by Marius
96	Rome acquires Cyrenaica by bequest
90–89	'Social War': unsuccessful revolt against Rome by the central Italians
89–85	Roman war with Mithradates, king of Pontus
88–83	Civil war at Rome, ending with the triumph of Sulla
74	Rome acquires Bithynia by bequest. Start of another war with Mithradates
67	Roman conquest of Crete
67–62	Campaigns of Pompey in the east. Mithradates defeated and finally killed (63). Conquest of Pontus, Cilicia, Syria and Palestine. End of the Seleucid kingdom
58–51	Campaigns of Julius Caesar in Gaul (highly successful) also in Germany and Britain (much less so)
53	Battle of Carrhae: Crassus and most of a Roman army wiped out by Parthian horse-archers
49	Caesar crosses the Rubicon, thereby starting civil war between himself and Pompey
48	Caesar victorious at Pharsalus. Death of Pompey in Egypt
46	Caesar in Africa, victorious at Thapsus. He makes plans to refound Carthage
45	Caesar in Spain, victorious at Munda
44	Murder of Caesar (15 March). Renewed civil strife
42	Battle of Philippi: Mark Antony and Octavian defeat Caesar's murderers
36	Campaigns of Antony in Armenia and Media
35	Campaigns of Octavian in Dalmatia
31	Battle of Actium: Octavian defeats Antony and Cleopatra
30	Suicide of Antony and Cleopatra. Octavian left as sole ruler of the Empire. End of Civil Wars. Rome acquires Egypt
27	Octavian takes title 'Augustus'
26	Aelius Gallus' unsuccessful expedition to Arabia
25	Roman annexation of Galatia (central Turkey)
19	Final conquest of all Spain by Agrippa. Cornelius Balbus awarded a triumph for campaigns in the Sahara
15	Conquest of the Alps and lands beyond them (Raetia, Noricum)

13 BC–AD 9	Roman conquest of Pannonia and Dalmatia
12 BC–AD 9	Campaigns in Germany beyond the Rhine
12	Building of the Via Julia Augusta (Genoa to the Rhône)
2	Building of a second Via Julia Augusta (Aquileia-Julium Carnicum-Drave valley)
AD 6	Provinces established in Moesia and Judaea.
9	Battle of the Teutoburger Forest: Romans disastrously defeated by Germans. End of Augustus' plan to conquer Germany. (Augustus' reign saw many cities founded, enlarged or improved, among them Ankara, Antioch-by-Pisidia, Aosta, Augst (near Basle), Beirut, Carthage, Corinth, Ljubljana, Lyons, Merida, Nicopolis-in-Epirus, Patras, Philippi, Salona, Saragossa, Tarragona, Zadar—and Rome itself.)
14	Death of Augustus. Tiberius succeeds him
14–37	Reign of Tiberius. Peace and consolidation. Ineffectual campaigns in Germany (15–16). Cappadocia annexed (17).
37–41	Reign of Caligula
41–54	Reign of Claudius. Conquest of Mauretania (42): Suetonius Paullinus leads an army across the Atlas. Conquest of South-East England (43). Annexation of Lycia (43) and Thrace (46). Building of the Via Claudia Augusta (Verona-Resia Pass-Epfach-Augsburg). New harbour at Ostia. New towns developed, among them Colchester, Cologne, Salzburg and Tangier
54–68	Reign of Nero. War on Rome's eastern frontier (58–66). Revolt of Boudica in Britain (60). Great fire at Rome (64): much rebuilding thereafter. Proposals for a Saône-Moselle canal in France and a Corinth Canal in Greece: neither ever materialised. Expedition to the source of the Nile turned back by swamps
69	'Year of the Four Emperors' at Rome. Galba, Otho, Vitellius each in turn have short reigns. Final triumph of Vespasian with the army of the East
70	Sack of Jerusalem by Titus. Jews dispersed over the world
69–96	Reigns of the Flavian dynasty (Vespasian 69–79, Titus 79–81, Domitian 81–96). Eastern provinces reorganized. Conquest of the Agri Decumates, between Rhine and Danube. Eruption of Vesuvius: destruction of Pompeii, death of Pliny the Elder (79). Conquest of northern England, Wales and finally Scotland (Roman victory at Mons Graupius, 84). Wars on the Danube prevent this from being followed up. Towns developed include Lincoln, Avenches (in Switzerland), Leibnitz (in Austria), Siscia and Sirmium (in Yugoslavia), Haïdra (in Africa) and a great number in Spain
96–98	Reign of Nerva. Cities founded at Gloucester and Djemila (in Africa)
98–117	Reign of Trajan. Conquest of Dacia and annexation of Arabia Petraea (106). Roman frontier in Britain withdrawn to the Stanegate line. Conquests of Parthian territory in the East. Building of the Via Traiana (an alternative to the Via Appia in S. Italy). Harbour facilities improved at Ostia, Civitavecchia, Ancona and Brindisi. Many towns founded in the Balkan regions
117–138	Reign of Hadrian. Trajan's Parthian conquests abandoned. Building of Hadrian's Wall, and similar works in Germany and Africa. Jerusalem re-founded under the name Aelia Capitolina: war with the Jews over this. Other

cities founded include one Hadrianopolis in Thrace, another in Cyrenaica, and Antinoöpolis in Egypt (linked to the Red Sea by the Via Hadriana)

138–161   Reign of Antoninus Pius. Renewed advance in North Britain and building of the Antonine Wall. Publication of Ptolemy's *Geographia*

161–180   Reign of Marcus Aurelius—last of the 'Five Good Emperors'. Conquest of Parthian territory. Antonine Wall abandoned. Great plague in the Empire. War with Germans and Sarmatians on the Danube frontier. Rome finally victorious (179): Marcus proposes to create two new provinces beyond the Danube

180–192   Reign of Commodus. Marcus's German conquests abandoned. War in Britain. Military advance in Africa

192–197   Civil war. Short reign of Pertinax and Didius Julianus, then conflict between Severus, Niger and Albinus for supreme power

193–211   Reign of Severus. Conquest of Parthian territory (for the third time in less than a century!). Expansion in Africa. Leptis Magna and other African cities enlarged and given new privileges. Victory in Britain, but no new territory annexed

211–235   Reigns of the 'Severan' emperors (Caracalla 211–217, Elagabalus 218–222, Severus Alexander 222–235). First mention of the Allemanni on the upper Rhine. Severus' African conquests given up. Wars on the Eastern frontier

235–284   Period of 'Military Anarchy' in the Roman Empire. Twenty emperors in fifty years, nearly all murdered by their own soldiers. Rhine frontier attacked by Allemanni and Franks, Danube frontier by Goths, East by Persians

284–305   Reign of Diocletian. Widespread administrative, military and financial reforms. This emperor's accession is generally taken to mark the end of the 'Early Empire' (to which the maps in this book refer) and the beginning of the 'Late Empire' (maps of which would look noticeably different)

APPENDIX II

The Roman Emperors

Augustus	31 BC–AD 14	
Tiberius	AD 14–37	
Gaius (Caligula)	37–41	**Julio–Claudian dynasty**
Claudius	41–54	
Nero	54–68	

Galba	68–69	
Otho	69	**Year of civil war**
Vitellius	69	

Vespasian	69–79	
Titus	79–81	**Flavian dynasty**
Domitian	81–96	

Nerva	96–98	
Trajan	98–117	
Hadrian	117–138	
Antoninus Pius	138–161	**'Antonine' emperors**
Marcus Aurelius	161–180	
Commodus	180–192	

Pertinax	192–193	
Didius Julianus	193	**Another year of civil war**

Septimus Severus	193–211	
Caracalla	211–217	
Macrinus	217–218	**Severan dynasty (except Macrinus)**
Elagabalus	218–222	
Severus Alexander	222–235	

Maximinus	235–238	

Gordian I	238		
Gordian II	238		
Pupienus	238		
Balbinus	238		
Gordian III	238–244		
Philip	244–249		
Decius	249–251		
Trebonianus Gallus	251–253		
Aemilian	253		
Valerian	253–260		**The 'Military Anarchy'**
Gallienus	260–268		
Claudius II	268–270		
Aurelian	270–275		
Tacitus	275–276		
Florian	276		
Probus	276–282		
Carus	282–283		
Carinus	283–284		
Numerian	283–284		

Diocletian	284–305		
Maximian	286–305, 306–308		
Galerius	305–311		
Constantius I	305–306		
Severus	306–307		**The 'Tetrarchy'**
Constantine I	306–337		
Maxentius	306–312		
Maximinus Daia	308–313		
Licinius	308–324		

Constantine I as sole emperor	324–337		
Constantine II	337–340		
Constans	337–350		**Constantinian dynasty**
Constantius II	337–361		
Julian	361–363		

Jovian	363–364		

Valentinian I	364–375	(West)	
Valens	365–378	(East)	**Valentinian dynasty**
Gratian	367–383	(West)	
Valentinian II	375–392		
Theodosius I	379–395		

Theodosius was the last emperor to rule both East and West.

Western Emperors:		**Eastern Emperors:**	
Honorius	395–423	Arcadius	395–408
Valentinian III	423–455	Theodosius II	408–450
Maximus	455	Marcian	450–457
Avitus	455–456	Leo	457–474
Majorian	457–461	Zeno	474–491
Severus	461–465	Anastasius	491–518
Anthemius	467–472	Justin I	518–527
Olybrius	472	Justinian	527–565
Glycerius	473–474		
Julius Nepos	474–480	and so on in succession	
Romulus Augustulus	475–476	to AD 1453.	

APPENDIX III

Geographical Sources for the Roman Empire

Strabo, a native of Amasia in Asia Minor, was a contemporary of the Emperor Augustus. His *Geographia* is one of the most accurate and reliable of all ancient geographical works, and gives us much information recorded nowhere else. His accounts of tribal customs, for example, are extremely valuable, and he is one of the very few authors who give us any idea of the relative size and importance of ancient towns. The chief drawback of his work is that it covers only a fairly restricted area: by far the greater part of it deals with the lands immediately adjoining the Mediterranean, and relatively little is said about remoter areas. It is an unfortunate fact that as in later years Roman geographical knowledge expanded, no writer comparable with Strabo came forward to record it for us.

> Strabo, *Geographia*, ed. C. Müller and F. Dübner, Paris, 1853.
> ed. F. Sbordone, Rome, 1963–.

Pomponius Mela, a Spaniard, wrote his geography in AD 43. It is a short work, telling us little that we do not know from other sources, and quoting several wild tales and erroneous beliefs about which the author should have been better informed—as, for example, the old Greek idea that a branch of the Danube flowed into the Adriatic Sea.

> Pomponius Mela, *De Chorographia*, ed. G. Randstrand, Göteborg, 1971.

Pliny the Elder, from Como in northern Italy, was killed in the eruption of Vesuvius in AD 79. He was among the most prolific of all ancient writers, but only one of his numerous works has survived: the monumental *Historia Naturalis*, a vast encyclopaedia of all human knowledge and a considerable amount of human misinformation. The geographical section of this consists largely of lists of place-names, sometimes ill-arranged and on occasion horribly muddled. Still, it is usually possible to sort the muddle out (in this respect Pliny is very much easier to deal with than, say, Ptolemy), and the work is of value because it gives us a picture of the Empire's *political* organization—something which Greek-speaking geographers cover only very sketchily or not at all.

> D. Detlefson, *Die geographischen Bücher der Naturalis Historia des C. Plinius Secundus,* Berlin, 1904.

218

Ptolemy (Claudius Ptolemaeus) lived at Alexandria in Egypt, and wrote his *Geographia* there in about AD 150. This is the most extensive of ancient geographical works; the area covered by it reaches from Ireland to China and from Sweden to Zanzibar, and many of the places mentioned in it are recorded nowhere else. Unfortunately, the work is a most maddening one to use: Ptolemy was not primarily a geographer at all, but a mathematician and astronomer. His *Geographia* is not a 'geography' in the usual sense of the word, but a collection of instructions for drawing maps; it consists almost entirely of lists of features with their various latitudes and longitudes. The trouble is that these figures are not accurate enough for us to locate the places to which they refer, unless we have some more usable information from another source; when we *do* have such information, it often turns out that Ptolemy's positions are hopelessly wrong. In his enthusiasm for mapping the Ancient World, he seems to have been very un-critical about the calibre of the information he used to produce the maps. What—if anything—he meant in his work is in many cases a matter for conjecture.

Ptolemy, *Geographia*, ed. C. Müller, Paris, 1883.

The *Antonine Itinerary* and the *Peutinger Table* are works of a somewhat different nature from any of the foregoing. Both are the work of several authors (all anonymous) of several different periods, so that it is impossible to assign a definite date to either of them; the bulk of the material in both works dates from the third century AD. Both are descriptions of the roads of the Roman Empire. The *Itinerary* describes these roads in tabular form; it names long lists of places with the distances between them, somewhat in the manner of a modern AA Route Guide. The *Peutinger Table* is in map form, though very much distorted in order to fit all the Ancient World on to a sheet 21 feet long and only 1 foot wide. Unlike the Itinerary, it does not confine itself to the Roman Empire, but shows roads running through Iran as far as India—though these last are very hard to interpret.

Both these works are of the highest importance to the historical geographer, because in them alone do we find actual measurements—the distances from one place to the next—in a form which we can use. Often it is possible to trace on the ground the Roman roads described in the text, after which identifying particular places is merely a matter of measurement and calculation. It is largely because of these two itineraries that our knowledge of the Roman Empire is more thorough than our knowledge of its immediate neighbours: when we leave the Roman Empire, to consider a territory such as Germany or Iran, our trouble is not so much lack of material (Ptolemy is most informative about both the above-mentioned areas) as lack of material *which we can understand.*

Itineraria Romana, ed. O. Cuntz, Leipzig, 1929.
K. Miller, *Die Peutingerische Tafel*, Stuttgart, 1962.

The *Notitia Dignitatum,* dating from the fourth century AD, lists the high officials of the later Empire, and also the forts which each one controls. It is of great value to the student of Roman military history, and identifies for us a considerable number of Roman military bases (as, for example, those on Hadrian's Wall).

Notitia Dignitatum, ed. C. Seeck, Berlin, 1876.

The *Ravenna Cosmography* was drawn up in the late seventh century AD, but most of the material in it dates from a much earlier period. The author (whose name is unknown) would appear to have had in front of him a road-map similar to the *Peutinger Table*: following the various roads, he copied down from the map long lists of place-names, but unfortunately omitted the all-important distances between one place and the next. Nevertheless, the work is of some value, particularly when considered in conjunction with the *Antonine Itinerary* and the *Peutinger Table*. It has perhaps not received from modern scholars all the attention which it deserves.

Ravennatis Anonymi Cosmographia, ed. M. Pinder and G. Parthey, Berlin, 1860.

These are the principal *major* sources for Roman geography—those which cover the Roman Empire as a whole. In addition, some writers have supplied us with valuable descriptions of various parts of the Ancient World: Julius Caesar, for example, is useful for the geography of Gaul; Tacitus, for Germany; Josephus, for Palestine. Other geographical works of relatively local interest are collected in *Geographi Graeci Minores*, ed. C. Müller, Berlin.

Inscriptions (milestones, tombstones, inscriptions on public buildings, and so forth) have a value of their own for the historical geographer. Though it is fairly uncommon for a place-name to be mentioned *only* in inscriptions, they very often enable us to pin down a particular place-name upon a particular site, where otherwise we should be reduced to conjecture. They are also most valuable in giving us the proper way to spell a name; some literary sources (Ptolemy, the *Peutinger Table* and the *Ravenna Cosmography*, to name three of the worst offenders) are extremely bad spellers. The chief sources for inscriptions are:
Corpus Inscriptionum Latinarum (CIL), Berlin, 1893–.
Inscriptiones Latinae Selectae ed. H. Dessau (ILS), Berlin, 1892–1916. A selection from the CIL.
Inscriptiones Graecae ad Res Romanas Pertinentes (IGR), Paris 1911–1927.

Finally, something must be said of *Archaeology* as a means for enlarging our geographical knowledge. It is a highly valuable technique. In the first place, most of the inscriptions described above have been recovered by archaeology. Secondly, archaeology often tells us what the historians omit—details like the relative size and importance of ancient towns, the location of industry, and sometimes the course of military campaigns. There are several periods of Roman history—the mid-second century, to which these maps refer, is one of them—for which the historical record is very sketchy, and archaeology can often put a little flesh on the bare bones of the literary sources. The reason why we, today, can claim to be better-informed than Gibbon was when he wrote his *Decline and Fall of the Roman Empire*, is not that we know much more about Pliny, Ptolemy or Tacitus, but rather that archaeology has revealed to us many sites that Gibbon knew only as names.

Still, there remain many questions that archaeology alone cannot answer. Despite all the effort of prehistorians, the archaeology of a literate society such as Rome, where we have written records to back us up, remains very different from the archaeology of a society without written records. When the historical records fail us, as for example during the collapse of Roman power in the West, we find ourselves plagued with a multitude of questions (Who was King Arthur? Did he really exist? What did he look like?) to which archaeology alone has no answer. Archaeology has its own goals, which are not the same as those of history: the two, in my opinion, go best hand in hand, but one cannot be made to do the work of the other.

BIBLIOGRAPHY

CHAPTER I—EUROPA

General works

The Cambridge Ancient History

Hammond, N. G. L., and Scullard, H. H. *The Oxford Classical Dictionary.* 2nd edition, Oxford, 1970

Von Pauly, A. F., Wissowa, G., Kroll, W., et al. *Real-Encyclopädie der Classischen Altertumswissenschaft.* Stuttgart, 1893–

Roman History

Aufstieg und Niedergang der Römischen Welt. Berlin, 1972–

Barrow, R. H. *The Romans.* London, 1961

Bickerman, E. J. *Chronology of the Ancient World.* London, 1968

Dudley, D. *The Romans.* London, 1970

Grant, M. *The Climax of Rome.* London, 1968

Jones, A. H. M. *The Later Roman Empire.* Oxford, 1964

Marsh, F. B. *A History of the Roman World from 146 to 30 B.C.* 2nd edition, London, 1953

Masson, G. *A Concise History of Republican Rome.* London, 1973

Millar, F. *The Roman Empire and its neighbours.* London, 1967

Mommsen, T. *The Provinces of the Roman Empire.* London, 1909

Parker, H. M. D. *A History of the Roman World from A.D. 138 to 337.* 2nd edition, London, 1958

Salmon, E. T. *A History of the Roman World from 30 B.C. to A.D. 138.* 3rd edition, London, 1957

Scullard, H. H. *A History of the Roman World from 753 to 146 B.C.* 3rd edition, London, 1961
From the Gracchi to Nero. 4th edition, London, 1976

Stobart, J. C. *The Grandeur that was Rome.* 4th edition, London, 1961

Travel, Geography and Exploration

Bunbury, E. H. *A History of Ancient Geography.* London, 1879

Carpenter, R. *Beyond the Pillars of Heracles.* Washington, D.C., 1966

Cary, M. *The Geographic Background of Greek and Roman History.* Oxford, 1949

Cary, M., and Warmington, E. H. *The Ancient Explorers.* London, 1929

Casson, L. *The Ancient Mariners.* London, 1959
Travel in the Ancient World. London, 1974

Hyde, W. W. *Ancient Greek Mariners.* New York, 1947

Thomson, J. O. *History of Ancient Geography.* Cambridge, 1948

Tozer, H. F. *A History of Ancient Geography.* 2nd edition, New York, 1964.

Atlases

Finley, M. I. (ed.). *Atlas of Classical Archaeology.* London, 1977

Grosser Historischer Weltatlas. Munich, 1953

Grundy, G. B. (ed.). *Murray's Small Classical Atlas.* London, 1904

Kiepert, H. *Atlas Antiquus.* Berlin, 1892

Reich, E. *Atlas Antiquus.* London, 1908

Shepherd, W. R. *Historical Atlas*. 8th edition, London, 1959

Smith, W., and Grove, G. *An Atlas of Ancient Geography*. London, 1875

Tabula Imperii Romani: a series of maps of parts of the Roman Empire, now in progress.

Thomson, J. O. *Everyman's Atlas of Ancient and Classical Geography*. 3rd edition, London, 1966

Treharne, R. F., and Fullard, H. (ed.) *Muir's Historical Atlas*. 6th edition, London, 1963

Van der Heyden, A. A. M., and Scullard, H. H. *Atlas of the Classical World*. London, 1959

Van der Meer, F., and Mohrmann, C. *Atlas of the Early Christian World*. London, 1959

Westermanns Grosser Atlas zur Weltgeschichte. Brunswick, 1969

Towns, Roads and Planning

Chevallier, R. *Roman Roads*. London, 1976

Dilke, O. A. W. *The Roman Land Surveyors*. Newton Abbot, 1971

Landels, J. G. *Engineering in the Ancient World*. London, 1978

Macaulay, D. *City*. Boston, U.S.A., 1974

Miller, K. *Itineraria Romana*. Stuttgart, 1916

Salmon, E. T. *Roman Colonization under the Republic*. London, 1969

Von Hagen, V. W. *The Roads that Led to Rome*. London, 1967

The Roman Army

Connolly, P. *The Roman Army*. London, 1975

Grant, M. *The Army of the Caesars*. London, 1974

Parker, H. M. D. *The Roman Legions*. 2nd edition, Cambridge, 1958

Ritterling, E. *Legio*. Stuttgart, 1924. (Reprinted from the Pauly-Wissowa encyclopaedia, vol. XII.)

Roman Frontier Studies: reports of periodic conferences on the Roman *limes*, held from 1949 onwards.

Watson, G. R. *The Roman Soldier*. London, 1969

Webster, G. *The Roman Imperial Army*. London, 1969

Economic Geography

Finley, M. I. *The Ancient Economy*. London, 1973

Frank, Tenney (ed.). *An Economic Survey of Ancient Rome*. Baltimore, 1933–40

Rostovtzeff, M. *The Social and Economic History of the Roman Empire*. 2nd edition, Oxford, 1957

Toutain, J. *The Economic Life of the Ancient World*. London, 1930

CHAPTER II—BRITANNIA

Birley, A. *Life in Roman Britain*. London, 1964

Birley. E. *Roman Britain and the Roman Army*. Kendal, 1953

Branigan, K., and Fowler, P. J. *The Roman West Country*. Newton Abbot, 1976

Collingwood, R. G., and Myres, J. N. L. *Roman Britain and the English Settlements*. 2nd edition, Oxford, 1941

Collingwood, R. G., and Richmond, Sir Ian. *The Archaeology of Roman Britain*. Revised edition, London, 1969

Crawford, O. G. S. *Topography of Roman Scotland*. Cambridge, 1949

Cunliffe, B. *The Regni*. London, 1973

Davies, H. *A Walk along the Wall*. London, 1976

Dudley, D. R., and Webster, G. *The Roman Conquest of Britain*. London, 1965
The Rebellion of Boudicca. London, 1969

Dunnett, R. *The Trinovantes*. London, 1975

Dyer, J. *Southern England: an Archaeological Guide*. London, 1973

Feachem, R. W. *The North Britons*. London, 1965

Frere, S. S. *Britannia*. 2nd edition, 1974

Henderson, I. *The Picts*. London, 1967

Houlder, C. *Wales: an Archaeological Guide*. London, 1974

Margary, I. D. *Roman Roads in Britain*. Revised edition, London, 1967

Nash-Williams, V. E. *The Roman Frontier in Wales*. 2nd edition, Cardiff, 1969

The Ordnance Survey Map of Hadrian's Wall. Chessington, 1964

The Ordnance Survey Map of the Antonine Wall. Southampton, 1969

The Ordnance Survey Map of Roman Britain. 4th edition, Southampton, 1978

Ramm, H. *The Parisi*. London, 1978

Richmond, Sir Ian. *Roman Britain*. London, 1963

Rivet, A. L. F. *Town and Country in Roman Britain*. 2nd edition, London, 1964.
'The British Section of the Antonine Itinerary.' *Britannia* I (1970) 34ff.

Sorrell, A. *Roman Towns in Britain*. London, 1976

Todd, M. *The Coritani*. London, 1973

Wacher, J. S. (ed.) *The Civitas Capitals of Roman Britain*. Leicester, 1966
The Towns of Roman Britain. London, 1974

Webster, G. *The Cornovii*. London, 1975

CHAPTER III—HISPANIA

Alarcão, J. de. *Portugal Romano*. Lisbon, 1973

Albertini, E. *Les Divisions Administratives de L'Espagne Romaine*. Paris, 1923

Alvarez, E. 'Vias Romanas de Galicia.' *Zephyrus* XI (Salamanca, 1960) 5–103

Balil, A. 'La Defensa de Hispania en el Bajo Imperio.' *Zephyrus* XI (1960) 179–197
Casa y Urbanismo en la España Antigua. 3 vols, Valladolid, 1972–3

Corchado y Soriano, M. 'Estudio sobre Vías Romanas entre el Tajo y el Guadalquivir.' *Archivo Español de Arqueologia* XLII (Madrid, 1969) 124–158

Galsterer, H. *Untersuchungen zum Römischen Städtewesen auf der Iberischen Halbinsel*. Berlin, 1971

Jones, R. F. J. 'The Roman Military Occupation of North-West Spain.' *Journal of Roman Studies* LXVI (London, 1976) 45–66

Livermore, H. V. *The Origins of Spain and Portugal*. London, 1971

MacKendrick, P. *The Iberian Stones Speak*. New York, 1969

Menendez Pidal, R. (ed.). *Historia de España* vol. II, *España Romana*. 3rd edition, Madrid, 1962

Richmond, Sir Ian. 'Five Town Walls in Hispania Citerior.' *Journal of Roman Studies* XXI (London, 1931) 86–100

Roldan Hervas, J. M. 'Fuentes Antiguas para el Estudio de los Vettones.' *Zephyrus* XIX (Salamanca, 1968) 73–106
'Fuentes Antiguas sobre los Astures.' *Zephyrus* XXI (1970), 171–238
Iter ab Emerita Asturicam. Salamanca, 1971

Sanchez-Albornoz, C. *Estudios Criticos sobre la Historia del Reino de Asturias*. Vol. I, Oviedo, 1972

Schulten, A. *Numantia*. 4 vols. Munich, 1914–29
Los Cantabros y Astures y su guerra con Roma. Madrid, 1943
Iberische Landeskunde. Strasbourg, 1955

Sutherland, C. H. V. *The Romans in Spain*. London, 1939

Thouvenot, R. *Essai sur la Province Romaine de Bétique*. Paris, 1940

Van Nostrand, J. J. 'Roman Spain.' *An Economic Survey of Ancient Rome*, ed. T. Frank, vol. III, Baltimore, 1937

Vazquez de Prada, V. (ed.). *Historia Economica y Social de España*. Vol. I, Madrid, 1973

Wattenberg, F. *La Region Vaccea*. Madrid, 1959

West, L. C. *Imperial Roman Spain: the Objects of Trade*. Oxford, 1929

Wiseman, F. J. *Roman Spain*. London, 1956

CHAPTER IV—GALLIA

Agache, R. *La Somme Pré-Romaine et Romaine d'après les Prospections Aériennes à Basse Altitude*. Amiens, 1978

Audin, A. *Lyon, Miroir de Rome dans les Gaules*. Paris, 1965

Blanchet, A. *Les Enceintes Romaines de la Gaule*. Paris, 1907

Blanchet, A. (ed.). *Carte Archéologique de la Gaule Romaine*. Paris, 1931–

Brogan, O. *Roman Gaul*. London, 1953

Chadwick, N. K. *Early Brittany*. Cardiff, 1969

Cumont, F. *Comment la Belgique fut Romanisée*. Brussels, 1914

Desjardins, E. *Géographie Historique et Administrative de la Gaule Romaine*. Paris, 1876–93

Duval, P.-M. *Paris Antique*. Paris, 1961

Ebel, C. *Transalpine Gaul: the Emergence of a Roman Province*. Leiden, 1976

Etienne, R. *Bordeaux Antique*. Bordeaux, 1962

Grenier, A. *Manuel d'Archéologie Gallo-Romaine*. Paris, 1931–60
'La Gaule Romaine'. *An Economic Survey of Ancient Rome*, ed. T. Frank, vol. III, Baltimore, 1937

Hatt, J. J. *Histoire de la Gaule Romaine*. Paris, 1959

Hyde, W. W. *Roman Alpine Routes*. Philadelphia, 1935

Johnson, S. 'A Group of Late Roman City Walls in Gallia Belgica.' *Britannia* IV (1973) 210–223

Jullian, C. *Histoire de la Gaule*. Paris, 1914–26

König, I. *Itinera Romana 3: die Meilensteine der Gallia Narbonensis*. Berne, 1970

Labrousse, M. *Toulouse Antique*. Paris, 1968

Lambert, A. M. *The Making of the Dutch Landscape*. London, 1971

Latouche, R. *Caesar to Charlemagne*. London, 1968

Longnon, A. *Atlas Historique de la France*. Paris, 1912

Lot, F. *Recherches sur la Population et la Superficie des Cités Remontant à la Période Gallo-Romaine*. Paris, 1945
La Gaule. Paris, 1947

MacKendrick, P. *Romans on the Rhine*. New York,

1970

Roman France. London, 1971

Prieur, J. *La Province Romaine des Alpes Cottiennes*. Lyon, 1968

Rice Holmes, T. *Caesar's Conquest of Gaul*. 2nd edition, London, 1951

Römer am Rhein (a symposium). Cologne, 1967

Staehelin, F. *Die Schweiz in Römischer Zeit*. Basle, 1948

Tabula Imperii Romani: sheets M32 (Mogontiacum), Frankfurt, 1940. L32 (Mediolanum), Rome, 1966. M31 (Lutetia-Atuatuca-Ulpia Noviomagus), Paris, 1975. M30 (Londinium-Lutetia) in preparation.

Vogt, E. (Festschrift). *Helvetia Antiqua*. Zürich, 1966

Van Es, W. A. *De Romeinen in Nederland*. 2nd edition, Bussum, 1972

Von Petrikovits, H. *Das Römischen Strassen in der Schweiz*. Berne, 1967

Wankenne, A. *La Belgique à l'Époque Romaine*. Brussels, 1972

West, L. C. *Roman Gaul: the Objects of Trade*. Oxford, 1935

Wightman, E. M. *Roman Trier and the Treveri*. London, 1970

CHAPTER V—GERMANIA

Bradley, H. *The Goths*. London, 1887

Brogan, O. 'Trade between the Roman Empire and the Free Germans.' *Journal of Roman Studies* XXVI (1926) 195ff.

The Cambridge Ancient History, vol. XI (Cambridge, 1936) pp. 46–76

Courtois, C. *Les Vandales et l'Afrique*. Paris, 1955

Hachmann, R. *The Ancient Civilization of the Germanic Peoples*. London, 1971

Hagen, A. *Norway*. London, 1967

Hellmich, M. *Die Besiedlung Schlesiens in vor- und frühgeschichtlicher Zeit*. Breslau, 1923

Jankuhn, H. *Vor- und Frühgeschichte vom Neolithikum bis zur Völkerwanderungzeit*. Stuttgart, 1969

Jażdżewski, K. *Poland*. London, 1965

Just, L. *Handbuch der Deutschen Geschichte*. Constance/Frankfurt, 1957–68

Krüger, B. (ed.). *Die Germanen: Ein Handbuch*. Vol. I, Berlin, 1976

Lambert, A. *The Making of the Dutch Landscape*. London, 1971

Millar, F. *The Roman Empire and its Neighbours* (London, 1967) chap. 17 pp. 294 ff

Much, R. *Die Germania des Tacitus*. 3rd edition, Heidelberg, 1967

Musset, L. *The Germanic Invasions*. London, 1975

Neustupny, E. and J. *Czechoslovakia before the Slavs*. London, 1961

Norden, E. *Die Germanische Urgeschichte in Tacitus Germania*. 4th edition, Darmstadt, 1959

Norkus, J. *Die Feldzüge der Römer in Nordwestdeutschland in den Jahren 9–16 n. Chr*. Hildesheim, 1963

Schreiber, H. *Teuton and Slav*. London, 1965

Schuchhart, C. *Vorgeschichte von Deutschland*. Munich, 1943

Schütte, G. *Ptolemy's Maps of Northern Europe*. Copenhagen, 1917

Šimek, E. *Velká Germanie Klaudia Ptolemaia*. Brno, 1949

Stenberger, M. *Sweden*. London, 1962

Tabula Imperii Romani: sheet M33 (Prague). Prague, 1955

Tacitus' *Germania*:
   ed. J. G. C. Anderson, Oxford, 1938
   translated by H. Mattingly as 'Tacitus on Britain and Germany', Penguin edition, London, 1948

Thompson, E. A. *The Early Germans*. Oxford, 1965

Todd, M. *Everyday Life of the Barbarians*. London, 1972

   The Northern Barbarians, 100 B.C.–A.D. 300. London, 1975

Wells, C. M. *The German Policy of Augustus*. Oxford, 1972

Wheeler, Sir Mortimer. *Rome beyond the Imperial Frontiers* (London, 1954) pp. 7–94

CHAPTER VI—ITALIA

Italy

Ashby, T. *The Roman Campagna in Classical Times*. London, 1927

Beloch, J. *Campanien*. Berlin, 1879

Calderini, A. *Aquileia Romana*. Milan, 1930

Carcopino, J. *Daily Life in Ancient Rome*. London, 1941

Chilver, G. E. F. *Cisalpine Gaul*. Oxford, 1941

Coarelli, F. (ed.). *Etruscan Cities*. Milan/London, 1973–5

Donati, A. *Aemilia Tributim Discripta*. Faenza, 1967

Frank T. *An Economic Survey of Ancient Rome*, vols. I (the Republic) and V (the Empire). Baltimore, 1933

Frothingham, A. L. *Roman Cities in Northern Italy and Dalmatia*. London, 1910

Gasparotto, C. *Padova Romana*. Padua, 1951

Grant, M. *Cities of Vesuvius*. London, 1971

Guido, M. *Southern Italy: an Archaeological Guide*. London, 1972

Lugli, G. *Itinerario di Roma Antica*. Milan, 1970

MacKendrick, P. *The Mute Stones Speak*. London, 1962

Magaldi, E. *Lucania Romana*. Rome, 1947

Marconi, P. *Verona Romana*. Bergamo, 1937

Meiggs, R. *Roman Ostia*. Oxford, 1960

Moro, P. M. *Iulium Carnicum*. Rome, 1956

Nissen, H. *Italische Landeskunde*. Berlin, 1883–1902

Paget, R. F. *Central Italy: an Archaeological Guide*. London, 1973

Salmon, E. T. *Samnium and the Samnites*. Cambridge, 1967

Scullard, H. H. *The Etruscan Cities and Rome*. London, 1967

Sorrell, A., and Birley, A. *Imperial Rome*. London, 1970

Tabula Imperii Romani: sheets L32 (Mediolanum), Rome, 1966; and L33 (Tergeste), Rome, 1961

Thomsen, R. *The Italic Regions*. Copenhagen, 1947

Woodhead, A. G. *The Greeks in the West*. London, 1962

The island provinces

Blanchet, A. *Carte Archéologique de la Gaule Romaine*, III (département de la Corse). Paris, 1933

Bouchier, E. S. *Sardinia in Ancient Times*. Oxford, 1917

Finley, M. I. *A History of Sicily: Ancient Sicily to the Arab Conquest*. London, 1968

Guido, M. *Sardinia*. London, 1963
Sicily: an Archaeological Guide. London, 1967

Meloni, P. *L'Amministrazione della Sardegna da Augusto all'Invasione Vandalica*. Rome, 1958

Scramuzza, V. M. 'Roman Sicily.' *An Economic Survey of Ancient Rome*. ed. T. Frank, vol. III, Baltimore, 1937

Verbrugghe, G. P. *Itinera Romana 2: Sicilia*. Berne, 1976

Von Stauffenberg, A. S. *Trinakria*. Munich, 1963

The Upper Danube provinces

Alföldy, G. *Noricum*. London, 1974

Ertl, F. *Topographia Norici*. Kremsmünster, 1965

Kellner, H. G. *Die Römer in Bayern*. Munich, 1971

Mocsy, A. *Pannonia and Upper Moesia*. London, 1974

Neumann, A. *Vindobona*. Vienna, 1972

Oliva, P. *Pannonia and the Onset of Crisis in the Roman Empire*. Prague, 1962

Pauly-Wissowa article *Pannonia* (Supp. IX, 1962, pp. 515–775)

Die Römer an der Donau (symposium). Petronell, 1973

Schreiber, G. *Die Römer in Österreich*. Frankfurt, 1974

Szilágyi, J. *Aquincum*. Budapest, 1956

Vorbeck, E., and Beckel, L. *Carnuntum—Rom an der Donau*. Salzburg, 1973

Wilkes, J. J. *Dalmatia*. London, 1969

Winkler, G. *Die Römer in Oberösterreich*. Linz, 1975

CHAPTER VII—MACEDONIA

Greece

Alexander, J. A. *Potidaea: its History and Remains*. Athens, 1963

Andrewes, A. *The Greeks*. London, 1967

Cary, M. *A History of the Greek World from 323 to 146 B.C.* 2nd edition, London, 1951

Casson, S. *Macedonia, Thrace and Illyria*. Oxford, 1926

Cawkwell, G. *Philip of Macedon*. London, 1975

Colocotronis, V. *La Macédoine et l'Hellénisme*. Paris, 1919

Cook, R. M. *The Greeks till Alexander*. London, 1961

Ellis, J. R. *Philip II and Macedonian Imperialism*. London, 1976

Glotz, G. *Ancient Greece at Work*. London, 1926

Hammond, N.G.L. *Epirus*. Oxford, 1967
A History of Macedonia. Oxford, 1972

Hopper, R. J. *The Acropolis*. London, 1971

Jones, A. H. M. *Sparta*. Oxford, 1967

Kalléris, J. N. *Les Anciens Macédoniens*. Athens, 1954

Kitto, H. D. F. *The Greeks*. Penguin edition, 1957

Larsen, J. A. O. *An Economic Survey of Ancient Rome*, ed. T. Frank, vol. IV, Baltimore, 1938

Lerat, L. *Les Locriens de l'Ouest*. Paris, 1952

MacKendrick, P. *The Greek Stones Speak*. London, 1962

O'Sullivan, F. *The Egnatian Way*. Newton Abbot, 1972

Pendlebury, J. O. S. *The Archaeology of Crete*. London, 1939

Philippson, A. *Die Griechischen Landschaften*. Frankfurt, 1950–9

Rostovtzeff, M. *Social and Economic History of the Hellenistic World*. Oxford, 1941

Schoder, R. V. *Ancient Greece from the Air*. London, 1974

Stählin, F. et al. *Pagasai und Demetrias*. Berlin, 1934

Stobart, J. C. *The Glory that was Greece*. London, 1929

Tomlinson, R. A. *Argos and the Argolid*. London, 1972

The Lower Danube provinces

Berciu, D. *Romania*. London, 1967

Carter, F. W. *An Historical Geography of the Balkans*. London, 1977

Condurachi, E., and Daicoviciu, C. *Romania*. London, 1972

Daicoviciu, C. *Dacica*. Cluj, 1969

Fol, A., and Marazov, I. *Thrace and the Thracians*. London, 1977

Gerov, B. *Prouchvaniya vurhu Zapadnotrakiskite Zemi prez Rimsko Vreme* (Western Thrace in Roman Times). Sofia, 1961

Hoddinott, R. F. *Bulgaria in Antiquity*. London, 1975

Jones, A. H. M. *The Cities of the Eastern Roman Provinces*. 2nd edition, Oxford, 1971: chapter I, pp. 1–27

Kahrstedt, U. *Beiträge zur Geschichte der Thrakischen Chersones*. Baden-Baden, 1954

MacKendrick, P. *The Dacian Stones Speak*. Chapel Hill, North Carolina, 1975

Marshall Lang, D. *The Bulgarians*. London, 1976

Mihailov, G. *Inscriptiones Graecae in Bulgaria Repertae*. Sofia, 1956–66

Mócsy, A. *Gesellschaft und Romanisation in der Römischen Provinz Moesia Superior*. Budapest, 1970

Pannonia and Upper Moesia. London, 1974

Pârvan, V. *Getica*. Bucharest, 1926

Dacia. Cambridge, 1928

Römer in Rumänien (a symposium). Cologne, 1969

Rossi, L. *Trajan's Column and the Dacian Wars*. London, 1971

Sulimirski, T. *The Sarmatians*. London, 1970

Tabula Imperii Romani: sheet L34 (Aquincum-Sarmizegetusa-Sirmium). Amsterdam, 1968

Sheet L35 (Romula-Durostorum-Tomis). Bucharest, 1969

Supplement sheet (Drobeta-Romula-Sucidava). Bucharest, 1965

Sheet K34 (Naissus-Serdica-Thessalonike) in preparation.

Tudor, D. *Oltenia Romana*. Bucharest, 1958

Velkov, V. *Cities in Thrace and Dacia in Late Antiquity*. Amsterdam, 1977

Vulpe, R. *Studia Thracologica*. Bucharest, 1966

Wiesner, J. *Die Thraker*. Stuttgart, 1963

CHAPTER VIII—AFRICA

Albertini, E. *L'Afrique Romaine*. Algiers, 1949

Bandinelli, R. B. *Leptis Magna*. Rome, 1963

Baradez, J. *Fossatum Africae. Vue Aérienne de l'Organisation Romaine dans le Sud-Algerien*. Paris, 1949

Compléments Inédits au 'Fossatum Africae'. Limes-Conference VI (Cologne, 1967) pp. 200–210

Bates, O. *The Eastern Libyans*, London, 1914

Cagnat, R. *L'Armée Romaine d'Afrique*. Paris, 1913

Camps, G. 'Massinissa ou les Débuts de l'Histoire.' *Libyca* VIII, Algiers, 1960

Carcopino, J. *Le Maroc Antique*. Paris, 1943

Charles-Picard, G. *La Civilisation de l'Afrique Romaine*. Paris, 1959

The Life and Death of Carthage. English translation, London, 1968

Castellum Dimmidi. Paris, 1969

Chatelain, L. *Le Maroc des Romains*. Paris, 1944

Courtois, C. *Timgad: Antique Thamugadi*. Algiers, 1952

Les Vandales et l'Afrique. Paris, 1955

Dahmani, S. *Hippo Regius*. Algiers, 1973

Daniels, C. *The Garamantes of Southern Libya*. London, 1970

De Roch, S. *Tébessa: Antique Theveste*. Algiers, 1952

Diesner, H-J. *Der Untergang der Römischen Herrschaft in Nordafrika*. Weimar, 1964

Duval, P. M. *Cherchel et Tipasa*. Paris, 1946

Euzennat, M. *Le Limes de Volubilis*. Limes-Conference VI pp. 194–9

Foucher, L. *Hadrumetum*. Paris, 1964

Gascou, J. *La Politique Municipale de l'Empire
Romaine en Afrique Proconsulaire de Trajan a
Septime-Sévère*. Rome, 1972

Goodchild, R. G. *Libyan Studies*—selected papers
ed. J. Reynolds. London, 1976

Gsell, S. *Histoire Ancienne de l'Afrique du Nord*.
Paris, 1920–28
Cherchel: Antique Iol-Caesarea. Algiers, 1953

Haynes, D. E. L. *Antiquities of Tripolitania*.
London, 1959

Jodin, A. *Mogador: Comptoir Phénicien du Maroc
Atlantique*. Tangier, 1966

Jones, A. H. M. *The Cities of the Eastern Roman
Provinces*. 2nd edition, Oxford, 1971, pp. 349–
362

Jones, G. D. B., and Little, J. H. 'Coastal Settlement in Cyrenaica.' *Journal of Roman Studies*
LXI (1971) 64–79

Julien, C-A. *Histoire de l'Afrique du Nord*. Paris,
1951

Lassere, J-M. *Ubique Populus*. Paris, 1977

Leschi, L. *Algérie Antique*. Paris, 1952
Djemila: Antique Cuicul. Algiers, 1953

Lézine, A. *Carthage. Utique. Etudes d'Architecture
et d'Urbanisme*. Paris, 1968

Poinssot, C. *Les Ruines de Dougga*. Tunis, 1958

Raven, S. *Rome in Africa*. London, 1969

Reynolds, J. 'Hadrian, Antoninus Pius and the
Cyrenaican Cities.' *Journal of Roman Studies*
LXVIII (1978) 111–121

Romanelli, P. *La Cirenaica Romana*. Verbania,
1943
Storia delle Province Romane dell'Africa. Rome,
1959
Enciclopedia Classica, sec. 3 vol. X book VII.
Turin, 1970

Salama, P. *Les Voies Romaines de l'Afrique du Nord*.
Algiers, 1951

Tabula Imperii Romani: sheets HI 33 (Lepcis
Magna) and HI 34 (Cyrene). Oxford, 1954

Teutsch, L. *Das Römische Städtewesen in Nordafrika*. Berlin, 1962

Tissot, C. *Géographie Comparée de la Province
Romaine de l'Afrique*. Paris, 1884–8

Trousset, P. *Recherches sur le Limes Tripolitanus*.
Paris, 1974

Ward, P. *Sabratha: a Guide for Visitors*. Harrow,
1970

Warmington, B. H. *Carthage*. London, 1969

Wheeler, Sir Mortimer. *Roman Africa in Colour*.
London, 1966

CHAPTER IX—AEGYPTUS

Ball, J. *Contributions to the Geography of Egypt*.
Cairo, 1939
Egypt in the Classical Geographers. Cairo, 1942

Bell, H. I. *Egypt from Alexander the Great to the
Arab Conquest*. Oxford, 1948

Bevan, E. *A History of Egypt under the Ptolemaic
Dynasty*. London, 1927

Bonneau, D. *La Crue du Nil*. Paris, 1964

Broderick, M., and Morton, A. A. *A Concise
Dictionary of Egyptian Archaeology*. London,
1922

Emery, W. B. *Egypt in Nubia*. London, 1965

Gauthier, H. 'Les Nomes d'Égypte, depuis
Hérodote jusqu'à la Conquête Arabe.' *Mémoires
de l'Institut d'Égypte*, XXV (Cairo, 1935)

Grant, M. *Cleopatra*. London, 1972

Hanoteaux, G. *Histoire de la Nation Egyptienne*.
Paris, 1931

Johnson, A. C. 'Roman Egypt.' *An Economic
Survey of Ancient Rome*, ed. T. Frank, vol. II,
Baltimore, 1936

Jones, A. H. M. *The Cities of the Eastern Roman
Provinces*. 2nd edition, Oxford, 1971, pp. 295–
348

Jouguet, P. *La Vie Municipale dans l'Égypte
Romaine*. Paris, 1911

Kees, H. *Ancient Egypt: a Cultural Topography*.
London, 1961

MacLennan, H. *Oxyrhynchus: an Economic and
Social Study*. Princeton, 1935

Marlowe, J. *The Golden Age of Alexandria*.
London, 1971

Milne, J. G. *A History of Egypt under Roman Rule*.
3rd edition, London, 1924

Préaux, C. *L'Économie Royale des Lagides*. Brussels,
1939

Stein, A. *Die Präfekten von Agypten in der
Römischen Kaiserzeit*. Berne, 1950

Tabula Imperii Romani: sheet NG 36 (Coptos).
Oxford, 1958

Wallace, S. L. *Taxation in Egypt from Augustus to
Diocletian*. Princeton, 1938

CHAPTER X—ASIA

Asia Minor

Akurgal, E. *Ancient Civilizations and Ruins of Turkey.* Istanbul, 1973

Bean, G. E. *Aegaean Turkey.* London, 1966
Turkey's Southern Shore. London, 1968
Turkey beyond the Maeander. London, 1971
Lycian Turkey. London, 1978

Broughton, T. R. S. 'Roman Asia Minor.' *An Economic Survey of Ancient Rome,* ed. T. Frank, vol IV, (Baltimore, 1938) pp. 505–916

Cadoux, C. J. *Ancient Smyrna.* Oxford, 1938

Calder, W. M., and Bean, G. E. *A Classical Map of Asia Minor.* London, 1958

Cook, J. M. *The Greeks in Ionia and the East.* London, 1962
The Troad. Oxford, 1973

Goldman, H. (ed.). *Tarsus.* Princeton, 1950

Habicht, C. 'New Evidence on the Province of Asia.' *Journal of Roman Studies* LXV (1975) pp. 64–91

Hanfmann, G. M. A. *Sardis und Lydien.* Mainz, 1960
From Croesus to Constantine. Ann Arbor, 1975

Hansen, E. V. *The Attalids of Pergamon.* Ithaca, N.Y., 1947

Hasluck, F. W. *Cyzicus.* Cambridge, 1910

Haspels, C. H. E. *The Highlands of Phrygia.* Princeton, 1971

Haynes, S. *Land of the Chimaera.* London, 1974

Heberdey, R., and Wilhelm, A. *Reisen in Kilikien.* Vienna, 1896

Janssens, E. *Trebizonde en Colchide.* Brussels, 1969

Jones, A. H. M. *The Cities of the Eastern Roman Provinces.* 2nd edition, Oxford, 1971, pp. 28–214

Karageorghis, V. *Cyprus.* London/Geneva, 1969

Kleiner, G. *Die Ruinen von Milet.* Berlin, 1968

Levick, B. *Roman Colonies in Southern Asia Minor.* Oxford, 1967

Lloyd, S. *Early Highland Peoples of Anatolia.* London, 1967

Magie, D. *Roman Rule in Asia Minor.* Princeton, 1950

Metzger, H. *Anatolia II.* London, 1969

Mitford, T. B. 'Some Inscriptions from the Cappadocian *Limes.' Journal of Roman Studies* LXIV (1974) pp. 160–175

Pliny the Younger, *Letters* (trans. B. Radice). Penguin edition, London, 1969

Ramsay, W. M. *The Historical Geography of Asia Minor.* London, 1890
The Cities and Bishoprics of Phrygia. Oxford, 1895–7

Reinbach, T. *Mithridate Eupator, Roi de Pont.* Paris, 1890

Robert, L. *Villes d'Asie Mineure.* 2nd edition, Paris, 1962

Rosenbaum, E., et al. *A Survey of Coastal Cities in Western Cilicia.* Ankara, 1967

Sherwin-White, A. N. 'Rome, Pamphylia and Cilicia.' *Journal of Roman Studies* LXVI (1976) pp. 1–14
'Roman Involvement in Anatolia.' Ibid., LXVII (1977) pp. 62–75

Stark, F. *Ionia: A Quest.* London, 1954
The Lycian Shore. London, 1956
Alexander's Path. London, 1958
Rome on the Euphrates. London, 1966

Wetherell, J. E. *The Land of Troy and Tarsus.* London, 1931

Wood, J. T. *Discoveries at Ephesus.* London, 1977

Syria and Palestine

Abel, F. M. *Histoire de la Palestine.* Paris, 1952
Géographie de la Palestine. 3rd edition, Paris, 1967

Avi-Yonah, M. *Map of Roman Palestine.* 2nd edition, Jerusalem, 1940

Baly, D. *The Geography of the Bible.* London, 1957

Bouchier, E. S. *Syria as a Roman Province.* Oxford, 1941

Bossert, H. *Altsyrien.* Tübingen, 1951

Bowerstock, G. W. 'A Report on Arabia Provincia.' *Journal of Roman Studies* LXI (1971) pp. 219–242

Brünnow, R. E., and Domaszewski, A. *Die Provincia Arabia.* Strasbourg, 1904–9

Chapot, V. *La Frontière de l'Euphrate.* Paris, 1907

Downey, G. *A History of Antioch in Syria.* Princeton, 1961

Dussaud, R. *Topographie Historique de la Syrie Antique et Médiévale.* Paris, 1927

Furneaux, R. *The Roman Siege of Jerusalem.* London, 1973

Glueck, N. *Deities and Dolphins.* London, 1965

Grant, M. *Herod the Great.* London, 1971
The Jews in the Roman World. London, 1973

Grollenberg, L. H. *Atlas of the Bible.* English edition, London, 1957

Harding, G. Lankester. *The Antiquities of Jordan.* 2nd edition, London, 1967

Heichelheim, F. M. 'Roman Syria.' *An Economic*

Survey of Ancient Rome, ed. T. Frank, vol. VI, (Baltimore, 1938) pp. 123–257

Hitti, P. K. *History of Syria*. London, 1951

Jones, A. H. M. *The Cities of the Eastern Roman Provinces*. 2nd edition, Oxford, 1971, pp. 226–294

Josephus, *The Jewish War* (trans. G. A. Williamson). Penguin edition, London, 1970

Kenyon, K. M. *Jerusalem*. London, 1967
Digging Up Jerusalem. New York, 1974

Kraeling, C. H. (ed.). *Gerasa: City of the Decapolis*. New Haven, 1938

Levine, L. I. *Caesarea under Roman Rule*. Leiden, 1975

Mouterde, R., and Poidebard, A. *Le Limes de Chalcis*. Paris, 1945

Noth, M. *The History of Israel*. 2nd edition, London, 1960

Perowne, S. *The Later Herods*. London, 1958

Poidebard, A. *La Trace de Rome dans le désert de Syrie*. Paris, 1934
Un Grand Port Disparu: Tyr. Paris, 1939

Poidebard, A., and Lauffray, J. *Sidon*. Beirut, 1951

Rey-Coquais, J-P. 'Syrie Romaine de Pompée à Dioclétien.' *Journal of Roman Studies* LXVIII (1978) pp. 44–73

Robinson, D. M. *Baalbek/Palmyra*. New York, 1946

Rostovtzeff, M. *Caravan Cities*. Oxford, 1932

Sauvaget, J. *Alep*. Paris, 1941

Smith, G. A. *The Historical Geography of the Holy Land*. London, 1894

Yadin, Y. *Masada*. London, 1966
Bar-Kokhba. London, 1971

INDEX

(Note: through lack of space it has not always been possible on the maps to give the full name of a place, or alternative names when more than one was used. Fuller forms are given in this Index. Thus Lutetia on the maps appears here as Lutetia Parisiorum, and Germanicopolis as Germanicopolis–Gangra.

Some tribes and regions, which also had to be left off the maps, are likewise listed here, and can be located by reference to their principal cities.)